What people are saying about …

COLD-CASE CHRISTIANITY

"Whether or not you see the movie *God's Not Dead 2*, carefully reading and studying this book will turn you into a catalyst for change in a world desperately in need of faith. Though Jim is definitely one of a kind, the lessons taught in *Cold-Case Christianity* can be grasped and retold by anyone desiring to bring the truth of the gospel of Jesus Christ to others."

Rice Broocks, author of *God's Not Dead: Evidence for God in an Age of Uncertainty*

"When my faith was in crisis, I needed evidence to convince me that Christianity was true. During that time, I read *Cold-Case Christianity* three times and it was instrumental in giving me confidence in the reliability of the Gospels. This new updated and re-illustrated version is even better! As a cold-case homicide detective, J. Warner Wallace applies his investigative skills to make the evidence accessible and understandable to everyone. I am so personally thankful for this book and recommend it to everyone who is open to discovering the case for Christianity."

Alisa Childers, host of *The Alisa Childers Podcast* and author of *Another Gospel?* and *Live Your Truth and Other Lies*

"*Cold-Case Christianity* is my go-to book for evidence that the New Testament is telling the historical truth. So how did J. Warner Wallace make my favorite book even better? He added 300 illustrations, exciting new archaeological discoveries, answered the top objections skeptics had to the first edition, and added personal reflections that will enhance your confidence in the Scriptures. Even if you own the original classic, get this brilliant book now!"

Dr. Frank Turek, president of CrossExamined.org and author of *I Don't Have Enough Faith to Be an Atheist*

"As a budding Christian apologist, *Cold-Case Christianity* played a crucial role in my spiritual formation. And I'm not the only one. This clear and accessible book has helped a generation become better Christian case makers. That's because J. Warner Wallace doesn't just tell you what to think; he shows you how to think. Combining logical reasoning, forensic insights, and cop stories, *Cold-Case Christianity* helps you learn to think like a seasoned detective. After reading this book, you will be equipped to articulate and defend the truth of Christianity."

Tim Barnett, speaker for Stand to Reason, creator of Red Pen Logic with Mr. B, and coauthor of *The Deconstruction of Christianity*

"*Cold-Case Christianity* is a fantastic book. I wish I had this resource when I first examined the Christian faith. It would have answered many of my questions and helped set me on the track to truth."

Josh McDowell, speaker and author of *Evidence That Demands a Verdict*

"What happens when an atheist cop takes the same forensic skills he uses to solve the toughest crimes—homicides with a trail that's been cold for decades—and applies them to the eyewitness testimony and circumstantial evidence for the life of Jesus of Nazareth? A fascinating new approach to the question of gospel credibility, that's what. *Cold-Case Christianity* is simply the most clever and compelling defense I've ever read for the reliability of the New Testament record. Case closed."

Gregory Koukl, president of Stand to Reason and author of *Tactics: A Game Plan for Discussing Your Christian Convictions*

"*Cold-Case Christianity* offers a fresh approach to biblical fact-finding that actually makes apologetics fun! I highly recommend it to anyone interested in the evidence that backs up the Christian faith, whether you're a skeptic, a spiritual seeker, or a committed believer. Everyone will benefit from reading J. Warner Wallace's powerful new book."

Mark Mittelberg, author of *The Questions Christians Hope No One Will Ask (with answers)* and coauthor of *Becoming a Contagious Christian*

"The moment I heard of J. Warner Wallace's idea for a book, I thought it was one of the freshest ideas I'd heard in a long time. And now seeing the book in hand, he totally delivers. This is one of the most fun and clever ways to learn just how strong and enduring the case for Christianity is. I've always maintained that if we apply standard tools of investigation in an unbiased way, Christian truth claims would be vindicated. Jim's 'cold-case' detective work shows this idea to be right on the money."

Craig J. Hazen, PhD, founder and director of the Christian Apologetics Program, Biola University, and author of *Five Sacred Crossings*

"Today Americans are searching for truth. The most fundamental truth is the reality of a sovereign God. During his journey from agnosticism to apologetics, J. Warner Wallace used his 'cold-case' investigative techniques to prove the reality of the divine. READ his book. You will not regret it."

William G. Boykin, LTG(R) US Army, executive vice president of Family Research Council, former deputy undersecretary of Defense for Intelligence, and founding member of US Army Delta Force

"*Cold-Case Christianity* reads like the fast-paced detective drama it actually is. The book is chock full of interesting evidence and arguments, and it is unique among the literature in exhibiting a legal-reasoning approach to the evidence for and against historic Christianity. I enthusiastically endorse this great book and thank J. Warner Wallace for his excellent work."

J. P. Moreland, Distinguished Professor of Philosophy, Biola University, and author of *The God Question*

"*Cold-Case Christianity* is one of the most insightful, interesting, and helpful books in defending the faith I have read in a long time. Whether you are a Christian or a skeptic, J. Warner Wallace will challenge you to consider the evidence through fresh eyes. I have been studying the evidence for the faith for many years, and yet Jim helped me look at the historical, scientific, and philosophical facts in a new way. I could not recommend it more highly."

Sean McDowell, educator, speaker, and author of *Is God Just a Human Invention?*

"J. Warner Wallace's *Cold-Case Christianity* offers a fascinating angle on the evidence for the resurrection of Jesus. While Wallace does have experience as a former atheist—a bonus feature—he brings his expertise as a cold-case detective to bear on the forensic aspects of the events surrounding the first Easter. This book is a unique contribution to the growing literature on Jesus's resurrection."

Paul Copan, professor and Pledger Family Chair of
Philosophy and Ethics, Palm Beach Atlantic University

"Detective J. Warner Wallace is as creative telling a story as he is solving a crime. This is his ultimate case, where he investigates his own personal transformation by applying many lessons he learned on the job."

Robert Dean, producer of *Dateline NBC*

"J. Warner Wallace, my colleague in the fraternity of law enforcement, has made a valuable contribution to this generation and those to come. His book has the potential of becoming a classic for those seeking truth. Jim does a superb job of using the discipline and logic of a police detective as a matrix through which to examine the evidence for God, Jesus, the reliability of Scripture, and the message of the gospel. Skeptics, seekers, and committed believers will all find his analysis interesting and compelling. Armchair detectives and scholars alike will treasure this work. This book will be an important resource in my personal library."

Robert L. Vernon, assistant chief of police (ret.) LAPD
and founder of Pointman Leadership Institute

"WARNING: Do not start reading this book unless you have time set aside. You will NOT be able to put it down. This is a one-of-a-kind, groundbreaking book that everyone should read. J. Warner is in a unique position to investigate the claims of Christianity. He is quickly becoming my favorite apologist. Twelve stars out of a possible ten!"

Don Stewart, speaker and author of over seventy books

"With his background as a detective, J. Warner Wallace is qualified to sift through evidence and reach well-reasoned conclusions. Warner's *Cold-Case Christianity* is therefore unique among apologetics resources available today: the historical facts and related evidence are examined via the same protocols that a professional investigator would follow in handling a case. Wherever one falls on the faith spectrum—Christian, skeptic, or somewhere in between—Warner's application of investigative principles in his examination of Christianity makes for a must-read contribution to the realm of apologetics."

Alex McFarland, speaker and author of the bestselling
10 Most Common Objections to Christianity

"I am fortunate to be both J. Warner Wallace's friend and former chief and thoroughly enjoyed reading *Cold-Case Christianity.* Jim is a seasoned and incredibly skillful investigator who has a real talent for uncovering the important pieces of evidence and logically linking them together to arrive at the truth. This book is a compelling investigative work paralleling the steps Jim takes while investigating a crime with the steps he has taken to reveal the truth about Christ. *Cold-Case Christianity* is a bright light that illuminates the truth in a persuasive and convicting style."

Jim Herren, chief of police (ret.), UCLA Police Department

"I have had the pleasure of working with J. Warner Wallace for the past twenty-five years, and it is what I have learned from him that I cherish the most. His brilliant work, *Cold-Case Christianity*, provides readers with an opportunity to learn from Jim's experiences as a cold-case detective and discover his true passion—a passion that is equally matched by his character, knowledge, and wisdom. *Cold-Case Christianity* has opened a new resource for all to see and displays the endless contributions Jim has made to Christianity."

John J. Neu, chief of police (ret.), Torrance Police Department

"The work of an investigator requires an eye for observation and a mind to recognize its relevance. God has blessed Jim Wallace with such gifts. Those gifts have been sharpened by years of use and proved in such works as this. In the tradition of the great Sir Robert Anderson of Scotland Yard, Wallace digs for the facts and presents them reasonably."

Ken Graves, speaker and pastor of Calvary Chapel, Bangor, Maine

J. WARNER WALLACE

COLD-CASE
CHRISTIANITY

UPDATED & EXPANDED EDITION

A HOMICIDE DETECTIVE INVESTIGATES
THE CLAIMS OF THE GOSPELS

DAVID C COOK®
transforming lives together

COLD-CASE CHRISTIANITY
Published by David C Cook
4050 Lee Vance Drive
Colorado Springs, CO 80918 U.S.A.

Integrity Music Limited, a Division of David C Cook
Brighton, East Sussex BN1 2RE, England

DAVID C COOK® and related marks are registered trademarks of David C Cook.

The website addresses recommended throughout this book are offered as a resource to you. These websites are not intended in any way to be or imply an endorsement on the part of David C Cook, nor do we vouch for their content.

Library of Congress Control Number 2023935700
ISBN 978-0-8307-8530-8
eISBN 978-0-8307-8656-5

© 2013, 2023 James Warner Wallace
Published in association with the literary agency of Mark Sweeney &
Associates, 302 Sherwood Drive, Carol Stream, IL 60188.
First edition published by David C Cook in 2013, ISBN 978-1-4347-0469-6.

The Team: Michael Covington, Stephanie Bennett, Jeff Gerke, Jack Campbell, Susan Murdock
Cover Design: James Hershberger

Printed in the United States of America
Second Edition 2023

3 4 5 6 7 8 9 10 11 12

012224

CONTENTS

SECTION 2
Examine the Evidence
Applying the principles of investigation to the claims of the New Testament

APPENDIX
Witnesses and Resources
Compiling the resources necessary to make the case

SPECIAL THANKS

My deepest thanks to the readers who made the original version of *Cold-Case Christianity* a "must-read classic Christian book."[1] I've reviewed every word of the original text, making several important additions and adding a new "afterword" to the original manuscript. I've also re-illustrated the book and redesigned the interior layout.

When I wrote the first edition ten years ago, I was humbled by those who offered support and wisdom. I continue to be grateful to Sean McDowell for motivating me to write the book and for being a true brother in the faith, to Craig Hazen for being the most enthusiastic encourager and connecting me to the people who made the book a reality, to Lee Strobel for having the heart and desire to support the work, and to my literary agent, Mark Sweeney, who took a chance on a cold-case detective and has been answering every phone call since.

This updated 10th-anniversary edition of *Cold-Case Christianity* is dedicated to my best friend, most trusted partner, truest inspiration, and smartest critic: my wife, Susie. Thanks for being the first person to read every word and for helping me to be the kind of man who would even dream about writing books.

Cold-Case Christianity

TEN YEARS LATER

I wrote *Cold-Case Christianity* during one of my busiest seasons as a cold-case detective. It launched a journey as a public speaker (including a small role in the feature film *God's Not Dead 2*) and provided an opportunity to meet seekers and Christians across the world. "Humbling" is a word often overused, but it's an appropriate descriptor for this season of my life. God found a way to use a detective with an art degree to make the case to an eager and gracious audience.

In the ten years of public interaction, one question emerges more than any other: "Jim, can you share your spiritual 'testimony'?" People want to hear my "salvation story," the personal events God used to draw me to Himself. Audiences ask this question even *after* they've heard me make the case publicly or *after* reading *Cold-Case Christianity*. But this book *is* my "salvation story." It describes (along with *God's Crime Scene* and *Person of Interest*) the evidential journey I took to become a follower of Jesus.

For some, that seems hard to believe.

Isn't true faith *blind*? Can someone come to a "saving faith" by following *evidence*? Do we, as fallen humans, possess the ability to properly reason from evidence and draw a conclusion about God's existence, the reliability of the Bible, or the truth of the resurrection? If we can use evidence to determine Christianity is true, why call it "faith"? I tackle these important theological questions in my third book, *Forensic Faith*, but the short answer is this: God used the evidence of the gospel eyewitness accounts to capture and record the truth about Jesus, and I examined this evidence as a skeptical detective and learned the truth about the Savior.

I'm not a Christian today because I was raised in the church. I wasn't. I also didn't become a Christian because my childhood friends were Christians. They weren't. I'm not a Christian today because I was searching for God or wanted to know Him. I was happy and content as an atheist. I didn't become a Christian because I wanted to go to heaven or was afraid of hell. I was comfortable with my own mortality. I'm not a Christian because I wanted to change my life. As an atheist, I had a meaningful and fulfilling career, a loving family, an incredible wife, and lots of friends.

I'm also not a Christian because it *"works for me."* Life on this side of my decision hasn't always been easy. It's been over twenty years since I first trusted Jesus as Lord and Savior. I still struggle to submit my prideful will and selfish desire. There are times when I think it would be simpler to do it the old way; more expedient or convenient to cut a corner or take a shortcut. There are many occasions when doing the *right* thing means doing the *most difficult thing possible.*

I am a Christian today for one reason: Christianity is *true.* I'm a Christian because I want to live in a way that reflects the truth, even if it's hard, inconvenient, or unpopular. I'm a Christian because my high regard for the truth leaves me no alternative. An inconvenient truth is preferable to a convenient lie.

Over the past ten years, hundreds of thousands of readers have examined the evidence offered in this book and have learned how to become better detectives along the way. Many are now Christians. Make no mistake about it: God first called these readers and softened their skeptical hearts. The Christian evidence then did what it has always done: the evidence demonstrated the truth of the resurrection and the deity of Jesus.

To God goes the glory.

J. Warner Wallace

LEE STROBEL

I loved hanging out with homicide detectives.

I started my journalism career as a general assignment reporter on the overnight shift at the *Chicago Tribune*, and that meant covering the frequent murders committed around the city—crime-syndicate hits, gang-related violence, domestic disputes gone awry, robberies that got out of hand. Later I was assigned to the criminal courts, where I reported on the major homicide trials from around Cook County.

All of which meant that I spent a lot of time interviewing and socializing with homicide detectives. I liked them because they were no-nonsense, get-to-the-point people, with an uncanny ability to cut through the fog of deception that defendants used to cover their tracks. These street-toughened investigators were seldom fooled by a phony alibi or a flimsy excuse as they systematically unraveled the mysteries that confounded everyone else. They were evidence-driven, and so was I, constantly checking and rechecking my information before publishing my reports for the city to see.

Back then, I was an atheist. I thought that faith in God was based on conjecture, wishful thinking, and emotions; in fact, the idea that there might be evidence supporting the existence of God was totally alien to me. And I wasn't alone.

J. Warner Wallace is a cold-case homicide investigator who also started out as an outspoken spiritual skeptic. He began with the assumption that the supernatural was impossible. Yet when he diligently applied his skills as a detective—allowing the evidence to take him wherever it would lead—he came to a far different conclusion. Assessing the evidence with razor-like precision, he solved the most important mystery of all time—whether Jesus of Nazareth is the unique Son of God.

In his savvy and captivating book, Jim will introduce you to the kinds of tools and techniques that he routinely uses to crack unsolved murders that have long baffled other cops. He will show you how this same analytical thinking can be used to crack the case of a long-ago killing on a cross—and the incredible resurrection that followed. It's a fascinating process, with Jim drawing on his quarter century of police experience to explain how and why the evidence of history decisively tips the scales in favor of Christianity.

If you're a spiritual skeptic like Jim and I were for many years, then you'll find this investigative adventure to be an irresistible, eye-opening, and potentially life-changing journey, full of helpful insights and wisdom. Like a good cop, I hope you'll pursue the evidence to the conclusion it ultimately supports. That verdict, in the end, will be yours to reach.

If you're a follower of Jesus, then Jim's account will not only bolster your own faith, but it will also sharpen your skills in explaining to others why so many incisive thinkers throughout history have concluded that Christianity is uniquely credible and trustworthy.

Undoubtedly, you've seen media stories that have traced how cold-case detectives have pieced together an evidential puzzle in order to solve the most perplexing of homicides. Perhaps one of those accounts was based on a case that Jim actually helped crack. But as important as these investigations are, none of them approach the significance of the case that this book tackles.

So get ready to shadow Jim as he probes the evidence for faith. You'll find his approach to be compelling, his logic to be sound, and his conclusions to be amply supported. Unravel with him the historical case for Jesus—and discover its eternal implications for you and all the people you know.

Lee Strobel
www.LeeStrobel.com
Author of *The Case for Christ* and *The Case for Faith*

THE DETECTIVE WAY

I got the call at about 1:00 a.m. Detectives who are assigned to the homicide unit also investigate officer-involved shootings (OISs), and all of us on the OIS team were called out for this one. When I arrived at the scene, Officer Mark Walker was standing by his patrol car talking with a sergeant and waiting for our arrival. I shook his hand, made sure he was ready to talk about the shooting, and began to walk through the events that precipitated our "callout."

Mark told me he was working patrol when he saw a man driving down the street, swerving from lane to lane as though he was drunk. He pulled the driver over and approached his car. When he leaned in to talk to the man, he could smell the alcohol on his breath. Mark asked the man to step out from the car, and the driver reluctantly complied. As the man stood outside his car, Mark could see that he was angry and defiant. Mark decided to conduct a quick pat-down search to make sure the irritated driver wasn't carrying any weapons. Mark had no idea the driver was Jacob Stevens, a parolee with a long arrest record in an adjacent city. Jacob had just been released from state prison. He was on parole for an assault charge, and tonight he was carrying a loaded Colt .45-caliber pistol hidden in his waistband. Jacob knew that he would go back to jail if the gun was discovered, and he was determined to stay out of jail.

When Mark asked Jacob to turn around so he could conduct the pat-down search, Jacob turned away for a moment, pulled his gun, and then turned back toward Mark, pointing the gun at Mark's chest.

"I knew he had the drop on me," Mark explained as he recalled the events. "His gun was already drawn and pointed at me before I could even get my hand on mine."

Jacob had no intention of discussing the situation with Mark. He'd already decided he wasn't going back to jail, even if it meant killing this police officer. Jacob pointed his gun at Mark and started to squeeze the trigger. Mark was about to enter the fight of his life, and he was starting off with a distinct disadvantage: he was already seconds behind his opponent.

All of us who work in law enforcement understand the importance of wearing our bullet-proof vests. When we first became officers, we were trained with these vests, and at some point, most of us were shown how the vests performed in *live-fire* tests. We knew they could stop a bullet, including a .45 round. On this night, Mark would put his vest to the test.

"I just tensed my stomach muscles and prepared to take the shot as I pulled my gun out of the holster. I knew he would get the first round off."

While Mark knew *that* his vest could sustain the impact of a .45-caliber round, tonight he trusted *in* the vest for the very first time. In that singular moment, Mark went from "belief that" to "belief in." It's one thing to believe *that* the vest can save a life; it's another thing to trust *in* the vest to save your life. Mark obviously survived the shooting and lived to describe it for us. The lesson I learned from Mark, however, had far more impact on my life than he would ever know.

This gave Mark "belief that"

This gave Mark "belief in"

FROM "BELIEF THAT" TO "BELIEF IN"

I was thirty-five years old before I first paid attention to a pastor's sermon. A fellow officer had been inviting me to church for many months, and while I was able to put him off for some time, I eventually acquiesced and attended a Sunday-morning service with my family. I managed to ignore most of what the pastor talked about until he began to paint a picture of Jesus that caught my attention. He characterized Jesus as a really smart guy who had some remarkably wise things to say about life, family, relationships, and work. I began to believe *that* this might be true. While I was uninterested in bowing my knee to Jesus as God, I was at least willing to listen to Jesus as a teacher. A week later I purchased my first Bible.

My friends knew me as an angry atheist, a skeptic who thoughtfully dissected Christians and the Christian worldview, yet I suddenly found myself reading the Gospels to hear what Jesus had to say. Something about the Gospels caught my attention, more as an investigator than as someone interested in the ancient philosophy of an imaginary sage. By this time in my life, I had already served as a patrol officer and a member of the Gang Detail, the Metro Team (investigating street narcotics), the SWAT Team, and the Crime Impact Team (investigating career criminals). I had interviewed hundreds (if not thousands) of eyewitnesses and suspects. I had become familiar with the nature of eyewitness statements, and I understood how testimony was evaluated in a court of law. Something about the Gospels struck me as more than mythological storytelling. The Gospels resembled ancient eyewitness accounts.

I'd conducted many interviews and had success getting suspects to "cop-out." As a result, my department sent me to several investigative schools to refine my skills; I was eventually trained in forensic statement analysis (FSA). By carefully employing this methodology and scrutinizing a suspect's choice of pronouns, use of tensed language, and compression or expansion of time (along with many other linguistic tendencies), I was typically able to determine if he or she committed the crime, and I could often establish the time of day when the crime actually occurred. If this technique could provide me with such incredible insight into the statements of suspects and witnesses, why couldn't it be used to investigate the claims of the Gospels? I began to use FSA as I studied the gospel of Mark. Within a month, and despite my deep skepticism and hesitation, I concluded that Mark's gospel was the eyewitness account of the apostle Peter. I was beginning to move from a belief *that* Jesus was a wise teacher to a belief *in* what He said about Himself. I began a journey from casual assent to committed trust, from *belief that* to *belief in*.

For most of my career, I investigated cold-case murders. Unlike other lesser crimes, an unsolved homicide never closes; there is no statute of limitations on a murder, and time doesn't run out on a homicide investigation. My agency has dozens of unsolved murders that remain open, waiting for someone to take the time to re-examine them.

There are many similarities between investigating cold cases and investigating the claims of Christianity. Cold-case homicides are events from the distant past for which there is often little or no forensic evidence. (That's why they were unsolved in the first place.) Sometimes eyewitness reports are taken by the first detectives, but by the time the case is reopened, these eyewitnesses and detectives are no longer alive. It's my job to evaluate the credibility of the original statements, even though I can't re-interview the eyewitnesses or the people who first chronicled their observations. In the end, a strong cumulative case can usually be made by collecting witness statements, testing their reliability, and verifying their observations with what little forensic evidence is available. By taking this approach, I have arrested and successfully prosecuted several cold-case suspects who thought they had gotten away with murder.

Christianity makes a claim about an event from the distant past for which there is little or no forensic evidence. Like cold cases, the truth about what happened can be discovered by examining the statements of eyewitnesses, even though we can't re-interview these witnesses or the people who first chronicled their observations. Our goal, once again, is to assemble a strong cumulative case by collecting witness statements, testing their reliability, and verifying these observations with what little forensic evidence is available.

These contain
eyewitness accounts

These also contain
eyewitness accounts

But are there any reliable eyewitness statements in existence to corroborate in the first place? This became the most important question I had to answer in my personal investigation of Christianity. Were the gospel narratives *eyewitness accounts* or were they only *moralistic mythologies*? Were the Gospels reliable or were they filled with untrustworthy, supernatural absurdities? The most important questions I could ask about Christianity just so happened to fall within my area of expertise.

I hope to share some of that expertise with you in this book. Somewhere on my journey from "belief that" to "belief in," a friend told me about C. S. Lewis. After reading *Mere Christianity*, I purchased everything Lewis had written. One quote from *God in the Dock* stuck with me through the years. Lewis correctly noted, "Christianity is a statement which, if false, is of no importance, and, if true, is of infinite importance. The one thing it cannot be is moderately important."[1] Christianity, if it is true, is worthy of our investigation. Over the years I've retained my skepticism and my desperate need to examine the facts, even as I've journeyed from "belief that" to "belief in." I am still a detective, after all. I think I've learned a few things that may help you investigate the truth claims of the Bible.

I will tell you up front I am going to provide you with several examples from my career as a homicide and cold-case detective as I share what I've learned over the years; I will be telling some *cop stories*. I've carefully edited these examples, however, changing the names of those who were involved and modifying the details of each case slightly to protect the officers and victims. I've had the privilege of investigating some of the most important and well-publicized cases our city has encountered in the past twenty years. While I want you to learn from what we did right and what we did wrong, I want to respect the privacy of the detectives (and victims' families) along the way.

If you're a skeptic who rejects the Bible like I did, my experiences and insights might help you to assess the gospel writers in a new light. If you're someone who has encountered Christians who were unprepared to defend what they believe, I'd like to encourage you to be patient with us because the Christian tradition is *intellectually robust and satisfying*, even if we believers are occasionally unable to respond to your challenges. The answers are available; you don't have to turn off your brain to be a believer. Yes, it is possible to become a Christian *because* of the evidence rather than *despite* the evidence. Many of us have done just that.

If you're already a believer, my experiences might provide you with a few tools that can help you defend your faith in a more vigorous and informed way. You may learn something new about the history of Christianity or the nature and power of evidence. I want to encourage you to become an informed Christian, to worship God with your mind, and to prepare yourself as a Christian *case maker*. Let's start by examining ten simple principles of evidence that may change the way you look at Christianity forever.

LEARN TO BE A DETECTIVE

Ten important principles every aspiring detective needs to master

Chapter 1
Principle #1:

DON'T BE A "KNOW-IT-ALL"

"Jeffries and Wallace," Alan barked impatiently as a young officer scrambled to write our names on the crime-scene entry log. Alan lifted the yellow tape and passed beneath it, crouching painfully from the stress he had to place on his bad knee. "I'm getting too old for this," he said as he unbuttoned the coat of his suit. "The middle of the night gets later every time they call us out."

This was my first homicide scene, and I didn't want to make a fool of myself. I had been working robberies for many years, but I had never been involved in a suspicious death investigation before. I was worried my movements in the crime scene might contaminate it in some way. I took small, measured steps and followed Detective Alan Jeffries around like a puppy. Alan had been working in this detail for over fifteen years; he was only a few years short of retirement. He was knowledgeable, opinionated, confident, and grumpy. I liked him a lot.

We stood there for a moment and looked at the victim's body. She was lying partially naked on her bed, strangled. There was no sign of a struggle and no sign of forced entry into her condominium, just a forty-six-year-old woman lying dead in a very unflattering position. My mind was racing as I tried to recall everything I had learned in the two-week homicide school I recently attended. I knew there were important pieces of evidence requiring collection and preservation. My mind struggled to assess the quantity of "data" at the scene. What was the relationship between the evidence and the killer? Could the scene be reconstructed to reveal his or her identity?

"Hey, wake up!" Alan's tone shattered my thoughts. "We got a killer to catch here. Go find me her husband; he's the guy we're lookin' for."

What? Alan already had this figured out? He stood there looking at me with a sense of impatience and disdain. He pointed to a framed picture toppled over on the nightstand. Our victim was in the loving embrace of a man who appeared her age. He then pointed to some men's clothing hanging in the right side of her closet. Several items appeared missing.

"I've been doing this for a long time, kid," Alan said as he opened his notebook. "Stranger murders are pretty rare. That guy's probably her husband, and in my experience, spouses kill each other." Alan systematically pointed to several pieces of evidence and interpreted them in light of his proclamation. There was no forced entry, the victim didn't appear to put up much of a fight, the picture had been knocked over on the nightstand, men's clothing appeared to be missing from the closet; Alan saw all of this as confirmation of his theory. "No reason to make it complicated, newbie; most of the time it's real simple. Find me the husband, and I'll show you the killer."

As it turned out, it was a little more difficult than that. We didn't identify the suspect for another three months, and it turned out to be the victim's twenty-five-year-old neighbor. He barely knew her but managed to trick the victim into opening her door on the night he raped and killed her. She turned out to be single; the man in the photograph was her brother (he visited occasionally from overseas and kept some of his clothing in her closet). All of Alan's presuppositions were wrong, and his assumptions colored the way we were seeing the evidence. Alan's *philosophy* was hurting his *methodology*. We weren't following the evidence to see where it led; we had already decided where the evidence would lead and were simply looking for affirmation. Luckily, the truth prevailed.

All of us hold presuppositions impacting the way we see the world around us. I've learned to do my best to enter every investigation with my eyes and mind open to all the reasonable possibilities. I try not to *bite* on any particular philosophy or theory until one emerges as the most rational, given the evidence. I've learned this the hard way; I've made more than my share of mistakes. There's one thing I know for sure (having worked both fresh and cold homicides): you simply cannot enter an investigation with a philosophy that dictates the outcome. Objectivity is paramount; this is the first principle of *detective work* each of us must learn. It sounds simple, but our presuppositions are sometimes hidden in a way that makes them hard to uncover and recognize.

 ## SPIRITUAL PRESUPPOSITIONS

When I was an atheist, I held many presuppositions that tainted the way I investigated the claims of Christianity. I was raised in the *Star Trek* generation (the original cast, mind you) by an atheist father who was a cop and detective for nearly thirty years before I got hired as a police officer. I was convinced by the growing secular culture that all of life's mysteries would eventually be explained by science, and I was committed to the notion we would ultimately find a *natural* answer for everything we once thought to be *supernatural*.

My early years as a homicide detective only amplified these presuppositions. After all, what would my partners think if I examined all the evidence in a difficult case and (after failing to identify a suspect) concluded a ghost or demon committed the murder? They would surely think I was crazy. All homicide investigators presume supernatural beings are not reasonable suspects, and many detectives also happen to reject the supernatural altogether. Detectives must work in the real world, the "natural world" of material cause and effect. We presuppose a particular philosophy as we begin to investigate our cases. This philosophy is called "philosophical naturalism" (or "philosophical materialism").

Most of us in the *Star Trek* generation understand this philosophy, even if we can't articulate it perfectly. Philosophical naturalism rejects the existence of supernatural agents, powers, beings, or realities. It begins with the foundational premise that natural laws and forces alone can account for every phenomenon under examination. If there is an answer to be discovered, philosophical naturalism dictates that we must find it by examining the relationship between material objects and natural forces; that's it, nothing more. Supernatural forces are excluded *by definition*. Most scientists begin with this presupposition and fail to consider any answer that is not strictly physical, material, or natural. Even when a particular phenomenon cannot be explained by any natural, material process or set of forces, most scientists will refuse to consider a supernatural explanation. Richard Lewontin (an evolutionary biologist and geneticist) once famously wrote a review of a book written by Carl Sagan and admitted science is skewed to ignore any supernatural explanation, even when the evidence might indicate natural, material explanations are lacking:

> We take the side of science in spite of the patent absurdity of some of its constructs, in spite of its failure to fulfill many of its extravagant promises of health and life, in spite of the tolerance of the scientific community for unsubstantiated just-so stories, because we have a prior commitment, a commitment to materialism. It is not that the methods and institutions of science somehow compel us to accept a material explanation of the phenomenal world, but, on the contrary, that we are forced by our *a priori* adherence to material causes to create an apparatus of investigation and a set of concepts that produce material explanations, no matter how counterintuitive, no matter how mystifying to the uninitiated. Moreover, that materialism is an absolute, for we cannot allow a Divine Foot in the door.[1]

Scientists aren't alone; many historians are also committed to a naturalistic presupposition. Most historical scholars, for example, accept—*in a limited way*—the historicity of the New Testament Gospels, in so far as they describe the life and teaching of Jesus and the condition of the first-century environment in which Jesus lived and ministered. In fact, if the ancient accounts related to Jesus didn't include any descriptions of miraculous events (no virgin birth, no resurrection, no miraculous healings, nor demonstrations of supernatural power), I doubt any significant scholar would doubt the accuracy of the Gospels in their *entirety*. But the miraculous claims of the gospel authors provoke historians to separate what they believe is fact from what they believe is fiction. Mind you, many of these same historians simultaneously accept the historicity of the non-miraculous events described in the New Testament, even as they reject the miracles described *alongside* these events. Why do they accept some events and reject others? Because they have a presuppositional bias against the supernatural.

Bart Ehrman (the famous agnostic professor of religious studies at the University of North Carolina, Chapel Hill) was once in a radio debate with Michael Licona (associate professor in theology at Houston Baptist University) on the British radio program *Unbelievable?*[2] While debating the evidence for the resurrection, Ehrman revealed a naturalistic presupposition that is common to many historians. He said, "The bottom line, I think, is one we haven't even talked about, which

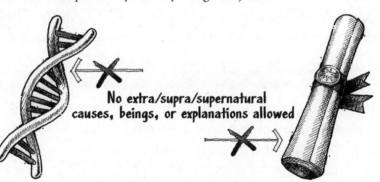

Philosophical Naturalism

The presuppositional belief that only natural laws and forces (as opposed to supernatural forces) operate in the world. Philosophical naturalists believe nothing exists beyond the natural realm.

is whether there can be such a thing as historical evidence for a miracle, and, I think, the answer is a clear no, and I think virtually all historians agree with me on that." Ehrman rejects the idea that any historical evidence could demonstrate a miracle because, in his words, "it's invoking something outside of our natural experience to explain what happened in the past." It shouldn't surprise us that Ehrman rejects the resurrection, given this presupposition; he arrived at a particular natural conclusion because he would not allow himself any other option, even though the evidence might be better explained by the very thing he rejects.

No extra/supra/supernatural causes, beings, or explanations allowed

MENTAL ROADBLOCKS

I began to understand the hazard of philosophical presuppositions while working as a homicide detective. Alan and I stood at that crime scene, doing our best to answer the question "Who murdered this woman?" One of us already had an answer. Spouses or lovers typically commit murders like this; case closed. We simply needed to find this woman's husband or lover. It was as if we were asking the question "Did her husband kill her?" after first excluding any suspect other than her husband. It's not surprising that Alan came to his conclusion; he started with it as his premise.

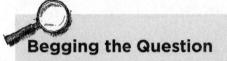

Begging the Question

When we smuggle our conclusions into our investigation by beginning with them as an initial premise, we are likely to beg the question and end up with conclusions that match our pre-suppositions rather than reflect the truth of the matter.

When I was an atheist, I did the very same thing. I stood in front of the evidence for God, interested in answering the question "Does God exist?" But I began the investigation as a naturalist with the presupposition that nothing exists beyond natural laws, forces, and material objects. I was asking the question "Does a supernatural being exist?" after first excluding the possibility of anything supernatural. Like Alan, I came to a particular conclusion because I started with it as my premise. This is the truest definition of bias, isn't it? Starting off with your mind already made up.

ENTER WITH EMPTY HANDS

Christians are often accused of being "biased" simply because they believe in the supernatural. This accusation has power in our current pluralistic culture. Biased people are seen as prejudicial and unfair, arrogant, and overly confident of their position. Nobody wants to be identified as someone who is biased or opinionated. But make no mistake about it, all of us have a point of view; all of us hold opinions and ideas that color the way we see the world. Anyone who tells you he (or she) is completely objective and devoid of presuppositions has another more important problem: that person is either astonishingly naive or a liar.

The question is not whether we have ideas, opinions, or pre-existing points of view; the question is whether we will allow these perspectives to prevent us from examining the evidence objectively. It's possible to have a prior opinion yet leave this presupposition at the door to examine the evidence fairly. We ask jurors to do this all the time. In the state of California, jurors are repeatedly instructed to "keep an open mind throughout the trial" and not to "let bias, sympathy, prejudice, or public opinion influence your decision."[3] The courts assume people have biases, hold sympathies and prejudices, and are aware of public opinion. Despite this, jurors are required to "keep an open mind." Jurors must enter the courtroom with empty hands; they must leave all their *baggage* in the hall. Everyone begins with a collection of biases. We must (to the best of our ability) resist the temptation to allow our biases to eliminate certain forms of evidence (and therefore certain conclusions) before we even begin the investigation.

Dangerous Presuppositions for Jurors

Dangerous Presuppositions for Truth Seekers

As a skeptic, I was slow to accept even the slightest possibility miracles were possible. My commitment to naturalism prevented me from considering such nonsense. But after my experience with presuppositions at the crime scene, I decided to be cautious about my naturalistic inclinations. Rather than start the investigation as though I already knew the outcome, I chose to suspend my biases long enough to be fair. If the evidence pointed to the reasonable existence of God, this certainly opened the possibility of the miraculous. If God *did* exist, He was the creator of everything we see in the universe. He, therefore, created matter from nonmatter, life from nonlife; He created all time and space. God's creation of the universe would certainly be nothing short of … *miraculous*. If there was a God who could account for the beginning of the universe, lesser miracles (say, walking on water or healing the blind) might not be all that impressive. To learn the truth about the existence of a miraculous God, I would need to at least lay down my presuppositions about the supernatural. My experience at crime scenes has helped me do just that. This doesn't mean I now rush to supernatural explanations every time

I fail to find an easy or quick natural explanation. It simply means I am open to following the evidence wherever it leads, even if it points to the existence of a miraculous designer.

 ## A TOOL FOR THE CALLOUT BAG, A TIP FOR THE CHECKLIST

I keep a leather bag packed beside my bed. It contains all the gear I need when I'm called to a homicide scene in the middle of the night. My *callout bag* typically includes a flashlight, blank notepads, plastic gloves, a digital recorder, camera, and (of course) my gun and badge. My bag also contains an investigative *checklist* I created many years ago when I was a new detective. While I seldom need to refer to it anymore, it represents years of wisdom gleaned from partners, classes, training seminars, successful investigations, and failed efforts. You might be interested in assembling your own callout bag and checklist. If so, you may want to include this first principle related to presuppositions; it will serve you well as you investigate the Gospels.

When I was an atheist, I allowed the presupposition of naturalism to unfairly taint the way I looked at the evidence for God's existence. I failed to differentiate between *science* (the systematic, rational examination of phenomena) and *scientism* (the refusal to consider anything other than natural causes). I was thirty-five before I recognized how unreasonable it was for me to reject the possibility of anything supernatural *before* I even began to investigate the supernatural claims of Christianity. In those days, when I encountered phenomena that could not be explained *naturally*, I simply *dug in* and continued to reject the possibility something *extranatural* might be operating. I refused to begin the journey with empty hands or an open mind.

Even though I'm a Christian today, I understand much of the phenomena we observe can be explained satisfactorily by simple relationships between matter and the *laws of nature*. For this reason, I try to be careful not to jump to supernatural explanations when natural causes are supported evidentially. Not all of God's activity is overtly miraculous. God is still at work even in the interaction between the matter He created and the natural laws that reflect His nature (this is, in fact, miraculous enough).[4] As a result, I try to encourage my skeptical friends to re-examine their natural presuppositions, but I'm careful to respect the claims of naturalists when they are evidentially supported.

LEARN HOW TO "INFER"

"I hate these kinds of cases," Mark muttered as he carefully pulled back the sheet on the bed. Detective Mark Richardson had a child of his own about the same age as the victim. Nothing is more disturbing than the homicide of a small infant, and it was Mark's turn to handle this murder. Three of us stood there and examined the scene while we waited for the coroner's investigator to arrive. Two of us were glad it wasn't our turn.

"How do parents do this kind of thing to their own kids?" Mark posed the question rhetorically, as if he didn't know the kind of response he was going to get from our senior partner.

"Don't call this dirtbag a 'parent,'" Al responded, casting a look of disgust in the direction of the disheveled parolee sitting on the couch down the hall. "If he did this, he's nothing more than the sperm donor for this kid."

I often get called out to assist members of our homicide unit at suspicious death scenes such as these when the manner of death is not immediately obvious. Better safe than sorry; these scenes must be investigated as homicides (until we determine otherwise) or they may become cold cases on my list. The situation surrounding this death was suspicious, so I got called to lend a hand. The baby appeared to have asphyxiated as he was lying in his father's bed, just feet away from an unused crib located in the same room. Mom and Dad had recently separated, and the baby's father had a history of violence against his wife going back several years. The baby's mother was no longer living at the house, and she often worried about the safety of her child. Her husband refused to release the baby to her, and she was afraid to seek legal help to retrieve the infant, based on her husband's violent nature. To make matters worse, her husband made several threats about strangling the boy in an effort to terrorize her.

Cold-Case Homicides

While most felonious crime investigations are limited by a *statute of limitations* (a legislated period beyond which the case cannot be legally prosecuted), homicides have no such restriction. This means that *fresh* homicides, should they go unsolved, can be investigated many years after they were committed. Investigators who have experience with cold cases can sometimes recognize the investigative pitfalls that cause cases to go cold in the first place.

Inferences

To infer means "to gather in." In logic, inference refers to the process of collecting data from numerous sources and then drawing conclusions based on this evidence. In legal terms, an inference is a "deduction of fact that may logically and reasonably be drawn from another fact or group of facts found or otherwise established" (Cal Evid Code § 600 [b]).

We observed the house was generally filthy and unkempt, and there were signs of drug use in the living room. When we first spoke to the victim's father, he seemed nonresponsive and hostile. He initially refused to answer simple questions and displayed a general distrust of law enforcement personnel. He was a parolee with a history of drug use, domestic violence, and felonious behavior. At first glance, one might suspect this man was capable of doing the unthinkable.

We called the coroner as we began to collect evidence and photograph everything in sight, and we didn't touch the body until the coroner's investigator arrived. Only then were we able to get a clear picture of the baby's condition. As we removed the bedding around the body and examined the child more closely, we discovered he was surprisingly clean and tidy. He looked healthy and well fed. He was lying next to a bottle of fresh formula, cleanly dressed in a new diaper and pajama suit. His hair was washed, and he was lying next to a long pillow that was propped up against one side of his torso. A second long pillow appeared to have been propped against the other side of the baby, but this pillow was now lying on the floor. The baby was lying facedown on the bed a short distance from the first pillow. There were no signs of neglect or abuse on the child, not a single bruise or suspicious mark.

In our follow-up interview of the baby's father, Al came to learn the child was his greatest treasure. Despite his many admitted failures and his emotionless, hardened exterior, the baby was this man's one joy. He carefully slept with the infant every night and was so concerned about sudden infant death syndrome that he placed the child faceup between two large pillows next to him on the bed so he could monitor his breathing. On this particular night, one of the two pillows rolled off the bed and the baby managed to roll over on his stomach. Given everything we saw at the scene and the condition of the baby, we ruled his asphyxiation an accidental death. Al agreed this was not a homicide.

THINKING LIKE A DETECTIVE

As investigators, we just employed a methodology known as *abductive reasoning* (also known as "inferring to the most reasonable explanation") to determine what we had at this scene. We collected all the evidential data and made a mental list of the raw facts. We then developed a list of the possible explanations that might account for the scene in general. Finally, we compared the evidence to the potential explanations and determined which explanation was, in fact, the most reasonable inference considering the evidence.

As it turns out, detectives aren't the only people who use abductive reasoning to figure out what really happened. Historians, scientists, and all the rest of us (regardless of vocation or avocation) have experience as detectives. In fact, most of us have become accomplished investigators as a matter of necessity and practice, and we've been employing abductive reasoning without giving it much thought. I had a partner once who gave me a bit of parental advice. Dave was a few years older than I was, and he had been working patrol for many years. He was a seasoned and salty officer, streetwise, cynical, and infinitely practical. He had two children who were already married when mine were still in high school. He was full of sage advice (along with some other stuff).

Reasonable Inferences

Courts across the land instruct jurors to draw "reasonable inferences." These are described as "conclusions which are regarded as logical by reasonable people in the light of their experience in life" (Lannon v. Hogan, 719 F.2d 518, 521, 1st Cir. Mass. 1983).

"Jim, let me tell ya something about kids. I love my two boys. I remember when they were in high school and used to go out with their friends on the weekends. I would stay up late and wait for them to come home. As soon as they walked in the door, I would get up off the couch and give them a big hug."

This struck me as a bit odd, given what I knew about Dave. He seldom exposed a sensitive side. "Wow, Dave, I have to tell you that I don't usually think of you as a touchy-feely kind of guy."

"I'm not, you moron," Dave said, returning to form. "I hug them as tightly as possible so I can get close enough to smell them. I'm not a fool. I can tell if they've been smoking dope or drinking within seconds."

You see, Dave was an evidentialist, and he applied his reasoning skills to his experience as a parent. The smell of alcohol or marijuana would serve as evidence he would later take into consideration as he was evaluating the possible activities of his children. Dave was thinking *abductively*. I bet you've done something similar in your role as a parent, a spouse, a son, or a daughter.

DISTINGUISHING BETWEEN *POSSIBLE* AND *REASONABLE*

All of us have learned the intuitive difference between *possible* and *reasonable*. When it comes right down to it, just about anything is *possible*. You may not even be reading this book right now, even though you think you are. It's *possible* aliens covertly kidnapped you last night and have induced a dreamlike, out-of-body, extraterrestrial hallucination. While you think this experience of reading is real, you may wake up tomorrow morning to discover yourself in an alien spaceship. But let's face it, that's not reasonable, is it?

While it's interesting to imagine the *possibilities*, it's important to return eventually to what's *reasonable*, especially when the truth is at stake. That's why judges across the land carefully instruct juries to refrain from what is known as "speculation" when considering the explanations for what has occurred in a case. Jurors are told they "must use only the evidence that is presented"[1] during the trial. They are told to resist the temptation to consider the attorneys' opinions about unsupported possibilities and to ignore unsupported speculation wherever they may hear it.

We also tell jurors to resist the impulse to stray from the evidence offered by asking questions like "What if …?" or "Isn't it possible that …?" when these questions are driven by evidentially unsupported speculation. They must instead limit themselves to what's reasonable considering the evidence presented to them.

In the end, our criminal courts place a high standard on *reasonableness*, and that's important as we think about the process of abductive reasoning. This rational approach to determining truth will help us to come to the most reasonable conclusion in light of the evidence. It can

Speculation

By its very definition, speculation is dangerously non-evidential:

"Reasoning based on inconclusive evidence; conjecture or supposition" (*The American Heritage Dictionary of the English Language*, 4th ed., 2003).

"A hypothesis that has been formed by speculating or conjecturing, usually with little hard evidence" (*Collins Thesaurus of the English Language, Complete and Unabridged*, 2nd ed., 2002).

be applied to more than criminal cases; we can apply the process of *abduction* to our spiritual investigations as well. But first, let's examine the concept with a real-life example from the world of homicide investigations.

ABDUCTIVE REASONING AND DEAD GUYS

Let's use the example of another death scene to fully illustrate the process. You and I have been called out to a "dead-body scene"—a location where a deceased person was discovered, and the circumstances seemed rather suspicious. While scenes like this are sometimes homicides, they are often less sinister; there are a few other explanations. Deaths fall into one of four categories: natural deaths, accidental deaths, suicides, or homicides. It's our job to figure out which of the four explanations is the most reasonable in the following scenario.

We have been called to the scene of a DBR (a "Dead Body Report") to assist patrol officers who have already arrived and secured the location. Here are the facts we are given when we enter the room: A young man was discovered on the floor of his apartment when his roommate returned from work. The man was lying facedown. The man was cold to the touch, nonresponsive, and stiff. Okay, given these minimal facts, it seems clear we have a dead guy, but which of the four potential explanations is most reasonable, given the facts? Is this death a natural death, an accident, a suicide, or a homicide?

Dead Man
Lying Facedown

natural death
accidental death
suicide
homicide

Given the minimal facts so far, all four of the potential explanations are still in play, aren't they? Unless we have something more to add evidentially, it will be difficult to decide if this case should be *investigated* as a homicide or simply *documented* as something other than criminal.

Let's change the scenario slightly and add a new piece of evidence to see if it will make things clearer. Imagine we entered the room and observed the man was lying in a pool of his own blood and that this blood seemed to come from the area of his abdomen (under his body). These are the new minimal facts: (1) A man is dead, (2) lying facedown on the floor, (3) in a pool of blood coming from the front of the man's lower abdomen. Given this new set of facts, is there any direction our investigation might take? Are any of our four explanations now more or less reasonable?

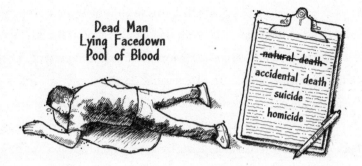

Dead Man
Lying Facedown
Pool of Blood

natural death
accidental death
suicide
homicide

Given the new evidence, we should be comfortable removing the *natural death* explanation from consideration. After all, what kind of natural event in the human body would cause someone to bleed from his lower abdomen? Without an orifice from which to bleed naturally, this does seem an unfounded conclusion to draw; a natural death might be *possible*, but it isn't *reasonable*.

What about the other three explanations? Could this still be an accidental death? Sure, the man could have tripped and fallen on something (we wouldn't know this until we turn him over). What about a suicide or a homicide? It seems these three remaining explanations are still reasonable considering what limited evidence we have about this case. Until we learn a bit more, it will be difficult to decide which of these final three options is the most reasonable.

Let's add a new dimension to the case. Imagine we enter the room and see the man lying on the floor in a pool of his own blood, but now we observe a large knife stuck in his lower back. This presents us with a new set of facts: (1) The man is dead, (2) lying facedown on the floor, (3) in a pool of blood, and (4) there is a knife stuck in the man's lower back.

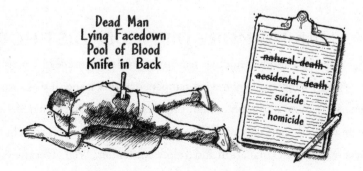

Dead Man
Lying Facedown
Pool of Blood
Knife in Back

natural death
accidental death
suicide
homicide

The presence of a knife in the victim's back seems to eliminate any reasonable inference he died *accidentally*. It's hard to imagine an accident that would account for this fact; an accidental death might be *possible* but it's not *reasonable*. More obviously, the presence of the knife most certainly affirms the unreasonable nature of a natural death, doesn't it? The most reasonable remaining explanations are either suicide or homicide, and suicide seems less and less likely, given the fact the victim's wound is located on his back. But since the wound is in the *lower* portion of his back (within his reach), let's leave this option on the table for now.

Imagine, however, a new fact exists in our scenario. Imagine that we discover three extra wounds on the victim's upper back, in addition to the one we observed earlier. Our fact list now includes: (1) A man who is dead, (2) lying facedown on the floor, (3) in a pool of blood, (4) with multiple knife wounds on his back. Our reasonable explanations are dwindling, aren't they?

In this situation, natural death, accidental death, and suicide seem out of the question. While someone may argue they are still *possible*, few would recognize them as *reasonable*. The most reasonable conclusion is simply *murder*. As responsible detectives, you and I would have no choice but to initiate a homicide investigation.

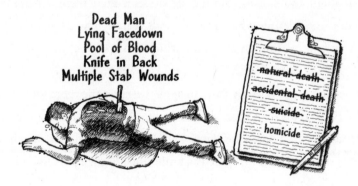

MAKING MORE DIFFICULT DISTINCTIONS

We just used abductive reasoning to determine which explanation most reasonably explained what happened at this scene. It was simple, right? But what if the scenario is more ambiguous than our dead-body scene? What if two competing explanations seem similarly reasonable? Are there any rules or principles to help us distinguish between the most reasonable explanation and a close contender? Well, over the years, I've given this a lot of thought as I've investigated potential homicide suspects in cold-case murders. When considering two or more closely competing explanations for a particular event (or suspects in a murder), I now assess the following factors (keep in mind these terms are mine and may not reflect the language of other philosophers or thinkers):

THE TRUTH MUST BE **FEASIBLE**
(The explanation has explanatory viability)

Before I even begin to think about the evidence related to a particular murder suspect, I need to make sure he or she was available to commit the crime in the first place. I investigate the *defenses* of potential suspects, eliminating those who cannot be involved based on confirmed alibis.

THE TRUTH WILL USUALLY BE **STRAIGHTFORWARD**
(The explanation demonstrates explanatory simplicity)

When considering several suspects, I look for the man or woman who most simply accounts for the evidence. If *one* person's actions can explain the evidence (rather than a theory requiring three or four different potential suspects to account for the same evidence), he or she is most likely the killer.

THE TRUTH SHOULD BE **EXHAUSTIVE**
(The explanation displays explanatory depth)

I also consider the suspect who most exhaustively explains the evidence I have in a case. While a particular suspect may explain one, two, or three pieces of evidence, the suspect who accounts for most (or all) of the evidence is typically the killer.

THE TRUTH MUST BE **LOGICAL**
(The explanation possesses explanatory consistency)

The truth is rational; for this reason, the truth about the identity of my killer must also *make sense*. Suspects commit murders for reasons of one kind or another, even if these reasons seem insufficient to you and me. The true killer will *make sense* to the jury once they understand his or her misguided motivation. Conversely, some candidates will appear logically inconsistent because they lack motive altogether.

5 *THE TRUTH WILL BE **SUPERIOR***
(The explanation achieves explanatory superiority)

Finally, I recognize that one of my suspects is unique in the superior way he or she accounts for the evidence. In essence, this suspect is a far better choice when compared to other candidates. The quality of his or her connection to the evidence is better. When I see this characteristic of *explanatory superiority*, I know I have my killer.

When a suspect meets these five criteria, I am confident I have reached the most reasonable conclusion; I know I have identified the killer.

AN ANCIENT DEATH-SCENE INVESTIGATION

Now it's time to apply this form of reasoning to a death scene that has been the topic of discussion for over two thousand years. What happened to Jesus of Nazareth? How can we explain His empty tomb? Did His disciples steal His body? Was He only injured on the cross and later recovered? Did He truly die and resurrect from the dead? We can approach these questions as detectives, using abductive reasoning.

The question of Jesus's fate might be compared to our dead-body investigation. We examined our death scene by first identifying its *characteristics* (the facts and evidence at the scene). We next acknowledged several potential explanations to account for what we observed. Let's apply this same approach to the alleged death and resurrection of Jesus.

Dr. Gary Habermas[2] and Professor Mike Licona[3] have taken the time to identify the "minimal facts" (or evidences) related to the resurrection. While there are many claims in the New Testament related to this important event, not all are accepted by skeptics and wary investigators.

The *Minimal Facts* Approach

Dr. Gary Habermas (Chair, Department of Philosophy and Theology at Liberty University) has popularized the "minimal facts approach" to examining the resurrection by identifying those aspects of the resurrection story accepted by most scholars and experts (from Christians to nonbelievers). This list of accepted "minimal facts" can then be used as the basis for our process of abductive reasoning.

Habermas and Licona surveyed the most respected and well-established historical scholars and identified several facts *accepted* by most researchers in the field.

They limited their list to those facts that were strongly supported (using the criteria of textual critics) and to those facts that were granted by virtually all scholars (from skeptics to conservative Christians). Habermas and Licona eventually wrote about their findings in *The Case for the Resurrection of Jesus.*[4]

As a skeptic myself, I formed a list of New Testament claims as I first investigated the resurrection. My list was much shorter than the list assembled by Habermas and Licona. As a non-Christian, I only accepted four truths related to the death of Jesus:

1. Jesus died on the cross and was buried.
2. Jesus's tomb was empty, and no one ever produced His body.
3. Jesus's disciples believed they saw Jesus resurrected from the dead.
4. Jesus's disciples were transformed following their alleged resurrection observations.

You'll notice none of these "minimal evidences" necessitate Jesus truly rose from the dead, and I certainly did not believe the resurrection was true. In my view as an atheist, any number of explanations could account for these facts. As I examined these *bare-bones* claims related to the resurrection, I assembled the possible explanations for each assertion (employing the process of abductive reasoning). I quickly recognized every one of these explanations had its own deficiencies and liabilities (including the classic Christian account). Let's examine the potential explanations and list their associated difficulties:

THE DISCIPLES WERE WRONG ABOUT JESUS'S DEATH

Some skeptics believe the disciples were mistaken about Jesus's death on the cross. They propose Jesus survived the beating (and the crucifixion) and simply appeared to the disciples after He recovered.

THE PROBLEMS:

While this proposal seeks to explain the empty tomb, the resurrection observations, and the transformation in the lives of the apostles, it fails to satisfactorily explain what the disciples observed and experienced when they pulled Jesus from the cross. It's been my experience that witnesses who first come upon the dead body of someone they care about quickly check for the most obvious sign of life. Is my friend or loved one *still breathing*? This test is simple and effective; everyone can perform it, and even those who know nothing about human biology have instinctively (and historically) relied on it. The disciples of Jesus would have reasonably checked to see if He was breathing.

In my experience as a homicide detective, I've also observed three conditions common to the bodies of dead people (known as the "Mortis Triad"). When your heart stops pushing warm blood through your body, you begin to lose warmth until you eventually reach the temperature of your environment. Dead people begin to feel "cold to the touch." This condition (known as "algor mortis") is often reported by those who discover the dead. In addition, chemical reactions begin to take place in the muscles after death occurs, resulting in stiffening and rigidity (known as "rigor mortis"). Dead people become rigid, retaining the shape they were in when they died. Finally, when the heart stops pushing your blood, gravity begins to draw it. Blood begins to pool in the bodies of dead people, responding to the force of gravity. As a result, purple discoloration begins to become apparent in those areas of the body closest to the ground (a phenomena known as "livor mortis").

In essence, dead bodies look, feel, and respond differently from living, breathing humans. Dead people, unlike those who are slipping in and out of consciousness, never respond to their injuries. They don't flinch or moan when touched. Is it reasonable to believe those who removed Jesus from the cross, took possession of His body, carried Him to the grave, and spent time treating and wrapping His body for burial would not have noticed any of these conditions common to dead bodies?

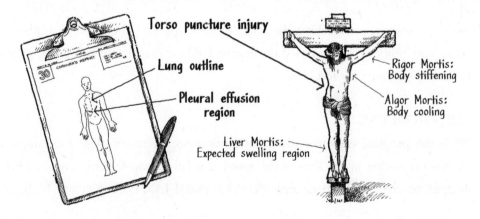

Torso puncture injury

Lung outline

Pleural effusion region

Rigor Mortis: Body stiffening

Algor Mortis: Body cooling

Liver Mortis: Expected swelling region

In addition to this, the Gospels report the guard stabbed Jesus and observed both blood and water pour from his body (refer to John 19:34). That's an important observation, given John was not a coroner or medical doctor. I've been to my share of coroner's autopsies, and I've spoken at length with coroner investigators at crime scenes. When people are injured to the point of death (such as the result of an assault or traffic accident), they often enter some form of "circulatory shock" prior to dying (because their organs and body tissues are not receiving adequate blood flow). This can sometimes result in either "pericardial effusion" (increased fluid in the membrane surrounding the heart) or "pleural effusion" (increased fluid in the membrane surrounding the lungs). When Jesus was pinned to the cross in an upright position following the terrible flogging He received, it's reasonable to expect this kind of effusion might have taken place in response to the circulatory shock He suffered prior to dying. These fluids would certainly pour out of His body if He were pierced with a spear.

While John might expect to see blood, he knew nothing about effusion, and at this point in medical history, his readers were equally unknowledgeable. Perhaps this is why many of the early-church fathers interpreted John's passage *allegorically* or *metaphorically*.[5] Given their limited understanding, they simply could not comprehend how water could literally emerge from the side of Jesus. But if Jesus was already dead when the soldier stabbed Him with the spear, the appearance of water makes sense. This observation by John (made well before effusion was understood medically) is strong evidence Jesus was dead before He was removed from the cross. It is unlikely (and equally unreasonable) John inserted this confusing forensic detail to convince his readers.

In addition to these concerns from the perspective of a homicide detective, there are other problems with the proposal Jesus didn't die on the cross:

1. Many first-century and early second-century *unfriendly* Roman sources (e.g., Thallus, Tacitus, Mara Bar-Serapion, and Phlegon) along with Jewish sources (e.g., Josephus and the Babylonian Talmud) affirmed and acknowledged Jesus was crucified and died.

2. The Roman guards faced death if they allowed a prisoner to survive crucifixion. Would they really be careless enough to remove a living person from a cross?

3. Jesus would need to control His blood loss from the beatings, crucifixion, and stabbing to survive, yet was pinned to the cross and unable to do anything that might achieve this goal.

4. Jesus displayed wounds following the resurrection but was never observed to behave as though He was wounded, even though He appeared only days after His beating, crucifixion, and stabbing.

5. Jesus disappeared from the historical record following His reported resurrection and ascension and was never sighted again (as one might expect if He recovered from His wounds and lived much beyond the young age of thirty-three).

 ## THE DISCIPLES LIED ABOUT THE RESURRECTION

Some non-Christians claim the disciples stole the body from the grave and later fabricated the stories of Jesus's resurrection appearances.

THE PROBLEMS:

While this explanation accounts for the empty tomb and the resurrection observations, it fails to account for the transformed lives of the apostles. In my years working robberies, I had the opportunity to investigate (and break) several conspiracy efforts, and I learned about the nature of successful conspiracies. We'll examine the challenge of conspiracy theories in chapter 7, but until then, let me simply say I am hesitant to embrace any theory requiring the conspiratorial effort of (1) large numbers of people who, (2) don't have significant familial relationships, nor (3) sufficient means by which to communicate, and (4) must sustain the lie over an unreasonably long timespan, while (5) enduring unimaginable pressure. The notion that the resurrection is simply a conspiratorial lie on the part of the apostles requires us to believe these men were transformed and emboldened not by the miraculous appearance of the resurrected Jesus, but by an elaborate conspiracy created without any benefit to those who were perpetuating the hoax.

Too many unrelated conspirators, over an unreasonable timespan, without sufficient communication, and under severe pressure

In addition to this concern from the perspective of a detective, there are other factors to consider when evaluating the claim that the disciples lied about the resurrection:

1. The Jewish authorities took many precautions to make sure the tomb was guarded and sealed, knowing the removal of the body would allow the disciples to claim Jesus had risen (see Matt. 27:62–66).

2. The people local to the event would have known it was a lie (remember Paul told the Corinthians in 1 Corinthians 15:3–8 there were still five hundred people who could testify to having seen Jesus alive after His resurrection).

3. The disciples lacked the motive to create such a lie (more on this in chapter 14).

4. The disciples' transformation following the alleged resurrection is inconsistent with the claim the appearances were only a lie. How could their own lies transform them into courageous evangelists?

 THE DISCIPLES WERE DELUSIONAL

Some skeptics believe the disciples, due to their intense grief and sorrow, only *imagined* seeing Jesus alive after His death on the cross. These critics claim the appearances were simply hallucinations resulting from wishful thinking.

THE PROBLEMS:

This only accounts for the resurrection experiences at first glance and fails to account for the empty tomb or the diversity of the resurrection observations. On those occasions and cases when I suspect someone may have imagined (or simply misinterpreted) an observation, I rely on a *cumulative* approach to establish the truth. Are there additional accounts I can compare to corroborate the statement? What is the most reasonable inference based on all available sources?

The resurrection accounts, for example, are diverse and robust. Jesus appeared to groups of varying sizes, at a variety of locations and times, involving both friends and strangers, for differing purposes and varying periods of time, as recorded by multiple authors.[6] It's unlikely these diverse observations are all simply hallucinations.

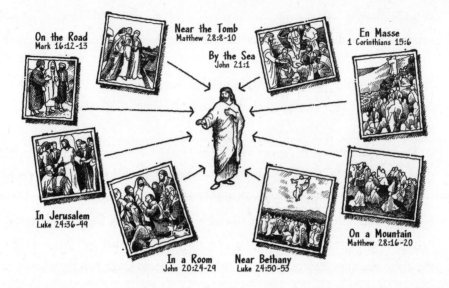

I frequently encounter witnesses who are related in some way to the victim in my case. These witnesses are often profoundly impacted by their grief following the murder. As a result, some allow their sorrow to impact what they remember about the victim. They may, for example, suppress all the negative characteristics of the victim's personality and amplify all the victim's virtues.

Let's face it, we all tend to think the best of people once they have died. But these imaginings are typically limited to the nature of the victim's character and not the elaborate and detailed events that involved the victim in the past. Those closest to the victim may be mistaken about his or her nature, but I've never encountered loved ones who have collectively imagined an identical set of fictional *events* involving the victim.

It's one thing to remember someone with fondness, another to imagine an elaborate and detailed history that never occurred.

In addition to these observations from the perspective of a detective, there are other reasonable concerns when considering the explanation that the disciples hallucinated or imagined the resurrection:

1. While *individuals* hallucinate, there are no examples of large *groups* of people having the exact same hallucination.

2. While a short, momentary group hallucination may seem reasonable, long, sustained, and detailed hallucinations are unsupported historically and intuitively unreasonable.

3. The risen Christ was reportedly seen on more than one occasion by several different groups (and subsets of groups). It's unreasonable these diverse sightings were additional group hallucinations of one nature or another.

4. Not all the disciples were inclined favorably toward such a hallucination. The disciples included people like Thomas, who was skeptical and did not expect Jesus to come back to life.

5. If the resurrection was simply a hallucination, what became of Jesus's corpse? The absence of the body is unexplainable under this scenario.

THE DISCIPLES WERE FOOLED BY AN IMPOSTER

Some nonbelievers have argued an imposter tricked the disciples and convinced them Jesus was still alive; the disciples then unknowingly advanced the lie.

THE PROBLEMS:

While this explanation accounts for the resurrection observations and transformed apostles, it requires an additional set of conspirators (other than the apostles who were later fooled) to accomplish the task of stealing the body.

Many of my partners spent several years investigating fraud and forgery crimes prior to joining us on the homicide team. I've learned a lot from these investigators, including what it takes to pull off a successful con. Accomplished con artists must (1) win the confidence of those they are trying to fool (hence the title "con" artist), and (2) know more about the subject of the deception than the person being deceived. The less the victim understands about the specific topic and area in which they are being "conned," the more likely the con artist will be successful. Victims are often fooled and swindled out of their money because they have little or no expertise in the area in which the con artist is operating. The perpetrator can use sophisticated language and make claims outside the victim's expertise. The crook *sounds* legitimate, primarily because the victim doesn't really know what truly *is* legitimate. When the targeted victim knows more about the subject than the person attempting the con, the odds are good the perpetrator will fail at his attempt to fool the victim.

Win their confidence:
Ponzi: YES
Imposter: No

**Know more than
they do:**
Ponzi: YES
Imposter: No

Charles Ponzi
A Famous Con Artist

An Alleged Imposter
An Unreasonable Con Artist

For this reason, the proposal that a sophisticated first-century con artist fooled the disciples seems unreasonable. There are many concerns with such a theory:

1. The impersonator would need to be familiar enough with Jesus's mannerisms and statements to convince the disciples. The disciples knew the topic of the con better than anyone who might con them.

2. Many of the disciples were skeptical and displayed none of the necessary naïveté that would be required for the con artist to succeed. Thomas, for example, was openly skeptical from the beginning.

3. The impersonator would need to possess miraculous powers; the disciples reported the resurrected Jesus performed many miracles and "convincing proofs" (Acts 1:2–3).

4. Who would seek to start a world religious movement if not one of the hopeful disciples? This theory requires someone *other* than the disciples to impersonate Jesus.

5. This explanation also fails to account for the empty tomb or missing body of Jesus.

5 THE DISCIPLES WERE INFLUENCED BY LIMITED SPIRITUAL SIGHTINGS

More recently, some skeptics have offered the theory that one or two of the disciples had a *vision* of the risen Christ and then convinced the others these spiritual sightings were legitimate. They argue additional sightings simply came as a response to the intense influence of the first *visions*.

THE PROBLEMS:

This proposal may begin to explain the transformation of the apostles, but it fails to explain the empty tomb and offers an explanation inconsistent with the biblical record. It's not unusual to have a persuasive witness influence the beliefs of other eyewitnesses (we'll discuss this in greater detail in chapter 4). I've investigated several murders in which one emphatic witness has persuaded others something occurred, even though the other witnesses weren't even present to see the event for themselves. But these persuaded witnesses were easily distinguished from the one who persuaded them once I began to ask for their account of what happened. Only the persuader possessed the details in their most robust form. For this reason, his or her account was typically the most comprehensive, while the others tended to generalize since they didn't see the event for themselves. In addition, when pressed to repeat the story of the one persuasive witness, the other witnesses eventually pointed to that witness as their source, especially when pressured. While it's possible for a persuasive witness to convince some of the other witnesses his or her version of events is the true story, I've never encountered a *persuader* who could convince *everyone*. The more witnesses involved in a crime, the less likely all of them will be influenced by any one eyewitness, regardless of that witness's charisma or position within the group.

This theory also suffers from all the liabilities of the earlier claim that the disciples imagined the resurrected Christ. Even if the *persuader* could convince everyone of his or her first observation, the subsequent group *visions* are still unreasonable for all the reasons we've already discussed. There are many concerns related to the claim that a select number of *persuaders* convinced the disciples of resurrection:

1. The theory fails to account for the numerous, diverse, and separate group sightings of Jesus that are recorded in the Gospels. These sightings are described specifically with great detail. It's not reasonable to believe all these disciples could provide such specified detail if they were simply repeating something they didn't see for themselves.

2. As many as five hundred people were available to testify to their observations of the risen Christ (according to Paul in 1 Cor. 15:3–8). Could all these people have been influenced to imagine their own observations of Jesus? It's not reasonable to believe someone could persuade all these disciples to proclaim something they didn't truly see.

3. This explanation also fails to account for the empty tomb or the missing corpse.

 ## THE DISCIPLES' OBSERVATIONS WERE DISTORTED LATER

Some unbelievers claim the original observations of the disciples were amplified and distorted as the legend of Jesus grew over time. These skeptics believe Jesus may have been a wise teacher, but argue the resurrection is a legendary and historically late exaggeration.

THE PROBLEMS:

This explanation may account for the empty tomb (if we assume the body was removed), but it fails to explain the early claims of the apostles related to the resurrection (more about this in chapters 11 and 13). Cold-case detectives investigate the possibility of "legendary" distortions more than other types of detectives. Given the passage of time, it seems possible witnesses may now amplify their original observations in one way or another. Fortunately, I have the record of the first investigators to assist me as I try to separate what the eyewitnesses truly saw (and reported at the time of the crime) from what they might recall today. If the original record of the first investigators is thorough and well documented, I will have a much easier time discerning the truth about what each witness saw. In my experience, the first recollections of the eyewitnesses are usually more detailed and reliable than what they might offer thirty years later. Like other cold-case detectives, I rely on the original reports as I compare what witnesses once said to what these witnesses are saying today.

The reliability of the eyewitness accounts related to the resurrection, like the reliability of the cold-case eyewitnesses, must be confirmed by the early documentation of the *first investigators*. For this reason, the claim that the original story of Jesus was a late exaggeration is undermined by several concerns:

1. In the earliest accounts of the disciples' activity after the crucifixion, they are seen citing the resurrection of Jesus as their primary piece of evidence that Jesus was God. From the earliest days of the Christian movement, eyewitnesses were making this claim.

2. The students of the disciples also recorded the resurrection was a key component of the disciples' eyewitness testimony (more on this in chapter 13).

3. The earliest known Christian *creed* or oral record (as described by Paul in 1 Corinthians 15) includes the resurrection as a key component.

4. This explanation also fails to account for the fact the body of Jesus was not produced to demonstrate this late legend was false.

THE DISCIPLES WERE ACCURATELY REPORTING THE RESURRECTION OF JESUS

Christians, of course, claim Jesus truly rose from the dead and the Gospels are accurate eyewitness accounts of this event.

THE PROBLEM:

This explanation accounts for the empty tomb, the resurrection observations, and the transformation of the apostles. It would be naive, however, to accept this explanation without recognizing a liability highlighted by skeptics and nonbelievers. The claim Jesus truly rose from the dead presents the following concern and objection:

This explanation requires a belief in the supernatural: that Jesus had the supernatural power to rise from the dead in the first place.

ABDUCTIVE REASONING AND THE RESURRECTION

I limited the evidence to four modest claims about the resurrection and kept my explanatory options open to all the possibilities (both *natural* and *supernatural*). The last explanation (although it is a miraculous, supernatural explanation) suffers from the least number of liabilities and deficiencies, while retaining the greatest explanatory power.

Allow me to illustrate it a different way. When it comes down to the claims about the resurrection, there are just two possibilities: Jesus either (A) rose from the dead or (B) He didn't. It's really that simple.

As a committed philosophical naturalist who rejected supernatural explanations, I was inclined to select *option B*. But all the naturalistic theories typically offered to explain the evidence related to Jesus were fatally flawed. Each stood as an obstacle, preventing me from reasonably reaching the conclusion the resurrection was untrue.

The Christian explanation for the resurrection involved a far less encumbered path. It only required me to jump one hurdle: my presuppositional bias against the supernatural. If I was willing to enter the investigation without this pre-existing bias, the Christian explanation accounted for the evidence most simply and most exhaustively. It is logically consistent (if we simply allow for the existence of God in the first place). It is also superior to the other accounts (given it does not suffer from all the problems we see with the other explanations).

If we approach the issue of the resurrection in an unbiased manner (without the presuppositions described in the previous chapter) and assess it as we evaluated the dead-body scene, we can judge the possible explanations and eliminate those that are unreasonable. The conclusion that Jesus was resurrected (as reported in the Gospels) can be sensibly inferred from the available evidence. The resurrection *is reasonable*.

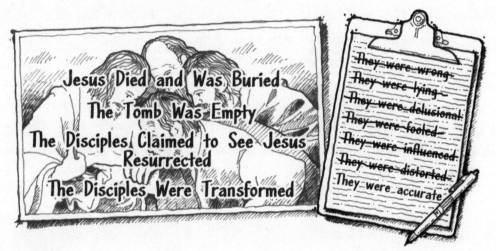

A TOOL FOR THE CALLOUT BAG, A TIP FOR THE CHECKLIST

Okay, let's add another tool to our callout bag: an attitude about *reason* that will help us as we examine and discuss the claims of Christianity. Like other nonbelievers in our world today, I used to think of *faith* as the opposite of *reason*. In this characterization of the dichotomy, I believed atheists were reasonable "freethinkers" while believers were simple, mindless drones who blindly followed the unreasonable teaching of their leadership. But if you think about it, *faith* is actually the opposite of *unbelief,* not *reason*. As I began to read through the Bible as a skeptic, I came to understand that the biblical definition of faith is a well-placed and reasonable inference based on evidence.[7] I wasn't raised in the Christian culture, and I think I have an unusually high amount of respect for evidence. Perhaps this is why this definition of faith comes easily to me. I now understand it's possible for reasonable people to examine the evidence and conclude that Christianity is true. While my skeptical friends may not agree on how the evidence related to the resurrection should be interpreted, I want them to understand I've arrived at my conclusions *reasonably.*

As I speak around the country, I often encounter devoted, committed Christians who are hesitant to embrace an *evidential* faith. In many Christian circles, faith that requires evidential support is seen as weak and inferior. For many, *blind faith* (a faith that simply trusts without question) is the truest, most sincere, and most valuable form of faith we can offer God. Yet Jesus seemed to have a high regard for evidence. In John 14:11, He told those watching Him to examine "the evidence of the miracles" (NIV) if they did not believe what He said about His identity. Even after the resurrection, Jesus stayed with His disciples for an additional forty days and provided them with "many convincing proofs" He was resurrected and was who He claimed to be (Acts 1:2–3 NIV). Jesus understood the role and value of evidence and the importance of developing an evidential faith. It's time for all of us, as Christians, to develop a similarly reasonable faith.

Chapter 3
Principle #3:

THINK "CIRCUMSTANTIALLY"

"I think we're done with this one," I said as I closed the cover of the red three-ring binder. I slipped it back onto the long shelf next to dozens of other *red books* in the homicide vault and looked at my partner. "Now I just have to tell Paula's family."

Our agency stores its cold cases next to our solved murders in a single storage room adjacent to the detective division. Solved homicides are stored in black binders, unsolved in red. The goal is to eventually fill the room with nothing but black binders. After a year with Paula's case, I was frustrated that it was still in a red book.

Paula Robinson was murdered in the spring of 1988. She was a junior in high school, and her murder was a true *whodunit*. The crime scene told us a lot about what happened prior to her death but little about who was responsible. We knew she voluntarily allowed the suspect to enter her parents' house. We knew she had a sandwich with the killer and he smoked a cigarette in the backyard. We also knew the killer was with her in her bedroom, where he tried to sexually assault her and eventually ended up killing her in a horrific rage. This crime scene was one of the worst in the history of our department.

While we knew a few things about the events leading up to the murder, we knew far less about the appearance and identity of the killer. Neighbors saw a young man leaving the residence following the crime, so we had a rough idea of how tall he was and about how much he weighed. But he was wearing a cap that covered his hair, and he fled so quickly that details related to his appearance were hard to come by. We did, however, recover a few of his hairs at the crime scene, and these hairs became our best lead.

The hair provided us with a partial DNA marker—not enough to submit to the statewide database, but enough to compare to anyone we might identify as a potential suspect. All we had to do was make a list of everyone and anyone who might be responsible for this, find them, and collect their DNA. Sounds easy, right? Well, we spent a year identifying, locating, and then traveling around the country to gather DNA swabs from every possible suspect. We swabbed thirty-four different men. All of them voluntarily agreed to be swabbed; we didn't have to write a single search warrant. Why? Because none of them murdered Paula Robinson; none of them had anything to fear. In the end, we ran out of potential suspects. Thirty years after the murder, we simply exhausted our leads in the case and found ourselves without any viable options. It was time to suspend the case once again.

I visited Paula's mother one last time. Her hopes had been elevated when we reopened the case (and she learned we might have a partial DNA marker). We tried to keep her expectations low, given the difficult nature of these kinds of cases, but she couldn't help but get excited about the possibilities.

"Sometimes we have a suspect that fits the evidence and we're able to put together a case, but this is not one of those situations," I tried to explain. "I don't need to have a DNA 'hit' to make a case, but in this situation, the DNA we *do* have has *eliminated* everyone under consideration. I'm sorry." Paula's mother simply sat and wept.

In all my years working cold-case homicides, I've yet to encounter a case I was able to solve with DNA.[1] Most cold-case teams make a living with *DNA hits*, capitalizing on the latest technology and applying new science to old cases. I haven't been that lucky. My experiences with the latest scientific advances have produced results like Paula's case: a lot of work with no progress. Instead, I've been successful assessing cases that have little or no forensic evidence but are replete with what we call *circumstantial* evidence. I only wish Paula's case was one such example.

DIRECT AND CIRCUMSTANTIAL EVIDENCE

Evidence typically falls into two broad categories. Direct evidence is evidence that can prove something all by itself. In California, jurors are given the example of a witness who saw it was raining outside the courthouse. Jurors are instructed, "If a witness testifies he saw it raining outside before he came into the courthouse, that testimony is direct evidence that it was raining."[2] This testimony (if it is trustworthy) is enough, in and of itself, to prove it is raining. On the other hand, circumstantial evidence (also known as *indirect evidence*) does not prove something on its own, but points us in the right direction by proving something *related* to the question at hand. This associated piece of evidence can then be considered (along with additional pieces of circumstantial evidence) to figure out what happened. Jurors in California are instructed, "For example, if a witness testifies that he saw someone come inside wearing a raincoat covered with drops of water, that testimony is circumstantial evidence because it may support a conclusion that it was raining outside."[3] The more pieces of consistent circumstantial evidence, the more reasonable the conclusion. If we observed several people step out of the courthouse for a second then duck back inside soaked with little spots of water on their clothing, or saw more people coming into the courthouse carrying umbrellas and dripping with water, we would have several additional pieces of evidence to make the case it was raining. The more cumulative the circumstantial evidence, the better the conclusion.

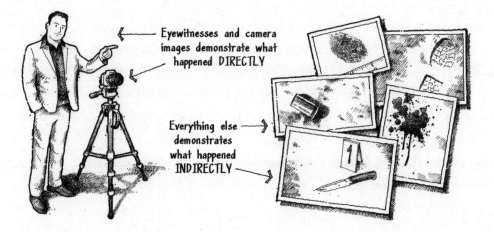

Eyewitnesses and camera images demonstrate what happened DIRECTLY

Everything else demonstrates what happened INDIRECTLY

So, before we go any further, let me dispel two common misperceptions about evidence. First, there is no such thing as "hard evidence." It's simply not a category. So, when someone says, "You don't have any 'hard evidence' this (or that) is true," take a moment to explain the two categories that do exist in criminal trials: *direct* and *indirect evidence*. Secondly, most people tend to think direct evidence is required to be certain about what happened. But what about cases that have no direct evidence connecting the suspect to the crime scene? Can the truth be proven beyond a reasonable doubt when all the evidence we have is circumstantial? Absolutely.

Jurors are instructed to make no qualitative distinction between direct and circumstantial evidence in a case. Judges tell jurors, "Both direct and circumstantial evidence are acceptable types of evidence to prove or disprove the elements of a charge, including intent and mental state and acts necessary to a conviction, and neither is necessarily more reliable than the other. Neither is entitled to any greater weight than the other."[4] Juries make decisions about the guilt of suspects in cases that are *completely* circumstantial every day, and I'm very glad they do; all my cold-case homicides were successfully prosecuted with nothing but circumstantial evidence. Let me give you an example of the power and role of circumstantial evidence in determining the truth of a matter.

MURDER, CIRCUMSTANTIAL EVIDENCE, AND CERTAINTY

Let's examine a hypothetical murder to demonstrate the power of direct and indirect (circumstantial) evidence. I want you to put yourself on the jury as the following case is being presented in court. First, let's lay out the elements of the crime. On a sunny afternoon in a quiet residential neighborhood, the calm was broken by the sound of screaming coming from a house on the corner. The scream was very short and was heard by a neighbor who was watering her lawn next door. This witness peered through the large picture window of the corner house and observed a man assaulting her neighbor in the living room. The man was viciously bludgeoning the victim with a baseball bat. The witness next saw the suspect open the front door of the house and run from the residence with the bloody bat in hand; she got a long look at his face as he ran to a car parked directly in front of the victim's residence.

An Eyewitness is 100%
Certain She Can Identify
the Suspect

If this witness was now sitting on the witness stand, testifying the defendant in our case was, in fact, the man she saw murdering the victim, she would be providing us with a piece of *direct evidence*. If we came to trust what this witness had to say, this one piece of direct evidence would be enough to prove the defendant committed the murder. But what if things had been a little bit different? What if the suspect in our case had been wearing a mask when he committed the murder? If this were the case, our witness would be unable to identify the killer directly (facially) and would only be able to provide us with scant information. She could tell us about the killer's general build and what kind of clothing he was wearing, but little more. With this information alone, it would be difficult to prove our defendant was the true killer.

The Eyewitness is now Unable to Identify the Suspect

Now, let's imagine detectives developed a potential suspect (named Ron Jacobsen) and began to collect information about his activity at the time of the murder. When detectives questioned Ron, he hesitated to provide them with an alibi. When he finally *did* offer a story, detectives investigated it and determined it was a lie. Based on the fact Ron lied, do you think he is guilty of this murder? He fits the general physical description offered by the witness and he has lied about his alibi. We now have two pieces of circumstantial evidence pointing to Ron as the killer, but without something more, few of us would be willing to convict him. Let's see what else the detectives were able to discover.

During the interview with Ron, they learned he had recently broken up with the victim after a tumultuous romantic relationship. He admitted to arguing with her recently about this relationship and was extremely nervous whenever detectives focused on her. He repeatedly tried to minimize his relationship with her. Are you any closer to returning a verdict on Ron? He fits the general description, lied about his alibi, and seems suspiciously nervous and evasive in the interview. It's not looking good for Ron, but there may be other reasonable explanations for what we've seen so far. Even though we have three pieces of circumstantial evidence pointing to Ron's involvement in this crime, there still isn't enough to be certain of his guilt.

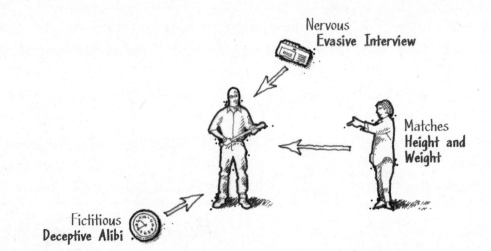

Nervous
Evasive Interview

Matches
Height and
Weight

Fictitious
Deceptive Alibi

The Sufficiency of Circumstantial Evidence

"Before you may rely on circumstantial evidence to conclude that a fact necessary to find the defendant guilty has been proved, you must be convinced that the People have proved each fact essential to that conclusion beyond a reasonable doubt. Also, before you may rely on circumstantial evidence to find the defendant guilty, you must be convinced that the only reasonable conclusion supported by the circumstantial evidence is that the defendant is guilty. If you can draw two or more reasonable conclusions from the circumstantial evidence, and one of those reasonable conclusions points to innocence and another to guilt, you must accept the one that points to innocence. However, when considering circumstantial evidence, you must accept only reasonable conclusions and reject any that are unreasonable" (Section 224, Judicial Council of California Criminal Jury Instructions, 2006).

What if I told you responding officers found that the suspect in this case entered the victim's residence and appeared to be waiting for her when she returned home? There were no signs of forced entry into the home, however, and detectives later learned Ron was one of only two people who had a key to the victim's house, allowing him access whenever he wanted. Ron certainly seems a "person of interest" now, doesn't he? Ron matches the general description, has lied to investigators, is nervous and evasive, and had a way to enter the victim's house. The circumstantial case is growing stronger with every revelation.

What if you learned the investigators were approached by a friend of Ron's who found a suicide note at Ron's house? This note was dated on the day of the murder and described Ron's desperate state of mind and his desire to kill himself on the afternoon that followed the homicide. Ron apparently overcame his desire to die, however, and never took his own life. The fact Ron was suicidal immediately following the murder adds to the cumulative case against him, but is it enough to tip the scales and convince you he is the killer? It was certainly enough to motivate the detectives to dig a little deeper. Given all this suspicious evidence, a judge agreed to sign a search warrant and detectives served this warrant at Ron's house. There they discovered several important pieces of circumstantial evidence.

The Cumulative Nature of Circumstantial Evidence

The nature of circumstantial evidence is such that any one piece may be interpreted in more than one way. For this reason, jurors must be careful not to infer something from a single piece of evidence. Circumstantial evidence usually accumulates into a powerful collection, however, and each additional piece corroborates those coming before until, together, they strongly support one inference over another.

An explanation derived from circumstantial evidence becomes more reasonable as the collection of corroborating evidence grows and the alternative explanations have been deemed unreasonable.

First, they discovered a baseball bat hidden under Ron's bed. This bat was dented and damaged in a way that was inconsistent with its use as a piece of sporting equipment, and when the crime lab did chemical tests, detectives learned that while the bat tested negative for the presence of blood, it displayed residue indicating it had been recently washed with bleach. In addition to this, investigators also discovered a pair of blue jeans that had been chemically spot-cleaned in two areas on the front of the legs. Like the bat, the jeans tested negative for blood but demonstrated some form of household cleaner had been used in two specific areas to remove something. Finally, detectives recovered a pair of boots from Ron's house. The witness described the boots she saw on the suspect and told responding officers these boots had a unique stripe on the side. The boots at Ron's house also had a stripe, and after some investigation with local vendors, detectives learned this unusual brand of boot was relatively rare in this area. Only two stores carried the boot and only ten pairs had been sold in the entire county in the past five years. Ron happened to own one of these ten pairs.

There are many pieces of circumstantial evidence now pointing to Ron as the killer. He had access to the victim's house, lied about his activity on the day of the murder, behaved suspiciously in the interview, appeared suicidal after the murder, and was in possession of a suspicious bat matching the murder weapon, a pair of questionably spot-cleaned pants, and a set of rare boots matching the suspect description. At this point in our assessment, I think many of you as jurors are becoming comfortable with the reasonable conclusion Ron is our killer. But there is more.

Our eyewitness at the crime scene observed the suspect as he ran to his getaway car, and she described this car to the detectives. The witness believed the suspect was driving a mustard-colored, early '70s Volkswagen Karmann Ghia. When executing the search warrant at Ron's house, detectives discovered (you guessed it) a yellow 1972 Karmann Ghia parked in his garage. After examining the motor vehicle records for the entire state, they discovered there was only one operational Karmann Ghia registered in the entire state.

Is Ron the killer? Given all we know about the crime, the only reasonable conclusion is that Ron is the man who committed the murder. Is it *possible* Ron is just unlucky enough to suffer from an unfortunate alignment of coincidences making him appear guilty when he is not? Yes, anything is *possible*. But is it *reasonable*? No. Everything points to Ron, and when the evidence is considered cumulatively, Ron's guilt is the only reasonable conclusion. While there may be other explanations for these individual pieces of evidence, they are not reasonable when considered as a whole. Remember that, as a juror, you are being asked to return a verdict based on what's reasonable, not what's possible.

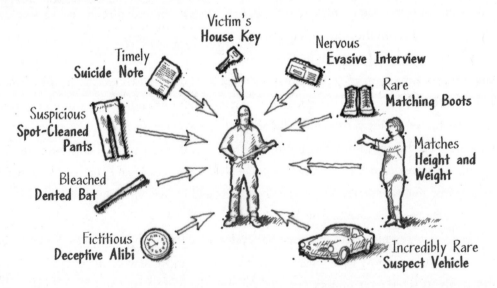

Victim's
House Key

Timely
Suicide Note

Nervous
Evasive Interview

Rare
Matching Boots

Suspicious
Spot-Cleaned
Pants

Matches
Height and
Weight

Bleached
Dented Bat

Fictitious
Deceptive Alibi

Incredibly Rare
Suspect Vehicle

Our case against Ron is entirely circumstantial; we don't have a single piece of forensic or eyewitness evidence linking him directly. These are the kinds of cases I assemble every year as I bring cold-case murderers to trial. The case against Ron is compelling and overwhelmingly sufficient. If you, as a juror, understand the nature and power of circumstantial evidence, you should be able to render a *guilty* verdict in this case.

THE COSMIC CIRCUMSTANTIAL CASE

The question of God's existence might be compared to our murder investigation. We assembled the circumstantial evidence and asked the question "How reasonable is it this evidence can be interpreted in any way *other* than to indicate Ron did this?" As the evidence set *grew*, the likelihood of Ron's innocence *shrank*. Similarly, we can look at the evidence in our world (and in the universe) and ask, "How reasonable is it this evidence can be interpreted in any way other than to confirm the existence of God?" We live in a universe filled with characteristics (evidence) demanding an explanation. Let's consider just a few of them:

A UNIVERSE WITH A BEGINNING

The vast majority of scientists continue to acknowledge the universe came into being from nothing at some point in the distant past. Many have articulated this as the "Big Bang" theory (commonly referred to as the Standard Model of Cosmology). But if the universe "began to exist," what "began" it? What caused the first domino to fall in the long sequence of cause-and-effect dominoes? If this first domino fell over as the result of being toppled by some other domino, how far back does this sequence go? Scientists understand the absurdity of an endless

"Causal" Evidence

The Cosmological Argument:

(1) Anything that begins to exist has a cause

(2) The universe began to exist

(3) Therefore, the universe must have a cause

(4) This cause must be eternal and uncaused

(5) God is the most reasonable explanation for such an uncaused first cause

sequence of dominoes spanning back into infinite eternity; everyone is looking for an "uncaused first cause" capable of starting the domino run all by itself. This "uncaused first cause" must exist outside of space, time, and matter (as nothing has ever been observed to cause itself to exist). What could be uncaused and powerful enough to cause the universe? If the *caused universe* once was *not*, why is it here at all? As Gottfried Leibniz famously wrote, "Why is there something rather than nothing?"[5]

We typically think of God as an eternal, all-powerful Being who exists outside of space, time, and matter. The evidence of the finite universe (a universe that has a beginning) points circumstantially to the existence of such a God. An incredibly powerful, uncaused first cause outside of space, time, and matter appears necessary to bring our universe into existence. If an eternal, all-powerful Being exists, Leibniz's famous question has an answer. A Being of this nature might freely choose to create a universe demonstrating His power and serving as a place where His cherished creatures could begin to understand His nature. The causal evidence of the universe is a significant piece of circumstantial evidence for God's existence.

A UNIVERSE WITH THE APPEARANCE OF DESIGN

Science has also helped us to understand the universe appears remarkably "fine-tuned" to support the existence of life. There are several forces in the cosmos precisely calibrated to work together to make life possible. The laws of electron mass, atomic mass, proton mass, strong nuclear force, weak nuclear force, speed of light, cosmological constant, gravity, mass of the universe, and many more are finely tuned to govern the universe and our world. Even within the atom itself, the precise relationship between protons, neutrons, and electrons appears fine-tuned and calibrated. According to Stephen Hawking, "if the proton-neutron mass difference were not about twice the mass of the electron, one would not obtain the couple of hundred or so stable nucleides that make up the elements and are the basis of chemistry and biology."[6] The forces in our universe, both small and large, appear fine-tuned to make life possible.

In addition to these cosmic and atomic forces, there are also specific conditions necessary for a planet to support life. If, for example, the size of the earth were altered slightly, life would not be possible on the planet. When a planet is too small, it loses internal heat and cannot keep its interior core active; if a planet is too large, it will likely possess an overabundance of water and an overly thick atmosphere. As it turns out, the characteristics of a planet must be *just so* for life to be possible. The presence of liquid water, the proper distance from a star, the existence of a terrestrial crust, a properly proportioned magnetic field, the correct ratio of oxygen to nitrogen in the atmosphere, the existence of a large moon, and a mother star of a specific size and type are all required. The path leading to life on earth seems narrow and difficult, yet the forces governing the universe (and our world) appear to have a goal in mind: the production of a universe in which carbon-based life can emerge.

How can random forces be so conspicuously aligned and organized to support life? Is it merely a coincidence? That's certainly *possible*, but is it *reasonable*? If God exists, He can fine-tune the universe, and He just might have a reason to do so. The Bible, for example, describes God as "the Maker of heaven and earth" (Ps. 115:15), and describes Him as the Being who designed and created the universe with the earth in mind. The fine-tuning of the universe is another important piece of circumstantial evidence pointing to the existence of an intentional, supernatural, powerful, and creative Being.

"Fine-Tuning" Evidence

The Anthropic Principle:

(1) The physical constants and laws of the universe appear uniquely and specifically related to one another (fine-tuned), making life possible on earth

(2) The fine-tuned relationships of these laws and constants appear designed (as their existence by natural, unguided means seems improbable and unlikely)

(3) A design requires an intelligent designer; an incredibly vast and complex design requires an incredibly intelligent and powerful designer

(4) God is the most reasonable explanation for such a vast, universal designer (and fine-tuner)

A UNIVERSE WITH COMPLEX LIFE

Scientists observe what they call the "appearance of design" in biological systems. Even Richard Dawkins (the renowned and vocal atheist and emeritus fellow of New College, Oxford) concedes that biological systems often appear designed[7] (although he proposes a blind, natural process can somehow account for this appearance). There are many examples of cellular biological *machines* possessing characteristics of "specified complexity" and bearing a striking resemblance to systems and structures designed by humans (intelligent agents). These characteristics lead many to the reasonable belief that unguided forces are simply insufficient to create such structures.

William Dembski (the well-known mathematician, statistician, theologian, and intelligent-design advocate) has argued specified complexity (and, therefore, the intervention of an intelligent agent) can be identified by using an "explanatory filter." If an object or event (1) cannot be explained by some natural law necessitating its appearance, (2) exists despite the high improbability it could occur as the result of chance, and (3) conforms to an independently existing and recognizable pattern, it is most reasonable to infer it is the product of an intelligent designer.[8]

"Design" Evidence

The Teleological Argument:

(1) Structures and systems that (a) cannot be explained by some natural law requiring their appearance, (b) exist despite the high improbability they could result from chance, and (c) conform to an independently existing and recognizable pattern are most reasonably explained as coming from the design efforts of an intelligent agent

(2) Biological systems possess characteristics (i.e., the information contained in the DNA code) that (1) cannot be explained by some natural law requiring their appearance, (2) exist despite the high improbability they could result from chance, and (3) conform to an independently existing and recognizable pattern of specified complexity

(3) Biological systems are, therefore, most reasonably explained as coming from the design efforts of an intelligent agent

(4) God is the most reasonable explanation for such an incredibly wise, all-powerful intelligent agent

Perhaps the most important evidence suggesting the involvement of an intelligent designer is the presence of DNA and the guiding role this DNA plays in the formation of biological systems. DNA is a digital code of sorts; it contains specified *information*. When examined through Dembski's explanatory filter, DNA is best explained by the creative activity of an intelligent designer.

Let me offer an illustration to make the point. Imagine we are still at the scene of our DBR ("Dead Body Report") from the prior chapter. All we have this time, however, is a young man, lying on the floor of his apartment, cold to the touch, non-responsive, with a large cut on his forehead. In this version of the death scene, the man is also lying next to a wall, and we find blood spatter on the surface of this wall, near the body. Once again, we are tasked with determining if this is a natural death, an accident, a suicide, or a homicide.

The blood spatter evidence may—*or may not*—tell us much about what happened here. The pattern on the wall may simply be the result of the chemical nature of blood and the physics of the event that led to his death. He may, for example, have simply stumbled after a heart attack or tripped accidentally on the carpet, hitting his head and accounting for the injury that led to the spatter.

Now let's change the scenario. Imagine this time we find the same man on the floor, but on the wall next to the body we find the words "he deserved it" written in the victim's blood. Should we start looking for a suspect, and if so, *why*? You know the answer *intuitively*. While natural forces like physics and chemistry might account for the spatter in the first scenario, the information and message in the second scenario is best explained by an *intelligent agent*. If you encountered that information in the death scene, you would immediately, and *reasonably*, infer the need to open a homicide investigation.

This same intuitive impulse can be applied to investigating the origin of the information we find in DNA. As Stephen C. Meyer argues in his book *Signature in the Cell*, "Intelligence is the *only known cause* of complex functionally integrated information-processing systems"

(italics original).[9] In other words, in the history of scientific and intellectual research, we can find no example in which information came from anything other than an intelligent source. If DNA is a form of specified information guiding the complex process of cellular formation and biological structures, "intelligent design stands as the best—most causally adequate—explanation for this feature of the cell, just as it stands as the best explanation for the origin of the information present in DNA itself."[10]

If biological systems display characteristics of *design* (in the form of specified complexity), it is reasonable to conclude a *designer* was involved in the process. What kind of designer could be responsible for the information, complexity, and specificity we see in biological systems? If God exists, He would certainly possess the characteristics and power to accomplish such a thing. The presence of specified information in biological systems is yet another piece of circumstantial evidence pointing to the existence of God.

A UNIVERSE WITH OBJECTIVE MORALITY

Each and every one of us feels a certain obligation to *moral duty*. We have an intuitive sense of moral *oughtness*; we recognize some things are right and some things are wrong, regardless of culture, time, or location. We understand it's never morally *right* to lie, steal, or kill for the mere *fun* of it. These moral laws are transcendent and objective: their truth is not a matter of subjective opinion. Regardless of how you or I might *feel* about these laws, the truth of their moral status lies in the actions themselves, not in our subjective opinions about the actions. We may discover moral truth, but we do not invent it. Because of this, we can look across history and culture and make meaningful judgments about the moral *rightness* or *wrongness* of any given set of actions. We recognize culture itself cannot be the source of moral law, and there is instead a "law above laws" transcending all of us. So, from where does transcendent, objective moral truth come?

All moral laws come from moral lawmakers. If there exists even one transcendent moral law (e.g., it's never morally *right* to kill someone for the mere *fun* of it), there must exist a transcendent moral *source*.

Darwinian evolution has great difficulty accounting for the existence of objective moral obligations for two reasons. First, if we live in a purely natural, physical world governed by the "cause and effect" relationships between chemical processes in our brains, "free will" is an illusion, and the idea of true moral choice is nonsensical. How can I, as a detective, hold a murderer accountable for a series of chemical reactions that occurred in his brain when he didn't have the freedom to escape the causal chain of biological events?

In addition to this, Darwinian evolution cannot produce truly objective morality. If moral truths are merely behavioral concepts humans created to aid their survival, morality is once again rooted in subjects (humans) rather than in the objective moral truth claim under consideration (e.g., whether it's ever morally *right* to kill someone for the mere *fun* of it). If morality is simply a convention of our species, we'd better hope science-fiction writers are wrong about the possibility of sentient life in other parts of the universe. Unless there is a "law above the laws," an entity such as *Star Trek*'s United Federation of Planets would be powerless to stop immoral behavior. Objective morality must be rooted in something bigger than the evolutionary development of any one species.

"Moral" Evidence

The Axiological Argument:

(1) There is an objective, transcendent moral law

(2) Every moral law has a moral law giver

(3) Therefore, there is an objective, transcendent moral law giver

(4) God is the most reasonable explanation for such a transcendent moral law giver

If God exists, He would certainly transcend all species, cultures, locations, and moments in time. For this reason, the existence of transcendent moral truth is best explained by the existence of God as the transcendent source of such truth. Once again, we have an important piece of circumstantial evidence.

The cumulative circumstantial case for God's existence is much like the circumstantial case we made in our murder investigation. The more evidence we gathered, the clearer was Ron's involvement as the killer. Ron was either incredibly unlucky or incredibly guilty. At some point we recognized the evidence made Ron's guilt the only reasonable inference, and we got there without a single piece of direct evidence.

In a similar way, the circumstantial evidence in our universe is consistent with God's existence and involvement as the uncaused first cause, the fine-tuner, the designer, and the moral law giver required to account for all the evidence we observe. As in the homicide investigation, the more evidence we gather, the more reasonable our conclusion becomes. We've only briefly described four lines of circumstantial evidence for God's existence. I've written about eight lines of evidence for God in *God's Crime Scene: A Cold-Case Detective Examines the Evidence for a Divinely Created Universe*, and I've listed several expert witnesses at the end of this book. In addition to the evidence I've offered, investigators and philosophers have proposed many additional arguments (including the Ontological Argument, the Transcendental Argument, the Argument from Religious or Aesthetic Experience, and many more).

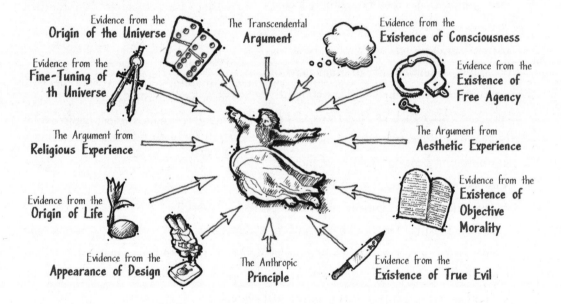

The cumulative circumstantial evidence pointing to God's existence is either incredibly coincidental or a compelling indication of the truth of the matter. At some point, God's existence is the only reasonable inference considering the evidence, and like our homicide, we can get there without a single piece of direct (or forensic) evidence.

As the circumstantial case against Ron grew, the likelihood of his guilt *also* grew. As the circumstantial case for God grows, the likelihood of His existence *also* grows. If the evidence for Ron's guilt is compelling enough to reasonably conclude he is guilty, the evidence for God's existence is compelling enough to reasonably conclude He exists.

A TOOL FOR THE CALLOUT BAG, A TIP FOR THE CHECKLIST

It's time to add another principle to our investigative checklist as we assemble the tools we'll need to investigate and communicate the claims of Christianity. Circumstantial evidence has been unfairly maligned over the years; it's important to recognize this form of evidence is *not* inferior in the eyes of the law. In fact, there are times when you can trust circumstantial evidence far more than you can trust direct evidence. Witnesses, for example, can lie or be mistaken about their observations; they must be evaluated before they can be trusted (we'll talk about that in the next chapter). Circumstantial evidence, on the other hand, cannot lie; it is what it is. You and I can assess and make an inference from the circumstantial evidence using our own reasoning power to come to a reasonable inference. It's not a coincidence that I was a nonbeliever before I learned anything about the nature of evidence. In those days, as I was evaluating the claims of Christianity, I demanded a form of evidence (direct evidence) that simply isn't available to anyone who is studying historical events. I failed to see that rejecting (or devaluing) circumstantial evidence would prevent me from understanding anything about history (once eyewitnesses of a particular event are unavailable for an interview). If I continued to reject (or devalue) circumstantial evidence, I would never have been able to successfully prosecute a single cold-case killer. All of us need to respect the power and nature of circumstantial evidence in determining truth so we can be fair when evaluating the role circumstantial evidence plays in making the case for Christianity.

I'm alarmed sometimes when I hear Christians make inaccurate statements related to the nature of evidence. When discussing evidence with skeptics, we don't need to concede that a particular fact related to the Christian worldview has no evidential value simply because it is not an example of *direct* evidence. Even though a particular fact may not have the individual power to prove our case in its *entirety*, it is no less valid as we assemble the cumulative evidence. When we treat circumstantial evidence as though it is not evidence at all, we do ourselves a disservice as ambassadors for the Christian worldview. Circumstantial evidence is powerful *if* it is properly understood. When defending our belief in the existence of God, the resurrection of Jesus, or the validity of the Christian worldview, we may need to take some time to explain the nature, role, and power of circumstantial evidence. It's time well spent, because most of our friends, family members, and coworkers have not given this much thought. We need to help people understand the depth and quantity of the evidence supporting our view. Remember, circumstantial cases are powerful when they are cumulative. The more evidence pointing to a specific explanation, the more reasonable the explanation (and the more unlikely the evidence can be explained away as coincidental). Take the time to discover and master the evidence for yourself so you can articulate the deep, rich, and robust evidential support for the claims of Christianity.

Chapter 4
Principle #4:

TEST YOUR WITNESSES

"Mr. Strickland, how can you be so sure this man is the same man who robbed you?" The defendant's attorney stood up as he examined the witness and pointed to the man sitting next to him at the defense table. His questions were becoming more accusatory. "Isn't it true the robbery occurred well after sunset?"

"Well, yes, it was about ten thirty at night." Jerry Strickland seemed to be preparing himself for an attack. He correctly interpreted the tone of the attorney's question and straightened himself in the witness box. He scratched his arm nervously. I knew Strickland was a smart guy, and I was curious to see how he would hold up under this pressure. I was working the robbery-homicide desk when I was assigned this case, and I knew it would all come down to Strickland's identification of the suspect.

"I notice you are wearing glasses today, but isn't it true you weren't wearing those glasses on the night of the robbery?" The defense attorney began to walk slowly toward Mr. Strickland, his arms crossed, his chin slightly elevated as he glanced briefly at the jury.

"I had my glasses on to start with, but I got punched and they flew off my head," replied Strickland as he pushed his glasses up on his nose. "After that I'm not sure what happened to them." Jerry's testimony started off calmly enough under the direct questioning of the deputy district attorney, but now he seemed to be losing his confidence under the pressure of the cross-examination.

"How long did this episode with your attacker last?" the defense attorney asked.

"Just a few seconds," replied Strickland.

"So let me get this right. You're willing to send my client to jail for years, yet you only saw the suspect for a few seconds, late at night, in the dark, without the benefit of your glasses?" The defendant's attorney was now facing the jury. His question was rhetorical; he made his point and was now watching the jury to see if it had the impact he intended.

"Well, I-I'm not sure what to say," Strickland stammered hesitantly as he sank in his chair.

The prosecutor was an energetic, competent attorney who understood the value of this victim's eyewitness testimony. She waited for the defense attorney to return to his seat and then prepared for her redirect. "Mr. Strickland, you said earlier you were robbed by this man. I want to ask you a question. Given your observations of the robber prior to the moment when he punched you; your observations of the suspect's height, the shape and features of his face, his body type, and the structure of his physique, I want you to rate your certainty about the identity of the suspect. On a scale of one to one hundred, how certain are you this man sitting here at the defendant's table is the man who robbed you?"

Jerry Strickland sat up in his chair and leaned forward. He paused just slightly before answering, "I am one hundred percent certain this is the man who robbed me. There is no doubt in my mind."

The jury returned a verdict in less than thirty minutes and convicted the defendant, largely on the strength of Strickland's eyewitness testimony. While the defense attorney did his best to illustrate the potential limits of the victim's ability to accurately describe the suspect, the jury was convinced Jerry Strickland was a competent eyewitness. They believed his testimony, and the rest was easy. Once you come to trust an eyewitness, you eventually must come to terms with the testimony that eyewitness has offered.

LEARNING TO TRUST AN EYEWITNESS

So, how do we come to trust what an eyewitness has to say? How can we evaluate a witness to make sure he or she is someone we can trust in the first place? Jurors are asked to evaluate witnesses in court cases every day. If you were sitting on a jury in the state of California today, the judge would advise you about assessing the witnesses who are about to testify before you. In fact, the judge would tell you to consider several factors and ask yourself the following questions:

1. How well could the witness see, hear, or otherwise perceive the things about which the witness testified?

2. How well was the witness able to remember and describe what happened?

3. What was the witness's behavior while testifying?

4. Did the witness understand the questions and answer them directly?

5. Was the witness's testimony influenced by a factor such as bias or prejudice, a personal relationship with someone involved in the case, or a personal interest in how the case is decided?

6. What was the witness's attitude about the case or about testifying?

7. Did the witness make a statement in the past that is consistent or inconsistent with his or her testimony?

8. How reasonable is the testimony when you consider all the other evidence in the case?

9. [Did other evidence prove or disprove any fact about which the witness testified?]

10. [Did the witness admit to being untruthful?]

11. [What is the witness's character for truthfulness?]

12. [Has the witness been convicted of a felony?]

13. [Has the witness engaged in (other) conduct that reflects on his or her believability?]

14. [Was the witness promised immunity or leniency in exchange for his or her testimony?][1]

These are the questions jurors are encouraged to ask as they evaluate witnesses who testify in court. Sometimes witnesses are testifying in trials that are a matter of life and death—trials involving defendants who may ultimately face the death penalty. In the end, there are four critical areas of concern when it comes to evaluating an eyewitness:

 WERE THEY EVEN THERE?

First, we've got to find out if the witness was even present to observe anything in the first place. This concern is captured by questions like, "How well could the witness see, hear, or otherwise perceive the things about which the witness testified?" You might think this is a silly issue to examine, but I can tell you from personal experience there are times when people claim to be a witness or participant in a case when they, in fact, were nowhere near the event. I reopened a case from the early 1970s my father helped investigate when he was working homicides. I remembered the case as a boy and the stress it caused my dad when it went unsolved. The case was well known in the region and received an incredible amount of publicity.

Assume the Witness Is Trustworthy

Jurors have a duty to take an unbiased look at witnesses and assume the best in them until they have a reason to do otherwise. Jurors are told to "set aside any bias or prejudice (they) may have, including any based on the witness's gender, race, religion, or national origin." In addition, jurors are instructed: "If the evidence establishes that a witness's character for truthfulness has not been discussed among the people who know him or her, you may conclude from the lack of discussion that the witness's character for truthfulness is good" (Section 105, Judicial Council of California Criminal Jury Instructions, 2006).

As I examined the cold case thirty years later, I discovered the original investigators had been deceived by a man who came forward and confessed to being the killer. He sat with detectives over the course of many days and offered just enough detail to convince them he had murdered the victim. In truth, he had nothing to do with the crime, but was seeking the attention and twisted fame it brought him. He was eventually exposed as a fraud, but his involvement in the case distracted the investigators long enough to take them off the trail of the real killer. This kind of thing happens in high-profile cases offering fifteen minutes of fame. This is why we need to make sure an eyewitness was truly present to see what he or she claims to have seen.

HAVE THEY BEEN HONEST AND ACCURATE OVER TIME?

The primary concern most of us have when evaluating witnesses is the issue of *credibility*. A witness who was present at the time of the crime but who is lying about what happened is of no value. The jury instructions address this issue with questions like, "Did the witness make a statement in the past that is consistent or inconsistent with his or her testimony?" In recent years, with the large number of court cases publicized and broadcast nationally, we've all seen examples of witnesses who were discredited as liars.

Robert Durst, for example, was an American real-estate heir suspected of killing his wife, Kathleen McCormack, in 1982. He was also believed to be involved in the murder of Susan Berman in 2000 and was later tried for the murder of Morris Black in 2001. His famous story was chronicled in the Hollywood movie *All Good Things* and in the HBO documentary

The Jinx: The Life and Deaths of Robert Durst. He was eventually charged with the murder of Susan Berman (at the time a cold case in Los Angeles County) and stood trial in 2021. The prosecutor in the case, John Lewin, was my partner throughout my career as a cold-case detective. In fact, the Durst case was John's first case without me, following my retirement.

Durst took the stand as a witness during this trial and attempted to describe several events from his past, including the events surrounding the death of Susan Berman. During John's cross-examination, however, Durst admitted to having lied repeatedly about the same events when he testified under oath in the Morris Black trial years earlier. When the jury discovered Durst had lied previously, they doubted anything he had to say presently. When a witness is caught lying in the past, his or her testimony about the case can be called into question. It's important, however, to remember jurors are also given this instruction by the judge:

> If you decide that a witness deliberately lied about something significant in
> this case, you should consider not believing anything that witness says. Or, if
> you think the witness lied about some things, but told the truth about others,
> you may simply accept the part that you think is true and ignore the rest.[2]

There may be a good reason for a witness to lie about something unrelated to the case (perhaps to avoid embarrassment or to protect the privacy of a loved one), yet still tell the truth about what he or she saw in the crime under consideration. Let's face it, all of us have lied in the past for one reason or another. Jurors must decide if a witness has simply lied on occasion (for some understandable reason) or is an untrustworthy, habitual liar. In the Robert Durst case, the jurors decided the witness was the latter.

CAN THEY BE VERIFIED?

It's fair to ask if a witness's observations can be verified by some other piece of evidence or testimony. This concern is captured in questions like, "How reasonable is the testimony when you consider all the other evidence in the case?" or "Did other evidence prove or disprove any fact about which the witness testified?" If a witness tells you the defendant committed a robbery at a bank teller's counter, and you learn the defendant's fingerprints were discovered on the counter, this corroborating fingerprint evidence will help you verify what the eyewitness has to say. The direct evidence of additional eyewitnesses can also verify a statement, and circumstantial evidence (forensic or otherwise) can help validate what a witness has offered.

DO THEY HAVE AN ULTERIOR MOTIVE?

Finally, jurors must decide if a witness has a motive to lie. That's why the jury instructions include questions like, "Was the witness's testimony influenced by a factor such as bias or prejudice, a personal relationship with someone involved in the case, or a personal interest in how the case is decided?" I've investigated several assault cases involving friends, family members, and spouses. In many of these cases, *both* parties exhibited injuries of one kind or another. Trying to get to the truth of the matter was extremely difficult. Both sides were angry enough to do or say anything to get the other person in trouble. Each appeared to have a motive to lie or exaggerate, and jurors had difficulty discerning the truth amid all the anger and embellishment.

These four critical areas should be examined before we trust an eyewitness. If we can establish a witness was present, has been accurate and honest over time, is verified by additional evidence, and has no motive to lie, we can trust what the witness has to say.

his statement is accurate

his statement is verified

The Witness is Reliable

his statement is timely

his statement is attested

SO, WHY CAN'T THEY AGREE?

If there's one thing my experience as a detective has revealed, however, it's this: multiple witnesses often make conflicting and inconsistent statements when describing what they saw at a crime scene. They frequently disagree with one another and either fail to see something obvious or describe the same event in seemingly conflicting ways. In fact, the more witnesses involved in a case, the more likely there will be points of disagreement.

Many years ago, a murder occurred in the parking lot of an Italian restaurant in our city. It happened late at night during a rainstorm, well after our homicide team went home for the day. Patrol officers responded to the scene and discovered the suspect was already long gone. The officers located three witnesses and interviewed them very briefly. They quickly recognized the murder investigation would require the involvement of our team. Radio dispatch called our sergeant, and he began waking us up by telephone, summoning four of us to handle the investigation. It took me nearly an hour to get into a suit and drive to the location of the crime. When I got there, I discovered the officers had gathered the witnesses and put them in the back seat of their police unit so they wouldn't get drenched in the rain. This simple act of kindness nearly ruined the case.

The murder at the Italian restaurant taught me a valuable lesson. From that point on, whenever I got called in the middle of the night to the scene of a murder, there was one request I made of the dispatcher: tell the officers on scene to separate the eyewitnesses immediately. When eyewitnesses are quickly separated from one another, they are far more likely to provide an uninfluenced, pure account of what they saw. Yes, their accounts will inevitably differ from the accounts of others who witnessed the same event. Every witness is influenced by his or her personal experiences, geographic location related to the crime, likes and dislikes, perspective, and worldview. I can deal with the inconsistencies; I expect them. But when witnesses are allowed to sit together (prior to being interviewed) and compare notes and observations, I'm likely to get one harmonized version of the event. Everyone will offer the same story. While this may be tidier, it will come at the sacrifice of some important detail each witness is inclined to forfeit to align his or her story with the other witnesses. I'm not willing to pay that price. I would far rather have three messy, apparently contradictory versions of the event than one harmonized version eliminating some important fact. I know in the end I'll be able to determine the truth of the matter by examining all three stories. The apparent contradictions are usually easy to explain once I learn something about the witnesses and their perspectives (both visually and personally) at the time of the crime.

Let me give you an example. Many years ago, I investigated a robbery in which a male suspect entered a small grocery store, walked up to the counter, and calmly spoke to the cashier. The suspect removed a handgun from his waistband and placed it on the counter. He pointed it at the cashier, using his right hand to hold the gun on the counter, his finger on the trigger. The suspect quietly told the cashier to empty the register of its money and place it in a plastic bag. The cashier complied and gave the robber all the money in the drawer. The robber then calmly walked from the store. This robbery was observed by two witnesses, who were properly separated and interviewed apart from each other. When the crime report was assigned to me as the investigator, I read the officer's summary and wondered if the witnesses were describing the same robber:

Sylvia Ramos
38-yr-old Female
Married with Kids
Interior Designer
Picking Up Milk on the
Way Home from Work

Paul Meher
23-yr-old Male
Single, No Kids
Apprentice Plumber
Visiting the Cashier on
His Day Off

How They Described the Suspect

Younger Boy in His Teens	Man about 24-25 Years Old
Very Polite with Sweet Voice	Threatening Scowl
Did Not Have a Gun	Had a Ruger P95 9mm Handgun
Bought Something at the Store	Bought Nothing at the Store
Wore an Izod Polo Shirt	Might Have Worn a T-Shirt
Had No Vehicle	Ran to a '90s Tan Nissan

At first, these statements seemed to describe two different men committing two different crimes. But the more I spoke with the witnesses, the more I realized both were reliable despite the fact they seemed to be saying different things about the suspect. Sylvia Ramos was hurrying home from work and stopped at the store to purchase some milk and a few small items. She stood in line behind the suspect as he calmly committed the robbery. While she heard the tone of his voice, she never heard his words distinctly, and she never saw a gun. She described him as a polite young man in his teens. Based on the way the cashier handed the robber the bag, Sylvia believed the robber made a purchase prior to committing the crime. Sylvia immediately recognized the suspect's blue shirt as a classic IZOD polo because many of the men in her office wore this style of shirt when she first started her career as a designer. In fact, she had recently purchased one for her husband. Sylvia watched the robber walk slowly out of the business and across the parking lot as he left the area. She was sure he didn't have a "getaway" car.

Paul Meher was visiting the cashier when the robbery occurred. The cashier was an old friend from high school, and Paul was standing behind the counter with his friend at the time of the crime. Paul couldn't remember many details related to the suspect's clothing, but believed he was wearing a T-shirt. He was certain, however, the robber pointed a gun at his friend, and he recognized this pistol as a Ruger P95 because his father owned one that was identical. Paul focused on the gun during most of the robbery, but he also observed the suspect scowling with a menacing expression on his face. The robber spoke his words slowly and deliberately in a way Paul interpreted as threatening. Paul described the man as just slightly older than him, at approximately twenty-four to twenty-five years of age. He was certain that the suspect made no effort to purchase anything prior to the crime, and afterward, Paul had a visual angle through the glass storefront allowing him to see the robber as he walked to the end of the parking lot, then ran to a tan-colored, 1990s Nissan four-door.

Once I interviewed these two witnesses, I understood why they seemed to disagree on several key points. In the end, many things impact the way witnesses observe an event. A lot depends on where a witness is located in relationship to the action. We've also got to consider the personal experiences and interests that cause some witnesses to focus on one aspect of the event and some to focus on another. Sylvia was older and had difficulty estimating the age of the suspect, but her design interests and experience with her husband helped her to correctly identify the kind of shirt the robber wore. Paul had personal experience with pistols and was standing in a position that gave him an entirely different perspective as he watched the robbery unfold. As the detective handling the case, it was my job to understand each witness well enough to take the best they had to offer and make a proper inference about what really happened. Every case I handle is like this; witnesses seldom agree on every detail. In fact, when two people agree completely on every detail of their account, I am inclined to believe they have either contaminated each other's observations or are working together to pull the wool over my eyes. I expect truthful, reliable eyewitnesses to disagree along the way.

THE LAST WITNESS INTERVIEWED

It's important to add one final observation. I've investigated several murder cases involving multiple eyewitness interviews. While at the scene, I took each witness off to the side to get their account without the input of other eyewitnesses. On one occasion, I discovered an additional, previously unidentified witness was quietly standing within earshot of my interviews, waiting for an opportunity to talk to me. Up to this point, none of the officers or detectives knew this person had seen anything, so while I was eager to hear what she had to say, it was clear she had not been isolated. She was already aware of what others had described. When interviewed, she surprisingly provided important information the other witnesses had missed completely. I was grateful she had been patient and waited to identify herself to us.

I observed something interesting about her statement, however. Because she had been eavesdropping on the interviews we were conducting and heard what others said, she was inclined to skip over the details offered by the first witnesses. She did an excellent job of *filling in the blanks*, but a poor job of covering the essential details of the crime others had already described. If I had not repeatedly asked her to start at the beginning and tell me everything she saw, she would undoubtedly have given me an incomplete account that, if compared to the first statements of eyewitnesses, would have looked like a contradiction. In my years of collecting eyewitness statements, I've observed something important: witnesses who are aware of what has been previously offered are far more likely to simply supply the *missing details*. While this witness may provide previously unknown (even *critical*) data, he or she may also offer a less detailed version.

THE GOSPEL WRITERS AS EYEWITNESSES

Growing up as a skeptic, I never thought of the biblical narrative as an eyewitness account. Instead, I saw it as something more akin to religious mythology—a series of stories designed to make a point. But when I read through the Gospels (and then the letters following them), it seemed clear the writers of Scripture identified themselves as eyewitnesses and viewed their writings as testimony. Peter called himself a "witness of Christ's sufferings" (1 Pet. 5:1) and one of many "eyewitnesses of his majesty" (2 Pet. 1:16–17). The apostle John claimed he was writing as an eyewitness when he described the life and death of Jesus. He identified himself as "the disciple who testifies to these things and who wrote them down" (John 21:24), and said he was reporting that "which we have heard, which we have seen with our eyes, which we have looked at and our hands have touched" (1 John 1:1). The apostles saw themselves first and foremost as a group of eyewitnesses, and they understood their shared observations were a powerful testimony to what they claimed to be true. When Judas left the group, they quickly replaced him and demonstrated the high value they placed on their status as eyewitnesses. They set out to "choose one of the men who have been with us the whole time the Lord Jesus went in and out among us, beginning from John's baptism to the time when Jesus was taken up from us" (Acts 1:21–22). They replaced Judas with another eyewitness.

As I read through the book of Acts, I realized the apostles repeatedly identified themselves as eyewitnesses and called upon their testimony as the foundation for all their preaching and teaching. In Peter's very first sermon at Pentecost, he told the crowd the disciples "are all witnesses of the fact" of the resurrection (Acts 2:32), and he repeated this

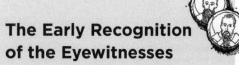

The Early Recognition of the Eyewitnesses

The early-church fathers and leaders recognized the Gospels were the eyewitness testimony of the apostles, and they set the Gospels apart for this reason. The ancient Christian author Tertullian wrote in AD 212: "The same authority of the apostolic churches will afford evidence to the other Gospels also, which we possess equally through their means, and according to their usage—I mean the Gospels of John and Matthew—whilst that which Mark published may be affirmed to be Peter's whose interpreter Mark was. For even Luke's form of the Gospel men usually ascribe to Paul" ("Against Marcion" 4:5, as translated in *Anti-Nicene Fathers*, vol. 3, p. 350).

claim later at Solomon's Colonnade (Acts 3:15). When Peter and John were eventually arrested for testifying about the resurrection, they told the members of the Sanhedrin "we cannot help speaking about what we have seen and heard" (Acts 4:20), and they promptly returned to the streets where they "continued to testify to the resurrection of the Lord Jesus" (Acts 4:33). The apostles clearly and repeatedly identified themselves as "witnesses of everything he [Jesus] did in the country of the Jews and in Jerusalem" (Acts 10:39) and used this status as the foundation for everything they taught. Even Paul relied on his status as an eyewitness. When Christian communities began to blossom across Asia Minor, Paul wrote to many of them and identified himself as both an apostle and as someone who could testify as an eyewitness. Paul said Jesus "appeared to James, then to all the apostles, and last of all he appeared to me also" (1 Cor. 15:7–8).

As the apostles began to write out their eyewitness observations, early Christians gave these accounts great authority and respect. As the "canon" of emerging New Testament Scripture was examined by the church fathers (the early leaders of the growing Christian community), the issue of *apostolic authority* was the first and foremost criteria for whether a particular writing made it into the collection. Was the text written by an apostolic eyewitness (Matthew, John, Peter, Paul, James, Jude, et al.) or by someone who at least had meaningful access to one or more of these eyewitnesses (e.g., Mark and Luke)? Only the accounts of the original eyewitnesses were given serious consideration, and the Gospels have always been understood as a set of eyewitness accounts.

The question, of course, is whether they can be trusted, and that's the focus of the second section of this book. We'll investigate the Gospels as eyewitness accounts, asking the same kinds of questions judges encourage jurors to consider when evaluating witnesses in criminal proceedings. We'll ask if the apostolic eyewitnesses were present when the events were recorded. We'll ask if they were accurate and honest over time. We'll ask if their testimony can be verified in some way. Finally, we'll investigate whether they had an ulterior motive. When a jury concludes a witness can be trusted, they must accept what the witness has to say and use this testimony as the foundation for future decisions they may make about the truth of the case. If the gospel writers are found reliable, we can accept their statements as the foundation for future decisions we make about the truth of Jesus's life and God's existence.

THE EXPECTATIONS FROM EXPERIENCE

Before I ever examined the reliability of the gospel accounts, I had a reasonable expectation about what a dependable set of eyewitness statements might look like, given my experience as a detective. When more than one witness observes a crime, I expect to see the following characteristics in their statements:

THEIR STATEMENTS WILL BE PERSPECTIVAL

Each eyewitness will describe the event from his or her spatial and emotional perspective. Not everyone will be in the same position to see the same series of events or the same details. It will be my job to puzzle together seemingly contradictory statements colored by the personal experiences and worldviews of the witnesses.

THEIR STATEMENTS WILL BE PERSONAL

Each eyewitness will describe the event in his or her own language, using his or her own expressions and terms. As a result, the same event may be described with varying degrees of passion or with divergent details resulting from the individual tastes and interests of the witness.

THEIR STATEMENTS MAY CONTAIN AREAS OF AGREEMENT

Some aspects of each eyewitness statement may be completely identical. This is particularly true when witnesses describe dramatic or important aspects of the crime or sequence of events. It's also true when later witnesses are aware of what others have offered and simply affirm the prior description by telling me, "The rest occurred just the way he said."

LATER STATEMENTS MAY FILL IN THE GAPS

Finally, as described earlier, I expect late witnesses who are aware of prior statements to simply *fill in* what has not been said previously.

It turns out my expectations of true, reliable eyewitness accounts were met (at least preliminarily and superficially) by the Gospels. All four accounts were written from different perspectives containing unique details specific to the eyewitnesses. They can, however, be assembled and connected to get a robust *picture* of what occurred. All four accounts are highly personal, utilizing the distinctive language of each witness. Mark is far more passionate and active in his choice of adjectives, for example. Several of the accounts (Mark, Matthew, and Luke) contain blocks of identical (or nearly identical) descriptions. This may be the result of common agreement at particularly important points in the narrative, or (more likely) the result of later eyewitnesses saying, "The rest occurred just the way he said." Finally, the last account (John's gospel) clearly attempts to *fill in* the details neglected by the prior eyewitnesses. John, aware of what the earlier eyewitnesses had already written, appears to make little effort to cover the same ground. Even before examining the Gospels with the rigor we will apply in section 2, I recognized they were consistent with what I would expect to see, given my experience as a detective.

The Committed Biblical Witnesses

The New Testament accounts repeatedly use words translated as "witness," "testimony," "bear witness," or "testify." They are translated from versions of the Greek words *marturia* or *martureo*. The modern word for *martyr* finds its root in these same Greek words; the terms eventually evolved into describing anyone who (like the apostolic eyewitnesses) remained so committed to their testimony concerning Jesus that they would rather die than recant.

THE *RELIABLE* BIBLE

In the end, it all comes down to the reliability of these accounts. When I was a nonbeliever, I heard Christians talk about the *inerrancy* or *infallibility* of the Bible, at least as these terms are typically applied to the original manuscripts composed by the authors. I examined these concepts in depth in seminary many years later, but as I first read the accounts in the Gospels, I was far more interested in evaluating their *reliability* as eyewitness accounts than their *inerrancy* as divine communiqués. I knew from my experience as a detective the best eyewitness accounts presented points of disagreement and that this did not automatically invalidate their reliability.

If it was God's desire to provide us with an accurate and reliable account of the life of Jesus, an account we could trust and recognize as consistent with other forms of eyewitness testimony,

God surely accomplished it with the four gospel accounts. Yes, the accounts are *messy*. They are filled with idiosyncrasies and personal perspectives along with common retellings of familiar stories. There are places where critics can argue the appearance of a contradiction, and places where authors focused on something they thought important while ignoring details of importance to others. But would we expect anything less from true, reliable eyewitness accounts? I certainly would not, based on what I've seen professionally.

Surely these apparent "contradictions" and curious peculiarities were present in the early texts and obvious to the earliest of Christians. The oldest gospel manuscripts we have display this sort of *eyewitness variability*, and there is no reason to think the originals were any less unique or idiosyncratic. The early believers could have destroyed all but one of the accounts, changed the *conflicting* details, or simply *harmonized* the Gospels. But these diverse accounts were preserved (as they are) because they are true; they display all the earmarks we would expect in true eyewitness testimony. If the early church had eliminated the four eyewitness perspectives and limited us to one tidy version, we would inevitably have missed some significant detail. If I had tried to *clean up* the apparent contradictions between Sylvia's and Paul's testimonies, I may have ignored the clear descriptions of the gun and the shirt. Instead, I took Sylvia and Paul at their word, learned about their personal perspectives, and wrote a search warrant for these two items. I recovered both the shirt and the pistol and eventually used these pieces of evidence to convict the robber in this case.

Sylvia added a detail missed by Paul

Paul added details missed by Sylvia

NOT ALL MEMORIES ARE CREATED EQUAL

Sylvia and Paul were reliable eyewitnesses, even though their individual perspectives framed their observations of the robbery in unique ways. But what if many years passed before their testimony was required in court? Couldn't the passage of time impact their memories of the event? We've all forgotten details from past events. Isn't it possible, reasonable in fact, that Sylvia and Paul might forget or confuse some important detail of this robbery?

Much has been written about the "unreliability" of eyewitness testimony over time, especially as cases previously hinging on eyewitness identification have been overturned by new DNA evidence. In fact, the New Jersey Supreme Court recently pointed to cases such as these and cited a "troubling lack of reliability in eyewitness identifications." As a result, the court issued new rules to make it easier for defendants to challenge eyewitness evidence in criminal cases.[3] Given some eyewitness identifications have been overturned by DNA evidence, why should we trust eyewitness testimony about an event in the past?

In my experience as a cold-case detective, I've learned not all memories are created equally. Let me give you an example. If you asked me what I did five years ago on Valentine's Day (February 14 here in the United States), I may or may not be able to remember many of the details. I probably took my wife out for dinner or maybe a short vacation. I could probably tax my memory and recall the day with some accuracy, but I may confuse it with other Valentine's Day memories; after all, I've got more than forty memories of Valentine's Day with my wife to sift through (we started dating in 1979). This day was important to me, so it may *stick out* in my memory a bit more than other days in February, but if you ask me for specific chronological details, I may struggle to recall the particulars from Valentine's Day five years ago.

But if you ask me to recall the specifics of Valentine's Day in 1988, I can provide you with a much more accurate recollection. This was the day Susie and I were married. It *sticks out* in my mind. I can remember the details with much more precision because this event was unequaled in my life and experience. It's the only time I've ever been married, and the excitement and importance of the event were unparalleled for me. Valentine's Day stands out when compared to other days in February, but that Valentine's Day was even more special. Not all memories are equally important or memorable.

| September 11 | January 28 | November 22 | December 7 | April |
| 2001 | 1986 | 1963 | 1941 | 33 |

We remember unique, unrepeated, and emotionally powerful events

When eyewitnesses encounter a similarly unique, unrepeated, and powerful event, they are far more likely to remember it and recall specific details accurately. Sylvia and Paul had never observed a robbery prior to the one they observed in the liquor store. It was a unique, unrepeated event. As such, it stuck out in their minds and memories. This doesn't mean their testimonies ought to be accepted without testing; the four criteria we've already described in this chapter must still be applied to Sylvia and Paul. We still must determine if they were present to see the robbery and have a history of honesty and accuracy. We still need to determine if their testimonies can be corroborated by additional evidence and examine their motives to make sure they are not lying. If these criteria can be met, we have good reason to trust their testimonies as reliable.

THE UNEQUALED EVENTS OF THE NEW TESTAMENT

I remember the day I was married because it was unique, unrepeated, and personally important. Now put yourself in the shoes of the apostles as they witnessed the miracles and resurrection of Jesus. None of these eyewitnesses had ever seen anyone like Jesus before. He did more than teach them important lessons; He astonished the eyewitnesses with unique and personally powerful miracles.

Imagine, for example, you *like to fish*. Your fishing hobby compels you to sit in a boat at your local lake three or four times a week. If I asked, "How was the fishing on April 10th, 2019?" you might struggle to recall your activity. One day of fishing is much like the next. But if you're sitting on the lake one day and someone approaches your boat *walking on the water*, well, that's a day you are unlikely to forget!

Ordinary day   Ordinary day   Ordinary day   Ordinary day   Extraordinary day

The apostles only experienced one Jesus in their lifetime; they only observed one man perform miracles and rise from the dead. The resurrection, for example, was unique, unrepeated, and powerful. The gospel eyewitnesses observed several powerful and memorable events and provided us with distinctive, idiosyncratic, personal, and reliable accounts. We simply must take the time to understand the perspective and character of each eyewitness and then determine if the accounts are trustworthy, given the four criteria we have described (more in section 2).

A TOOL FOR THE CALLOUT BAG, A TIP FOR THE CHECKLIST

This may be one of the most important principles we can tuck away in our callout bag. Unless you've worked a lot with eyewitnesses and have become familiar with the nature of apparent contradictions in eyewitness accounts, it's easy to assume people are lying (or are mistaken) simply because they don't agree on every detail or have ignored some facts in favor of others. If nothing else, we must remember an eyewitness account can be reliable despite apparent *contradictions*. While we might complain about two differing accounts, we would be even more suspicious if there were absolutely no peculiarities or differences. If this were the case with the Gospels, I bet we would argue they were the result of some elaborate collusion. As we examine the gospel accounts, we need to give the writers the same benefit of the doubt we would give other eyewitnesses. Human eyewitnesses produce human eyewitness accounts; they are often idiosyncratic and personal, but reliable, nonetheless.

As a Christian, I recognize the Bible is *God's Word*, but I also recognize it was delivered to us through the observations and recollections of human eyewitnesses. Before I share *that* the Bible has something important to offer, I typically take the time to make a case for *why* the Bible has something important to offer. It's important for people to understand the writers identified themselves as *eyewitnesses*. They weren't writing *moral fiction*. They were recording what they saw with their own eyes, heard with their own ears, and touched with their own hands. Let's recognize the importance of biblical *reliability* and help our skeptical friends recognize the nature of personal, reliable eyewitness testimony. Many of us have seen or heard something forever changing the way we thought about the world around us. That's precisely what happened to the gospel writers. Their observations changed them forever, and their testimony can change the world we live in.

Chapter 5

Principle #5:

HANG ON EVERY WORD

After an exhausting day of interviews, we were no closer to having a suspect in view. We were still looking for a *trailhead*, a direction leading us to the suspect who killed a young woman in our city in 1981. We managed to locate all the men and women who had been suspected of this crime many years ago and arranged interviews with them. Eight hours into these meetings, I was still undecided about who might be the most likely candidate for the murder. Then Scott Taylor said something that caught my attention.

Scott dated the victim about one year prior to the murder. He was interviewed in 1981, along with many other men who dated or knew her. The original investigators were unable to single out any one of these men as a primary suspect. Today, Scott said something unusual. It wasn't anything big. In fact, my partner didn't catch it at all.

We asked each candidate how he or she "felt" about the victim's murder. We were careful to ask the question the same way each time; the responses were important to us as we tried to understand the relationships between the potential suspects and the victim. One responded, "I'm shocked someone could have killed her." Another told us, "It's tragic; I hope you guys catch the killer." A third said, "Although we had problems, I was devastated when I learned about it." Scott said something very different.

"Let me ask you, Scott, how did you feel about her death? Did you have any feelings about it one way or the other?" I asked him casually, hoping to gauge his response.

Scott paused for a second, choosing his words. He shrugged his shoulders slightly and said, "Well, I was sorry to see her dead, you know. We didn't always get along, but it's never good to see anyone die."

Of all the possible responses Scott could have offered, this one struck me as odd and a bit telling. It may have simply been a common figure of speech for Scott. If so, a more thorough interview might provoke a similar response about something else. But Scott's first reply to our question was he was "sorry to see her dead." We knew the killer stood over the victim's body and made sure she was dead by nudging her (based on blood smears). It could reasonably be said the killer "saw her dead" prior to leaving the scene. Was Scott inadvertently telling us something about his involvement in this crime?

It would be another year before we would complete our investigation. Ultimately, we learned a lot more about Scott's relationship with the victim and we eventually determined he killed her because he didn't want anyone else to date her following their breakup. We assembled cumulative, circumstantial evidence to make our case. Scott's statement about "seeing her dead" pointed us in his direction and was eventually used in court (along with everything else we learned) to convict him. Was this statement enough, on its own, to make our case? Of course not. But it was consistent with Scott's involvement and truly reflected the way he felt in the moments following the murder.

Scott's case taught me the value of paying close attention to every word a suspect might offer. We all choose the words we use. Sometimes we choose as a matter of habit. Sometimes we choose words reflecting, either consciously or subconsciously, the truth about how we feel or the truth about what really happened. I've learned to hang on every word.

 ## THE ART OF FORENSIC STATEMENT ANALYSIS

In my first years as an investigator, my department sent me to several classes, seminars, and training exercises to improve my skills. One of these classes was a course in forensic statement analysis (FSA). There I learned to refine my ability to hear and interpret every word offered by a suspect in a case. I began to employ FSA techniques almost immediately. I routinely asked suspects to write down what they did on the day of the murder, accounting for their activity from the time they got up in the morning to the time they went to bed. I provided each suspect a blank piece of lined paper and a *pen*. Any alterations would therefore be unerasable, allowing me to see what they initially wrote and where they were uncomfortable with their original choice of words. I would then examine this statement, asking several important questions: What kinds of words did the suspect use to describe the victim? Does the suspect ever inadvertently slip from the present to the past tense, giving away his or her presence or involvement at the scene of the crime? Does the suspect compress or expand the description of events to hide something or lie about how something occurred? Does the suspect over- or under-identify the victim in an effort to seem friendlier or disinterested in the victim? In

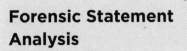

Forensic Statement Analysis

The careful study and analysis of the words (both written and spoken) provided by a suspect, witness, or victim. The purpose of forensic statement analysis is to determine truthfulness or deception on the part of the person making the statement.

essence, I examined every word to see if it provided any clue related to the suspect's involvement in the crime.

Let me give you an example. Imagine we asked a suspect about his activity last night with his wife (who is now the victim of a murder). In describing what happened, the man responded:

"I took Amy, my beautiful wife of thirty-one years, out to dinner and a movie."

I've already learned something about their relationship in just this one sentence. Notice the suspect told us his wife's name and was apparently proud enough of her (or their relationship) to mention how long they had been together. Notice also the suspect used the possessive expression "my beautiful wife" when he could easily have described her in some other way. Imagine, for example, if he had said this:

"I took my wife out to dinner and a movie."

While he still used a possessive expression ("my wife") in this response, he did not describe her as beautiful, and he reserved the information about her name and the length of their relationship.

Maybe he's a private person who was uncomfortable with revealing personal details. Maybe he was not as proud of his wife or wanted to distance himself from her. We'd need to spend some time with him to learn more. Let's now imagine he said this in response to our questioning:

> *"I took the wife out to dinner and a movie."*

The suspect dropped the possessive language and described his wife as "the wife." Hmm. Why would he do that? Maybe this was just a figure of speech he always used in describing anyone he had a relationship with, whether good or bad. Maybe he was distancing himself from his wife for some reason. Once again, we'd have to investigate this further. Finally, let's imagine he said something like this:

> *"I took the old lady out to dinner and a movie."*

Here, the suspect may simply have used a figure of speech common to his region or his culture or even his family. He might, however, have revealed something about his feelings toward his wife. He did not use possessive language, he gave us very little information about her, and he described her in a less-than-flattering manner. We would have to look at other areas of his statement to see if he used similar language when describing others or if he reserved these kinds of words for his wife alone. In any case, his use of words told us something important.

Clearly, this sort of word examination is more an *interpretive art* than a *hard science*, but the more we understand the importance of words, the better we become at discerning their meanings. Remember, all of us choose the words we use, and we have lots of words to choose from. Our words eventually give us away.

THE FORENSIC GOSPELS

I had been interviewing and studying suspect and eyewitness statements for many years before I opened my first Bible. I approached the Gospels like I would any other forensic statement. Every little idiosyncrasy stood out for me. Every word was important. The small details interested me and forced me to dig deeper. As an example, the fact John never mentioned the proper name of Jesus's mother (Mary) was curious to me. In his gospel, John repeatedly referred to Mary as "Jesus's mother" or "the mother of Jesus" but never referred to her by name (as did the other gospel writers). Why would this be the case?

The answer might be found in the nineteenth chapter of John's gospel when Jesus entrusted Mary to John at the crucifixion. Jesus told John that Mary was now his mother, and He told Mary that John was now her son. John took Mary and cared for her (as he would his own mother) from this point on. Writing the gospel of John many years later, John may have been uncomfortable calling his own mother by her formal name. I'm sure by this time in his life, John was referring to Mary as "my mother." It doesn't surprise me John would hesitate to call his adopted mother by her proper name in the gospel.

The more I read the Gospels, the more interested I was in taking a forensic approach to *read between* the lines of the gospel writers. My interest reached its peak in the gospel of Mark.

What Is the Forensic Statement Analyst Trying to Achieve?

Forensic statement analysts carefully examine the words offered by witnesses and suspects to determine:

1. Is the writer (or speaker) more involved in the event than they might like us to believe?

2. Are there relational problems between the writer (or speaker) and the victim who is the subject of the case?

3. What are the hidden difficulties between the writer (or speaker) and the victim in the investigation?

4. Was the writer (or speaker) doing what they claimed at the time of the crime?

5. Should the writer (or speaker) be considered as a suspect in the crime under consideration?

INVESTIGATING THE WORDS OF MARK

One of my Christian friends told me Mark's gospel was really the eyewitness account of the apostle Peter. The early church seemed to agree. Papias (ca. AD 70–163), an ancient bishop of Hierapolis (located in western Turkey), claimed Mark penned his gospel in Rome as Peter's scribe. He reported "Mark, having become the interpreter of Peter, wrote down accurately, though not indeed in order, whatsoever he remembered of the things said or done by Christ."[1]

Irenaeus (ca. AD 115–ca. 202), a student of Ignatius and Polycarp (two students of the apostle John) and the eventual bishop of Lugdunum (now Lyon, France), repeated this claim. He wrote, "Mark, the disciple and interpreter of Peter, did also hand down to us in writing what had been preached by Peter."[2] Justin Martyr (ca. AD 103–ca. 165), the famous early-church apologist from Rome, also mentioned an early "memoir" of Peter and described it in a way unique to the gospel of Mark.[3]

In addition, Clement of Alexandria (ca. AD 150–ca. 215), the historic leader of the church in North Africa, wrote those who heard Peter's teaching "were not satisfied with merely a single hearing or with the unwritten teaching of the divine Gospel, but with all sorts of entreaties they besought Mark, who was a follower of Peter and whose Gospel is extant, to leave behind with them in writing a record of the teaching passed on to them orally."[4] These early-church leaders and students of the apostles (from diverse geographic regions) were "closest to the action." They repeatedly and uniformly claimed Mark's gospel was a record of Peter's eyewitness observations. But could a forensic statement analysis of the gospel of Mark verify these claims?

As I began to study Mark's gospel forensically, I observed several interesting anomalies related to Peter. These peculiarities seemed reasonable if Peter was, in fact, Mark's source for information. Let me share some of them with you.

MARK MENTIONED PETER WITH PROMINENCE

Peter is featured frequently in Mark's gospel. As an example, Mark referred to Peter twenty-six times in his short account, compared to Matthew, who mentioned Peter only three additional times in his much longer gospel.

MARK IDENTIFIED PETER WITH THE MOST FAMILIARITY

More importantly, Mark is the only writer who refused to use the term "Simon Peter" when describing Peter (he used either "Simon" or "Peter"). This may seem trivial, but it is important. Simon was the most popular male name in Palestine[5] at the time of Mark's writing,[6] yet Mark made no attempt to distinguish the apostle Simon from the hundreds of other Simons known to his readers (John, by comparison, referred to Peter more formally as "Simon Peter" seventeen times). Mark consistently used the briefest, most familiar versions of Peter's name.

MARK USED PETER AS A SET OF "BOOKENDS"

Unlike in other gospel accounts, Peter is the first disciple identified in the text (Mark 1:16) and the last disciple mentioned in the text (Mark 16:7). Scholars describe this type of "bookending" as "inclusio"[7] and have noticed it in other ancient texts where a piece of history is attributed to a particular eyewitness. In any case, Peter is prominent in Mark's gospel as the first and last disciple named in the narrative.

MARK PAID PETER THE UTMOST RESPECT

Mark also seemed to respect Peter more than any other gospel writer did; he repeatedly painted Peter in the kindest possible way, even when Peter made a fool of himself. Matthew's gospel, for example, describes Jesus walking on water and Peter's failed attempt to do the same (Matt. 14:22–33). In Matthew's account, Peter began to sink into the sea; Jesus described him as a doubter and a man "of little faith." Interestingly, Mark respectfully omitted Peter's involvement altogether (Mark 6:45–52). In a similar way, Luke's gospel includes a description of the "miraculous catch" of fish in which Peter was heard to doubt Jesus's wisdom in trying to catch fish when Peter had been unsuccessful all day. After catching more fish than his nets could hold, Peter said, "Go away from me, Lord; I am a sinful man!" (Luke 5:1–11). Mark's parallel account omits this episode completely (Mark 1:16–20). While other gospels mention Peter directly as the source of some embarrassing statement or question, Mark's gospel omits Peter's name specifically and attributes the question or statement to "the disciples" or some other similarly unnamed member of the group. When Peter made an embarrassing claim (like saying he would never leave Jesus in Matthew 16:21–23), the most edited and least embarrassing version can be found in Mark's account (Mark 8:31–33). Repeatedly, Mark offers a version of the story kinder to Peter.

MARK INCLUDED DETAILS BEST ATTRIBUTED TO PETER

Mark alone included several seemingly unimportant details pointing to Peter's involvement in the shaping of the text. Mark alone told us "Simon and his companions" were the ones who went looking for Jesus when He was praying in a solitary place (Mark 1:35–37). Mark is also the only gospel author who described Peter as the first to draw Jesus's attention to the withered fig tree (compare Matt. 21:18–19 with Mark 11:20–21). Only Mark identified the specific disciples (including Peter) who asked Jesus about the timing of the destruction of the temple (compare Matt. 24:1–3 with Mark 13:1–4). While Matthew told us (in Matt. 4:13–16) Jesus returned to Galilee and "went and lived in Capernaum," Mark said Jesus entered Capernaum and the people heard He had "come home" (Mark 2:1). Mark said this despite the fact Jesus wasn't born or raised there. Why would Mark call it "home," when Jesus appears to have stayed there for a very short time and traveled throughout the region far more than He ever stayed in Capernaum? Mark alone described Capernaum as *Peter's* hometown (Mark 1:21, 29–31) and the home of Peter's mother. Peter could most reasonably refer to Capernaum as "home."

MARK USED PETER'S ROUGH OUTLINE

Many scholars also observe Peter's preaching style (see Acts 1:21–22 and Acts 10:37–41, for example) consistently seems to omit details of Jesus's private life. When Peter talked about Jesus, he limited his descriptions to Jesus's public life, death, resurrection, and ascension. Mark also followed this rough outline, omitting the birth narrative and other details of Jesus's private life found in Luke's and Matthew's gospels.

Mark used specific titles to describe Peter, gave him priority in the narrative, uniquely included information related to Peter, and copied Peter's preaching outline when structuring his own gospel. These circumstantial facts support the claims of the early-church fathers who identified Peter as the source of Mark's information.

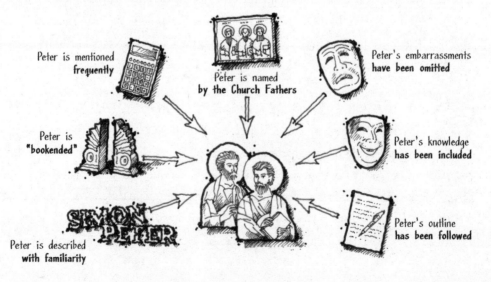

Peter is mentioned **frequently**

Peter is named **by the Church Fathers**

Peter's embarrassments **have been omitted**

Peter is **"bookended"**

Peter's knowledge **has been included**

Peter's outline **has been followed**

Peter is described **with familiarity**

SIMON PETER

By hanging on every word, we were able to construct a reasonable circumstantial case for the gospel of Mark as an eyewitness account. When combined with the testimony of the early church, this evidence becomes even more powerful.

 ## A TOOL FOR THE CALLOUT BAG, A TIP FOR THE CHECKLIST

Keep this principle in mind as you gather the tools in your *callout* bag and make your own investigative *checklist*. By paying close attention to the words witnesses use, we can learn a lot about the reliability and legitimacy of their statements. It's been fashionable recently to question the authenticity of the Gospels and the claims of the early-church fathers related to their authorship. Were the Gospels intentionally misattributed to the apostles or their associates? Was there a conspiracy of some sort to make the Gospels seem authoritative? The *forensic* internal evidence of language can help us to verify the claims of the early church related to these texts. The specific words used by the authors can teach us more than you might previously have thought possible. While it's been popular in the twenty-first century to try to cast doubt on what was so certain to those in the first and second centuries, thoughtful consideration of the words themselves will verify many of the claims of the early-church leaders. We need to do our best not to trust others (including me) for this careful analysis. Instead, read the Gospels for yourself and examine every word. Each of us has the obligation to *do the heavy lifting* for ourselves.

I recognize many of us, as Christians, are hesitant to treat *God's Word* as though it were a suspect or eyewitness statement requiring forensic dissection. It almost seems to disrespect the holy nature of the text. I've even known brothers and sisters in the faith who were hesitant to write on the pages of their Bibles out of love and respect for the Word. I certainly understand this kind of reverence, and I also understand it's tempting for us to leave this kind of analysis to *experts* in the field. But you'll be amazed at how rich and deep your faith will become after careful analysis and study. Some of us don't think we have enough training or experience to examine the language of Scripture. But imagine one of your sons wrote you a long letter describing something important to him. As an interested reader, you would find yourself intuitively measuring his choice of words. You would inevitably "read between the lines" and find yourself gleaning far more from the letter than the simple content intended. We all have enough *expertise* to begin to question the use of specific words and develop a richer understanding of the biblical text if only we will become interested readers of Scripture. There are several reliable experts in the field who can help us sort out the language. We simply need to *raise the bar* on our approach to the biblical text. Yes, it's hard work, but it's our duty as ambassadors for Christ and as defenders of the faith.

Chapter 6
Principle #6:

SEPARATE ARTIFACTS FROM EVIDENCE

"Ladies and gentlemen, the most important piece of forensic evidence the prosecution has in this case demonstrates the defendant had *nothing* to do with this murder." The defense attorney paused as his projector splashed an image of a cigarette butt on the courtroom screen. The jurors sat quietly with their eyes fixed on the photograph. Several jurors were taking notes.

I knew this cigarette butt was going to be a problem for our case from the moment I first saw it in the collection of evidence. The victim in this crime was murdered in his front yard in 1990. The murder occurred early in the morning, long before sunrise. When officers were called to the scene, they correctly taped off the area to preserve it for the criminalists. They were careful to *overestimate* the possible crime scene, capturing a large area within the tape, just to be sure they didn't miss anything. While it is always wise to tape off the biggest possible area, it often results in an excessive collection of items. Some of these items are related to the crime and can be correctly identified as evidence; some of these items are simply uninvolved *artifacts* collected incidentally. The jury will eventually decide which is which.

"The prosecution failed to perform a DNA test on this cigarette butt, even though they knew it was important to the case. They collected it, after all. Why would they do that unless they thought it was a piece of evidence?" The defendant's attorney paused with his hands on the podium, waiting for everyone on the jury to turn their eyes back toward him. "As you know, our team conducted the appropriate tests and learned there was, in fact, DNA on the cigarette, and this DNA, although it remains unidentified, does *not* belong to my client. The DNA belongs to the true killer. The police never even examined the DNA and missed the chance to find the real murderer."

It was true we never tested the cigarette for DNA. It was also true the partial DNA found by the defendant's team did not belong to the defendant and remained unidentified. But it was not true the cigarette butt was a piece of evidence. Yes, we collected it because it was inside the tapeline at the crime scene. But that yellow tape captured both evidence and *artifacts*.

The cigarette butt was discovered in a neighbor's side yard, approximately fifty feet from the point of the murder. It was at the outmost edge of the taped area. If the officers had taped an area just six inches smaller in radius, this butt would not even be part of our case. The defense argued the suspect was hiding in this location, fifty feet from the victim's front door, and must have smoked a cigarette while he was waiting for the victim to exit his house. They wanted the jury to view the cigarette butt as evidence of the killer's identity.

I knew better. The location of the cigarette was directly visible from the street and the front porch. If the suspect had been standing there, he would have been exposed and visible to anyone driving by (and to the victim as soon as he exited the front door). If the killer was relying on the darkness to hide his presence, the glowing ember of the cigarette and the smell of the smoke would be a sure giveaway. More importantly, I knew from the victim's family this area was used by his daughter's friends to smoke cigarettes while they were visiting and working on their cars in the driveway. We never tested the cigarette as evidence in this case because we never viewed it as evidence in the first place. It was simply an artifact at the scene.

Like all our cases, this investigation was built on circumstantial evidence. I had no direct evidence, and the defense knew it. The defendant had been very careful and got away without leaving a trace of his presence at the scene. While over thirty other pieces of circumstantial evidence pointed to the defendant as the killer, the only physical item collected at the scene happened to be an unrelated cigarette butt. The jury would now have to consider the circumstantial case surrounding the cigarette before they could consider the circumstantial case surrounding the defendant.

That's exactly what they did. The jury came back in less than three hours. They were able to distinguish between the evidence and the artifacts, and they properly kept the cigarette butt in its place as an artifact of the crime scene. They convicted the defendant of murder.

THE TEXTUAL ARTIFACTS OF THE BIBLE

Like crime scenes, historical scenes can be reconstructed with the evidence we have at our disposal. We must be careful, however, to distinguish between *evidence* and *artifacts*. The testimony of an eyewitness can be properly viewed as evidence, but anything added to the account after the fact should be viewed with caution as a possible *artifact* (something existing in the text when it shouldn't). The Gospels claim to be eyewitness accounts, but you may be surprised to find there are textual artifacts nestled in with the evidential statements. It appears scribes, in copying the texts over the years, added lines to the original narrative. Let me give you an example.

Most of us are familiar with the biblical story in the gospel of John in which Jesus was presented with a woman accused of committing adultery (John 8:1–11). The Jewish men who brought the woman to Jesus wanted her stoned, but Jesus refused to condemn her and told the men, "He who is without sin among you, let him be the first to throw a stone at her." When the men left, Jesus told the woman, "I do not condemn you, either. Go. From now on sin no more." This story is one of my favorite passages in all of Scripture. Too bad it appears to be an *artifact*.[1]

While the story may, in fact, be true, the earliest copies of John's gospel recovered over the centuries fail to contain any part of it. The last verse of chapter 7 and the first eleven verses of chapter 8 are missing in the oldest manuscripts available to us. The story doesn't appear until it is discovered in later copies of John's gospel, centuries after the life of Jesus on earth. In fact, some ancient biblical manuscripts place it in a different location in John's gospel. Some ancient copies of the Bible even place it in the gospel of Luke. While much about the story seems consistent with Jesus's character and teaching, most scholars do not believe it was part of John's original account. It is a biblical *artifact*, and it is identified as such in nearly every modern translation of the Bible (where it is typically noted in the margin or bracketed to separate it from the reliable account).

Should the existence of this textual artifact concern us? Do late additions to the biblical record disqualify the New Testament as a reliable manuscript? How can we call the Bible *inerrant* or *infallible* if it contains a late addition such as this? This passage is not the only textual artifact in the Bible. There are several additional verses considered artifacts by scholars and biblical experts. Let's look at a few of them to determine if their existence should cause us any alarm:

LUKE 22:43–44

"And there appeared an angel unto him from heaven, strengthening him. And being in an agony he prayed more earnestly: and his sweat was as it were great drops of blood falling down to the ground" (KJV).

The Story of the Woman Caught in Adultery

The famous story of the woman caught in adultery (known as *Pericope de Adultera*) is found today in John 7:53–8:11. It was not present in the earliest known manuscripts of John's gospel, however, including Papyri 66 (c. AD 200), Papyri 75 (early 3rd century), Codex Sinaiticus (4th century), and Codex Vaticanus (4th century). It first appears in its entirety in the 5th century in Codex Bezae, but there are several other codices from that time in history that do not contain the story (e.g., Codices Alexandrinus, Ephraemi, Washingtonianus, and Borgianus). It appears in a different location (after John 21:25) in many ancient copies of the text, including a set of ancient gospels written in Greek known as "Family 1," dating from the 12th to the 15th centuries. The story appears in the gospel of Luke (after Luke 24:53) in a group of Greek manuscripts known as "Family 13," dating from the 11th to 15th centuries.

These two verses do not appear in early manuscripts of Luke's gospel, and for this reason they have been omitted from some modern Bible translations (like the RSV). While the KJV does not isolate them as late additions, other translations (like the NIV, NASB, and NKJV) identify them as such in footnotes or special brackets.

JOHN 5:4

"For an angel went down at a certain season into the pool, and troubled the water: whosoever then first after the troubling of the water stepped in was made whole of whatsoever disease he had" (KJV).

Once again, this verse (along with the last few words of verse 3) does not appear in the best ancient manuscripts. Several modern translations have simply removed the verse (e.g., the NIV, RSV, and NRSV), while others have identified it in the footnotes (e.g., the NKJV and ESV).

1 JOHN 5:7

"For there are three that bear record in heaven, the Father, the Word, and the Holy Ghost: and these three are one" (KJV).

The second half of this verse ("the Father, the Word, and the Holy Ghost: and these three are one") does not appear in any manuscript of the Bible until the sixteenth century (and it only appears in two manuscripts at this point in history). It has been omitted from modern translations like the NASB and NIV and identified with a footnote in the NKJV.

ACTS 15:34

"Notwithstanding it pleased Silas to abide there still" (KJV).

The earliest and most reliable manuscripts do not contain this verse. Modern translations like the NIV, RSV, and NRSV have removed it, while the NASB, NKJV, and ESV have identified it with brackets or a footnote.

Skeptics point to passages like these in an effort to demonstrate the unreliability of the biblical text as an eyewitness account. If these lines are fiction, how many more verses are also false? When I was an atheist, this was one of my prime complaints about the Bible, and I discovered very few Christians knew these additions existed. I shook the faith of many of my Christian friends by simply demonstrating these passages were not in the original biblical text.

Evidence and Artifacts

Judges try to help jurors understand the difference between evidence and unrelated artifacts by instructing them to disregard anything other than what was presented as part of the case:

"You must decide what the facts are in this case. You must use only the evidence that was presented in this courtroom [or during a jury view]. 'Evidence' is the sworn testimony of witnesses, the exhibits admitted into evidence, and anything else I told you to consider as evidence ...

"You must disregard anything you saw or heard when the court was not in session, even if it was done or said by one of the parties or witnesses" (Section 222, Judicial Council of California Criminal Jury Instructions, 2006).

SEPARATING THE ARTIFACTS FROM THE EVIDENCE

It wasn't until years later I came to understand how to evaluate the existence of these late entries. I eventually learned every crime scene presents its own set of unique questions and difficulties. Every scene contains important evidence guiding us to the truth while also containing unrelated artifacts causing some uncertainty. I've never encountered a crime scene free of artifacts. Despite these unrelated items, we, as detectives, were able to evaluate the case and determine what belonged to the crime and what did not. Yes, there were always several questions to be answered. But our concerns were eventually resolved when we separated the artifacts from the evidence.

Doing this, of course, was sometimes quite difficult. Over the years, I've developed strategies to help me assess what is important in a crime scene and what is not. These principles can also be used to evaluate the textual artifacts in the biblical accounts.

IDENTIFY THE LATE ADDITIONS

Responding officers typically tape off crime scenes immediately in preparation for the criminalists. The criminalists then photograph everything and document the scene thoroughly. Years later, if an item of evidence is discovered and this item is not present in the original photographs, we have good reason to identify it as a late addition to the case. Once we are certain something is a late addition, we can simply ignore it as we assess the true evidence.

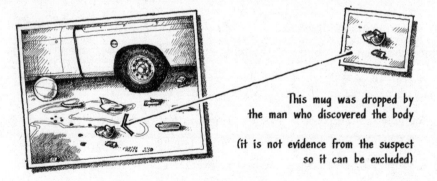

This mug was dropped by the man who discovered the body

(it is not evidence from the suspect so it can be excluded)

RECOGNIZE DIFFERENCES IN CHARACTER

But what if an item was at the scene from the very beginning? How can we determine if it is important to the case? There are some things we recognize as unrelated from the very first moment we arrive. I've investigated many cases in which paramedics reached the scene even before the police. They made a valiant effort to save the dying victim prior to the arrival of the first responding officers. By the time the police got there, the crime scene was littered with the paraphernalia from the paramedic team. Bandage packaging, tubing, syringes, and a variety of other obvious medical items were now part of the scene and were photographed by the criminalists before my arrival at the location. These items became a part of the case but were quickly and easily recognized as artifacts. They stood out like a sore thumb; they were evidence of the rescue effort, not the crime.

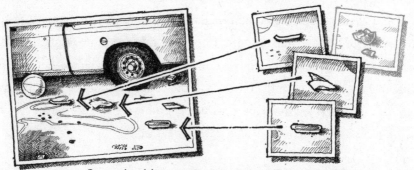

Paramedic debris is also not evidence from the suspect

3 LOOK FOR AN EXPLANATION

Many items at the scene may be explained by some unrelated cause accounting for their presence, which eliminates them as evidence. I once had a case in which a shoe print was photographed outside the victim's house. We initially thought it might belong to the killer until we matched it to the landlord who first discovered the victim when he entered the residence to check on her. Once we had an explanation for the existence of the print, we recognized it as an artifact.

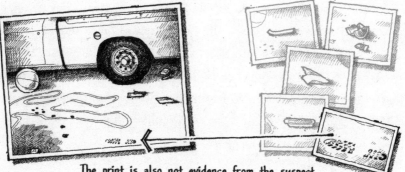

The print is also not evidence from the suspect

SEE WHAT HAPPENS IF YOU INCLUDE IT

There have been times when it was impossible for me to determine whether an item was a piece of evidence or simply an artifact of the scene. When this happens, I will sometimes imagine a hypothetical scenario including the item as evidence, just to see if its inclusion would change the outcome of the case. I once had a crime scene in which a pencil was recovered on the floor next to the victim. We weren't sure if it was part of the crime or if it belonged to the victim or the suspect. Forensic examinations provided nothing in the way of DNA or fingerprints. To be safe, I decided to consider it as evidence. I quickly realized the pencil had no impact on the case; when I later assembled the evidence pointing to a specific suspect, the presence of the pencil did nothing to either improve or weaken my case. There are times when we can be comfortable ignoring an item because it has no impact on the outcome, even if it were included.

RELY ON WHAT YOU KNOW

Some crime scene items present difficulties because they seem to contradict the larger group of confirmed items of evidence. Imagine we are investigating a homicide and have recovered forty-two pieces of evidence identifying a man named Ben Rogers as the killer. Many of these pieces of evidence came from the crime scene, including his DNA on the victim, several of Ben's personal items left behind at the location, and his fingerprints on the murder weapon. In addition to this, imagine we have an eyewitness who saw him running from the victim's home, covered in blood. Now imagine we also recovered a nametag belonging to Scotty Nichols, a man who worked with the victim. This nametag was sitting a few feet from the victim's body. When we question Scotty about the nametag, he tells us he lost the item a day before the murder occurred, and he offers us a verifiable alibi for the day of the crime. He has no idea why his nametag is in the victim's home. What are we to do with this item? In cases like this we must ask ourselves if the presence of the nametag impacts what we do know from the other evidence at the scene. When we have overwhelming evidence pointing in a particular direction, we may need to get comfortable with the fact there is some ambiguity related to other items at the scene.

The nametag remains unexplainable

SO, CAN WE TRUST THE BIBLICAL EVIDENCE?

We can apply these principles as we examine the New Testament and evaluate questionable passages to determine if they are evidence or artifacts. Luckily, we have "photographs" of the early crime scene to help us. We have hundreds of early, ancient manuscripts giving us a snapshot of what the text looked like before anyone added anything to the narrative. Once these late additions are exposed in this way, we can simply choose to ignore the passages as artifacts and focus on the remainder as evidence.

Some biblical passages appear suspicious even before we find they contain a variant. Some passages seem to reflect a different character or nature (like the paramedic paraphernalia at our murder scene). Textual critics examined the story of the adulterous woman, for example, and recognized the Greek words used in the narrative are far more like Luke's use of language than they are John's. The passage seems foreign to the gospel of John, even prior to discovering it was absent before the fifth century.

Next, we can look for reasonable explanations for the addition of these passages (just as we did with the landlord's shoe print). Let's look at the four examples I've given from the New Testament and think through some of the reasonable explanations. Each addition to the text appears to be an effort on the part of a scribe to make something clear, to emphasize a point, or to add some detail known to the scribe but omitted by the apostle. In Luke 22:43–44, Jesus's agony is emphasized by the unusual description of blood in his sweat. This may simply have been an effort to make the agony more vivid, or perhaps the scribe was borrowing from a literary style of the time to make the account more robust. In John 5:4, the detail related to the pool at Bethesda may simply have been added to explain John 5:7, a legitimate verse describing the stirring of the water without additional explanation. In 1 John 5:7, the scribe may have succumbed to the strong temptation to take the one verse most closely describing the Trinity and add a line making the doctrine irrefutable. While there are many verses point-

Reasons Why Scribes Sometimes Changed the Text

It's clear scribes occasionally changed the biblical manuscripts when copying them. Most of these changes were completely unintentional (simple misspellings or grammatical errors). Some, however, were intentional:

1. Some intentional alterations were performed in an effort to harmonize passages describing the same event in two separate gospels (parallel passages).

2. Some intentional alterations were done to add detail known to the scribe, but not clearly described by the apostolic author.

3. Some intentional alterations were made to clarify a passage of Scripture based on what a scribe thought the passage meant (the scribes were not always correct in their interpretation).

ing circumstantially to the Triune nature of God, this late insertion (if it were true) would remove all doubt. In Acts 15:34, the scribe adds a detail about Silas staying in Antioch. This fact may have been known to the scribe (if he was native to the area). As a result, he may have added it to the text to fill in a detail also known to local readers of the account.

Some biblical passages, however, are more difficult to assess as artifacts. They may appear in some ancient texts, but not in others from the same period. When this is the case, we can choose to hypothetically include the passage as though it were reliable evidence (like the pencil in our murder scene) to see what effect it has on the larger case. If we chose, for example, to include the story of the adulterous woman as a reliable part of the biblical narrative, would it change what we know about any of the central claims of the Bible? No, it wouldn't. The story seems consistent with what we know about Jesus's character and teaching. We can imagine Jesus doing something like this, given what we know about Him from other passages. The story of the adulterous woman does not change our final understanding of the teaching of Scripture, even if it is included. In most textual additions made to the Bible over the centuries, the changes were so insignificant as to have very little effect on the content of the narrative and virtually no impact on the important doctrinal claims of Christianity.

Finally, we must learn to be comfortable with some ambiguity. No scene is free of artifacts, and the biblical *crime scene* is no different. There may be a few passages of Scripture that seem *out of place* or difficult to understand (like Scotty Nichols's nametag). At times like these, we must ask ourselves if the reliable testimony of the biblical narrative is sufficient to accommodate an unexplained artifact. If we find the biblical text (with the artifacts removed) makes a strong and clear case (we'll discuss this more is the second section of this book), we can allow ourselves the minor discomfort of a few unanswered questions.

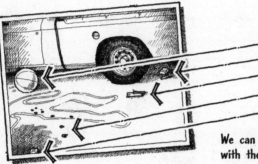

Separate the Artifacts from the Evidence:

Remove the evidence that's not involved in the crime, then build the case based on what remains

We can take a similar approach with the New Testament

PIECING TOGETHER THE PUZZLE

Let me give you an illustration to help you think about the relationship between evidence and artifacts. Imagine tomorrow you open a drawer in your family room and empty its contents onto the table. You find it contains all kinds of junk you haven't seen in quite some time, including keys, paper clips, batteries, and coins. You also discover it contains several *puzzle pieces*. In your curiosity about the puzzle, you begin to sift through the contents of the drawer, separating the puzzle pieces from the unrelated items. Some of these are obvious by their very nature. Like the paramedic paraphernalia, you immediately recognize batteries and coins are not part of the puzzle. As a result, you push these aside and start assembling.

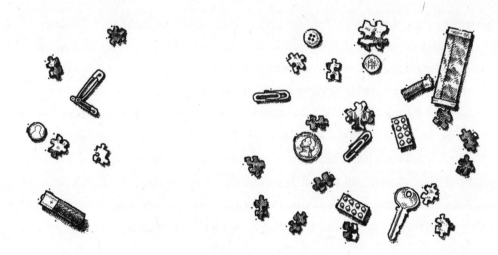

But it turns out there are two additional puzzle pieces in the drawer that simply don't match the others. As you begin to assemble the image, you can see these puzzle pieces don't fit; they seem to belong to a different puzzle.

Now let me ask you a few questions. Does the mere presence of the non-puzzle pieces in the drawer invalidate the reliability of the puzzle pieces? No, the non-puzzle pieces can be quickly and easily identified and set aside. Does the presence of the non-puzzle pieces change the resulting image you've pieced together? No, these additional "artifacts" are completely unrelated to the image on the puzzle. How about the two extra puzzle pieces that don't seem to match the rest? Does their presence in the drawer make the other puzzle pieces unreliable? No, most of the pieces fit together nicely and demonstrate a coherent relationship to one another (despite the presence of the two unmatching pieces). What if we accepted the two additional pieces as part of the puzzle and tried to force them in? Would they significantly change the final image? No, even if we were to accept these two pieces as part of the larger group and found a way to insert them into the puzzle, the image would still be obvious to us.

But here's an even more important question: What if there are still a few missing pieces once you're done assembling everything you find in the drawer? Do you have enough information from what you *do have* to identify the image in the puzzle? Yes, even with missing pieces from the puzzle, you have more than enough information to recognize the subject.

Crime scenes are a lot like this drawer full of items. Some "pieces" at the scene are evidence of the crime in question and some are extra artifacts having nothing to do with the crime. When we successfully separate the artifacts from the evidence, we can determine what happened. The mere presence of the artifacts is not an insurmountable obstacle for us. The biblical text is also much like the drawer full of items. Most passages in the text are evidence of the life of Jesus and there are extra textual artifacts requiring separation. When we successfully separate the textual artifacts from the biblical evidence, we can determine what happened over two thousand years ago. The mere presence of the textual artifacts is not an insurmountable obstacle for us.

A TOOL FOR THE CALLOUT BAG, A TIP FOR THE CHECKLIST

As you form your own checklist of evidential principles, be sure to include this important approach to *artifacts*. When I was an atheist, I believed the existence of *scribal alterations* in the Bible invalidated the evidential value of the text altogether. I now understand this is not the case. Every crime scene contains artifacts; if I refused to accept any explanation of the truth simply because an artifact existed alongside the reliable evidence, I could never convict anyone of a crime. All ancient documents also contain textual artifacts. If we reject the entirety of Scripture simply because it contains artifacts of one kind or another, we had better be ready to reject the ancient writings of Plato, Herodotus, Euripides, Aristotle, and Homer as well. The manuscripts for these texts are far less numerous, and they are far less reliable. If we apply the same standard of perfection some would demand of the Bible to other ancient histories, we would reject everything we thought we knew about the ancient past. More importantly, it's vital to recognize we possess a methodology to uncover the artifacts and separate them from the original text. The art of *textual criticism* allows us to compare manuscripts to determine what belongs and what does not. The same process I used (as a skeptic) to identify the few specious passages can also be used (now that I'm a believer) to identify the reliable passages. Textual criticism allows us to determine the nature of the original texts as we eliminate the textual artifacts. This should give us more confidence in what we read today, not less.

I have many Christian friends who are reluctant to admit the Bible contains *any* textual artifacts because they have always defended the Bible as either *inerrant* (containing no errors) or *infallible* (incapable of containing errors). But the presence of textual artifacts says nothing about the original text, and it's this original *autograph* we have in view when we talk about inerrancy and infallibility in the first place. When asked about my belief in the inerrancy of Scripture, I take the time to clarify this point: "I believe the original texts of the Bible—the 'autographs'—are the inerrant Word of God, and that we have the ability, by separating *artifacts* from *evidence*, to return to these autographs reliably."

God used humans to deliver His truth to His people. In the Old Testament, God used prophets to speak to the nation of Israel. In the New Testament, God used the apostolic eyewitnesses to testify of His Son. Christianity recognizes the inerrancy of the original documents these eyewitnesses provided, even though they were filled with idiosyncrasies and personal perspectives (as we described previously). Humans were also involved in the transmission of these eyewitness accounts. Like the authors, the scribes had personal perspectives and human idiosyncrasies impacting the way they copied the manuscripts. While they may have occasionally altered very minute portions of the text, we possess enough comparative copies of the ancient documents to identify these alterations and remove them from the reliable accounts. The textual artifacts testify to the gritty realism of the evidential account contained in the Bible. Like other real collections of evidence, there are artifacts embedded within the reliable evidence. Like crime scenes, these artifacts need not hinder our ability to determine (and defend) the truth.

Chapter 7

Principle #7:

RESIST CONSPIRACY
THEORIES

"Charlie, your roommate already told us where to find the green plaid shirt you were wearing last night." Charlie sat with his head down and his hands on his thighs. His body language communicated his continuing resistance to my questioning. This last statement, however, caused the first small reaction I had seen all afternoon. Charlie finally lifted his head and looked me in the eyes. "You and I both know I'm gonna find the victim's blood on that shirt." Charlie sat there quietly. I could tell he believed my lie about his roommate.[1]

Eighteen hours earlier, Charlie and his roommate, Vic, attempted to rob Dennis Watkins as he was walking home from his girlfriend's house. A simple street robbery turned into a homicide when Dennis decided he was bigger than Charlie and struggled with him for his knife. Charlie stabbed Dennis only once, but the resulting chest wound was fatal. The robbery took place late at night in an alley to the rear of a fast-food restaurant in our town. There were no witnesses and no one else was on the street at the time of the attack, but Charlie was unknowingly recorded by a surveillance camera located on a bank across the alley. While the camera was too far away to identify the killer facially, it did record the unusual green plaid shirt worn by one of the two attackers and captured an image of their general height and build. Several hours later (through a series of investigative efforts), we had Charlie and Vic in custody, but we had little evidence to corroborate their involvement. We needed a "cop-out" if we hoped to file the case with the district attorney.

We separated Charlie and Vic as soon as we arrested them; Vic was in a second interview room down the hall. I had not yet interviewed him; I lied to Charlie about the conversation. Vic didn't tell me where to find the plaid shirt. Charlie just happened to better match the physical build of the primary suspect I saw on the video, so I took a stab at him as the suspect who wore the shirt. I could tell I was right by Charlie's reaction. He was fidgeting in his chair and turned his gaze to the floor again. I stayed silent and let my statement hang in the air. Charlie finally looked up.

"Vic's lying about that. He's the one who gave me that shirt for my birthday, but he wears it more than I do." Charlie folded his arms again and leaned backward, trying to increase the distance between the two of us.

Some Popular Conspiracy Theories

Lee Harvey Oswald didn't act alone when he killed President Kennedy

The US government was involved in the 9/11 disaster

The 1969 Apollo moon landing was fabricated

A UFO crashed in Roswell, New Mexico

That was all I really needed—just another small piece of information. I left Charlie for a moment and entered the room with Vic. I pulled a chair up to the table separating us, introduced myself, and got down to business.

"Vic, I just got done talking to Charlie. Murder is a serious crime, and he told me *you* were the one who stabbed this guy. He told me about the green plaid shirt. He said you gave that shirt to him for his birthday, but you wear it more than he does. He told us where to find it. He said we'll find the victim's blood on the shirt and he's willing to testify against you, bud."

Within fifteen minutes, Vic told us all about the crime and confirmed what we had seen on the video. He provided many details about their prior plan to commit the robbery, and he confirmed his secondary involvement in the attack. He also told us Charlie was the man who stabbed Dennis, and he provided us with the location of the knife. Vic believed everything I said about Charlie. I had just enough true information to make my lies sound believable; the combination was powerful enough to convince Vic that Charlie had "ratted him out." Vic was now willing to return the favor.

RULES FOR SUCCESSFUL CONSPIRACIES

In my experience as a detective, I have investigated many conspiracies and *multiple-suspect* crimes. While successful conspiracies are the popular subject of many movies and novels, I've come to learn they are (in reality) very difficult to pull off. Successful conspiracies share several common characteristics:

1 *A SMALL NUMBER OF CONSPIRATORS*

The smaller the number of conspirators, the more likely the conspiracy will be a success. This is easy to understand; lies are difficult to maintain, and the fewer the number of people required to advance the lie, the better.

2 *THOROUGH AND IMMEDIATE COMMUNICATION*

This is key. When conspirators are unable to determine if their partners in crime have already given up the truth, they are far more likely to say something to save themselves from punishment. Without adequate and immediate communication, coconspirators simply cannot separate lies from the truth; they are easily deceived by investigators who can pit one conspirator against another.

3 *A SHORT TIMESPAN*

Lies are hard enough to tell once; they are even more difficult to repeat consistently over a long period of time. For this reason, the shorter the conspiracy, the better. The ideal conspiracy would involve only two conspirators, and one of the conspirators would kill the other right after the crime. That's a conspiracy that would be awfully hard to break!

4 *SIGNIFICANT RELATIONAL CONNECTIONS*

When all the coconspirators are connected relationally in deep and meaningful ways, it's much harder to convince one of them to "give up" the other. When all the conspirators are family members, for example, this task is nearly impossible. The greater the relational bond between the conspirators, the greater the possibility of success.

5 *LITTLE OR NO PRESSURE*

Few suspects confess to the truth until they recognize the jeopardy of failing to do so. Unless pressured to confess, conspirators will continue lying. Pressure need not be physical in nature. When suspects fear incarceration or condemnation from their peers, they often attempt to save face or save their own skin. This is multiplied as the number of coconspirators increases. The greater the pressure on coconspirators, the more likely the conspiracy is to fail.

Conspiracies

To prove that a defendant is part of a felonious conspiracy, prosecutors in the state of California must prove:

1. The defendant intended to agree and did agree with one or more of the other defendant(s) to commit alleged crime(s);

2. At the time of the agreement, the defendant and one or more of the other alleged member(s) of the conspiracy intended that one or more of them would commit alleged crime(s);

3. One of the defendants (or all of them) committed at least one of the alleged overt act(s) to accomplish the alleged crime (Section 415, Judicial Council of California Criminal Jury Instructions, 2006).

Charlie and Vic's conspiracy was difficult to maintain for several reasons. While there were only two conspirators, they were unable to communicate with each other. Once they were separated, they couldn't monitor what the other was saying to the police. We were, therefore, able to deceive each of them without detection. In addition to this, Charlie and Vic were only roommates. The more we talked to them, the more obvious it was they were willing to give each other up to avoid punishment. Neither Charlie nor Vic had ever been to state prison, but both had served time in the county jail system. They'd heard stories from other inmates about the nature of California prisons, and the fear of serving time there was a significant motivation for them to cooperate. Conspiracies are most successful when all the characteristics I've described are present. In this case, several key conditions were missing.

THE CHRISTIAN CONSPIRACY

When I was an atheist, I recognized the most significant claim of the alleged apostolic *eyewitnesses* was their assertion related to the resurrection. This was the big one; larger than any other alleged miracle ever performed by Jesus and the proof the apostles seemed to trot out every time they talked about Jesus. I always assumed it was a lie. Maybe it was just my skeptical nature or my prior experience with people on the job. I understand the capacity people possess to lie when it serves their purpose. In my view, the apostles were no different. In an effort to promote their cause and strengthen their own position within their religious community, I believed these twelve men concocted, executed, and maintained the most elaborate and influential conspiracy of all time. But as I learned more about the nature of conspiracies and had the opportunity to investigate and break several conspiracy cases, I started to doubt the reasonable nature of the alleged "Christian conspiracy."

To make the point, imagine playing a game of Clue, the classic Parker Brothers board game involving a murder and six suspects (I enjoyed this game as a boy, and often wonder if it was part of the reason I became a detective in the first place).

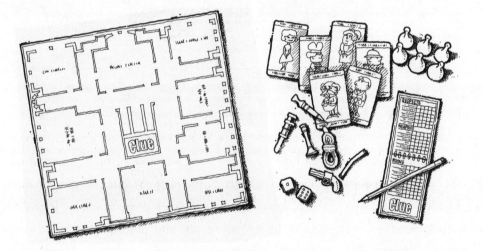

For the purposes of our illustration, let's change the location of the murder from the Tudor Mansion to the location of the crucifixion and the region surrounding it. We'll also change the game pieces from the six Clue suspects to the twelve disciples. With our new gameboard in place, let's investigate the possible "Christian conspiracy" considering the five principles for successful conspiracies I've already described. It's apparent from the start, the apostles faced far greater challenges than did Charlie and Vic two thousand years later. The number of conspirators required to successfully accomplish the Christian conspiracy would have been staggering.

The book of Acts tells us there were as many as 120 eyewitnesses in the upper room following Jesus's ascension (Acts 1:15). Let's assume for a minute this number is a gross exaggeration; let's work with a much smaller number to illustrate our point. Let's limit our discussion to the twelve apostles (adding Matthias as Judas's replacement). There are just too many game pieces on the gameboard.

This number is already prohibitively large from a conspiratorial perspective, and to make matters worse, none of the other characteristics of successful conspiracies existed for the twelve apostles. The apostles had little or no effective way, for example, to communicate with one another in a quick or thorough manner. Remember, the disciples didn't remain in a "holy huddle" in the center of the gameboard. Following their dispersion from Jerusalem, the twelve disciples were scattered across the Roman Empire and, according to the most ancient accounts, were ultimately interrogated and martyred far from one another. Methods of communication in the first century were painfully slow, and unlike Charlie and Vic, the apostles were separated by far more than a hallway. From Peter in Rome, to James in Jerusalem, to Thomas in Mylapore, the apostles appear to have been ultimately interrogated in locations preventing them from communicating with one another in a timely manner. They had no idea if any of their coconspirators had already "given up the lie" and saved themselves by simply *confessing* Jesus was never resurrected. While skeptics sometimes claim these recorded locations of martyrdom are unreliable because they are part of a biased Christian account, there isn't a single non-Christian record contradicting the claims of martyrdom offered by the local communities and historians.

In addition, the apostles would have been required to protect their conspiratorial lies for an incredibly long time. It's one thing to keep a secret for six minutes, six days, six weeks, six months, or even six years, but six *decades*? The apostle John, for example, appears to have lived the longest, surviving nearly sixty years after the resurrection. Charlie and Vic couldn't keep their conspiracy alive for thirty-six hours; the apostles allegedly kept theirs intact for many decades.

To complicate matters further, many of the disciples were complete strangers to one another prior to their time together as followers of Jesus. Some were indeed brothers, but many were added over the course of Jesus's early ministry and came from diverse backgrounds, communities, and families. While there were certainly pairs of family members in the group of apostolic eyewitnesses, many had no relationship to each other at all. Philip, Bartholomew, Thomas, Simon the Canaanite, and Matthias had no family relationship to any of the other apostles. Matthew also doesn't appear to have any familial relationship to other disciples and was, in fact, despised as a tax collector before joining the group. Whatever the relational connection between these men, the short years they spent together would quickly pale in comparison to the decades they would spend apart from one another prior to their final interrogations. At some point, the bonds of friendship and community would be tested if their individual lives were placed in jeopardy.

Perhaps the most important pieces in the game of Clue are the weapons used by the alleged killers. These weapons seem appropriate, given what the disciples endured for their resurrection claims. Remember, *successful* conspiracies are *unpressured* conspiracies. The apostles, on the other hand, were aggressively persecuted as they were scattered from Italy to India. According to the records and accounts of the local communities, each of them suffered unimaginable physical duress and died a martyr's death.[2] Ancient writers recorded Peter was crucified upside down in Rome, James was killed with the sword in Jerusalem, and Thomas was murdered by a mob in Mylapore. Each story of martyrdom is more gruesome than the prior as we examine the list of apostolic deaths. This pressure was far greater than the fear of state prison faced by Charlie and Vic, yet none of the Twelve recanted their claims related to the resurrection. Not one.

I can't imagine a less favorable set of circumstances for a successful conspiracy than those faced by the twelve apostles. Multiply the problem by ten to account for the 120 disciples in the upper room (Acts 1:15), or by forty to account for the five hundred eyewitnesses described by Paul (1 Cor. 15:6), and the odds seem even more prohibitive. None of these eyewitnesses ever recanted, none was ever trotted out by the enemies of Christianity to expose the Christian "lie."

Don't get me wrong, successful conspiracies occur every day. But they typically involve a small number of incredibly close-knit participants who are in constant contact with one another for a very short period without any outside pressure. That wasn't the case for the disciples. These men and women were either involved in the greatest conspiracy of all time or were simply eyewitnesses who were telling the truth. The more I learned about conspiracies, the more the latter seemed the most reasonable conclusion.

MARTYRDOM ISN'T ALWAYS A PROOF

Before I move on from this discussion of conspiracies, I want to address an issue sometimes raised related to the relationship between martyrdom and truth. History is filled with examples of men and women who were committed to their religious views and were willing to die a martyr's death for what they believed.

The Martyrdom Traditions of the Apostles

Andrew was crucified in Patras, Greece

Bartholomew (a.k.a. Nathanael) was flayed to death with a whip in Armenia

James the Just was thrown from the temple and then beaten to death in Jerusalem

James the Greater was beheaded in Jerusalem

John died in exile at the prison mines on the island of Patmos

Luke was hanged in Greece

Mark was dragged by horse until he died in Alexandria, Egypt

Matthew was killed by a sword in Ethiopia

Matthias was stoned and then beheaded in Jerusalem

Peter was crucified upside down in Rome.

Philip was crucified in Phrygia

Thomas was stabbed to death with a spear in India

The hijackers who flew the planes into the Twin Towers, for example, considered themselves religious martyrs. Does this martyrdom testify to the truth of their beliefs in a manner similar to the martyrdom of the twelve apostles? No, there is an important difference here. You and I might die for what we believe today, trusting in the testimony of those who were witnesses thousands of years ago. We were not there to see Jesus for ourselves, but we may believe we have good reason to accept their testimony. Our martyrdom would therefore be a demonstration of this trust, rather than a confirmation of the truth.

The original eyewitnesses, however, were in a very different position. They knew firsthand if their claims were true or not. They didn't trust someone else for their testimony; they were making a firsthand assertion. The martyrdom of these original eyewitnesses is in a completely different category from the martyrdom of those who might follow them. If their claims were a lie, they would know it personally, unlike those who were martyred in the centuries to follow. While it's reasonable to believe you and I might die for what we *mistakenly thought* was true, it's unreasonable to believe these men died for what they *definitely knew* to be untrue.

 ## A TOOL FOR THE CALLOUT BAG, A TIP FOR THE CHECKLIST

A healthy skepticism toward conspiracy theories is an important tool to include in our *callout* bag. We need to hesitate before we wholeheartedly embrace conspiratorial claims related to the apostles. Movies like *The God Who Wasn't There* and *Zeitgeist, the Movie*[3] have popularized the notion Jesus is simply a retelling of prior mythologies. In essence, these movies claim a group of conspirators assembled the fictional story of Jesus from several pre-existing mythologies (borrowing a little here and a little there) and perpetuated the elaborate lie until they died. While some of my skeptical friends may still reject the claims of Christianity, I hope I can at least help them recognize successful, large-scale conspiracies are rare and the notion of a "Christian conspiracy" is simply unreasonable.

As Christians, we need to recognize our culture is fascinated by conspiracy theories. Many of our friends and family members are quick to jump to elaborate conspiratorial possibilities even when there are simpler explanations on the table. Given what I now know about the difficult nature of successful conspiracies, I can help the skeptics in my world as they assess the claims of the apostles. You can too. We all need to take the time to understand the elements of successful conspiracies so we can communicate them to others. But to be consistent in our beliefs and explanations, we'll need to resist the temptation to see a conspiracy around every corner of current events. If it is unreasonable for the resurrection to be the product of a conspiracy, it is just as unreasonable other events requiring many conspirators and the perfect set of conditions would be the result of a conspiracy. Let's be careful not to unreasonably embrace conspiracy theories related to secular issues, while simultaneously trying to make a case against the alleged conspiracy of the apostles. If we are consistent in our understanding and rejection of unreasonable conspiratorial explanations, we'll successfully communicate the truth of the resurrection to a skeptical world.

Chapter 8

Principle #8:

RESPECT THE "CHAIN OF CUSTODY"

"Detective Wallace, isn't it true …"

Something told me the question I was about to hear was intended to criticize my cold-case investigation. One of the state's most capable defense attorneys stood behind the podium, glaring at me with a dramatic expression of suspicion as he began his sixth day of questioning. By now I was familiar with the approach he was taking; his questions were more rhetorical than probative. He was trying to make a point, and he was doing his best to vilify the original detectives in the process. When a defense attorney begins a question in this way, odds are good the next thing he says will be less than complimentary.

"Detective Wallace, isn't it true there isn't a single crime-scene photograph of the alleged button you say was left at the murder scene in 1985?" He stood a little straighter and adjusted the waist of his pants, revealing the suspenders he wore underneath his suit jacket. He was sporting the finest suit I had seen in a courtroom in quite some time, and he occasionally strutted back and forth behind the podium to model it for the jury.

"Sir, I do believe there was one photograph taken by the original crime-scene investigators," I responded. While this was true, I knew my response would not satisfy him; I could see where this was headed.

The button was a key piece of evidence pointing to the defendant. It was torn from his shirt during the murder and was discovered at the scene. Detectives later executed a search warrant and retrieved a shirt in the defendant's apartment. This shirt was missing a button. Forensic comparisons confirmed the button at the crime scene matched the defendant's shirt. But we had a problem.

The CSI officers were using a 35mm camera in 1985, and they were limited by their technology. They would typically use rolls of film with 12, 24, or 36 exposures each. As a result, I had fewer photographs than I would have liked (today our criminalists take hundreds of digital photographs with cameras capable of storing *thousands* of images). To make matters worse, photographers in 1985 had no way to preview the images they shot. They had to wait until the photographs were developed to determine if the images were clear and focused. As it turned out, one of the most important photographs taken in this crime scene was the photograph taken of the button, and it was one of three photographs out of focus. The CSI officers shot only forty-eight photographs in total, and none of them displayed a clear image of the button.

Evidence Tampering

Defense attorneys sometimes insinuate an officer has planted evidence in a case. In order to prove such an accusation, however, it must be demonstrated:

(1) The (officer) willfully and intentionally changed, planted, placed, made, hid, or moved (a piece of evidence). (2) The (officer) knew he or she was changing, planting, placing, making, hiding, or moving (a piece of evidence), and (3) When the (officer) changed, planted, placed, made, hid, or moved (the piece of evidence), he or she intended that his or her action would result in someone being charged with a crime or (the piece of evidence) being wrongfully produced as genuine or true in a court proceeding (Section 2630, Judicial Council of California Criminal Jury Instructions, 2006).

"Come now, Detective Wallace, you know as well as I do there isn't a single image of the button at the crime scene. You continue to point to these blurry images and expect the jury to believe they contain your most important piece of evidence?" He had a good point. We didn't have a clear image of the button from the crime-scene photographs. Despite this, we knew with certainty the button was part of the murder scene. The first responding officers reported seeing it, and the detectives who arrived later also documented the button in their notes. CSI officers collected the button and booked it into evidence later in the day, along with other items from the scene and several items collected in the search warrant.

"Isn't it true the first time this button was mentioned in a formal police report was in the property report completed by CSI officers *after* the search warrant was served?"

His implication was clear. If the button was not photographed at the scene, there was no way to be certain officers didn't collect it at the search warrant, pull it from the defendant's shirt, and later claim it first appeared at the murder scene. The attorney was carefully making the case detectives had lied about the button in an effort to tamper with the evidence and frame his client.

I was concerned the jury might accept this devious explanation of the button, but my fears were misplaced. After convicting the defendant, the jury later told us they believed the testimony of the responding patrol officers, CSI officers, and detectives who mentioned the button in their notes. The jury was unwilling to believe a conspiracy of this size (involving seven different officers from three divisions) came together to frame the defendant. They convicted him, despite the fact we didn't have a clear image of the button at the scene.

ESTABLISHING A "CHAIN OF CUSTODY"

Detectives quickly learn the importance of documenting and tracking key pieces of evidence. If the evidence isn't carefully handled, several questions will plague the case as it is presented to a jury. Was a particular piece of evidence truly discovered at the scene? How do we know it was actually there? How do we know an officer didn't "plant" it there? These kinds of questions can be avoided if we respect and establish the "chain of custody." Every crime scene contains important pieces of evidence, and these items of evidence must eventually be delivered to a jury for consideration when the case is brought to trial. Our button, for example, had to find its way from the crime scene to the courtroom. Along the way, it spent years sitting in our police property room and was also handled by several specialists until I eventually checked it out from property and transported it to court.

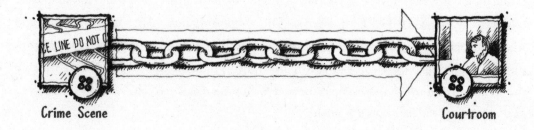

Crime Scene   Courtroom

Each step in this process is a link in the chain connecting the crime scene to the courtroom. If I can demonstrate the links are all connected and well documented, the jury will come to trust the button I am showing them in court is the same button we discovered at the crime scene. In an ideal investigation, the officer at the scene, after discovering the button, would document the discovery in his notes and ask a CSI officer to photograph the item. The CSI officer would then collect the button and book it into evidence, carefully packaging it and documenting his or her efforts in a report. The property room would then accept the button into evidence, citing the date and time it was booked in, along with the name of the officer who booked it. Every time the button was then removed from property to be examined by an expert, those handling it would document the movement of the button. Reports would be written, and property logs would be maintained to track the button's movement from the point when it was first booked into property until it was finally checked out for trial. If this is done properly, the defense will not be able to claim the button was planted.

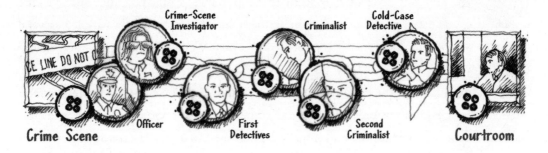

Many of us still remember the infamous O. J. Simpson trial. Simpson was accused of killing Nicole Brown and Ron Goldman, and his defense team claimed the police tampered with the evidence to implicate him. LAPD detective Mark Fuhrman testified he found a bloodstained glove at the location where Nicole Simpson and Ron Goldman were murdered. He also testified he traveled to O. J. Simpson's home later in the evening and found the matching bloodstained glove at Simpson's estate, along with several blood drops ultimately identified as Nicole's. The defense argued Fuhrman transported the items from the scene of the murder and planted them at Simpson's residence. The *chain of custody* was at the center of the defense's argument.

A NEW TESTAMENT "CHAIN OF CUSTODY"

Those who are skeptical of the New Testament Gospels offer a similar objection based on the *chain of custody*. The Gospels claim to be eyewitness accounts of the life and ministry of Jesus Christ. These accounts were eventually entered into the "court record" when they were established as Scripture at the Council of Laodicea in AD 363. It was here early Christian leaders first identified and codified the *canon* of the Christian Scripture, the official list of twenty-seven books and letters known as the New Testament. No council, prior to this meeting in the fourth century, formally acknowledged the list of accepted books and letters (including the Gospels); no "courtroom" recognized the evidence of the Gospels prior to this important church-council meeting. If the life of Jesus could be considered the Christian "crime scene," this council was undoubtedly the "courtroom" where the evidence of the eyewitness testimony was first formally acknowledged.

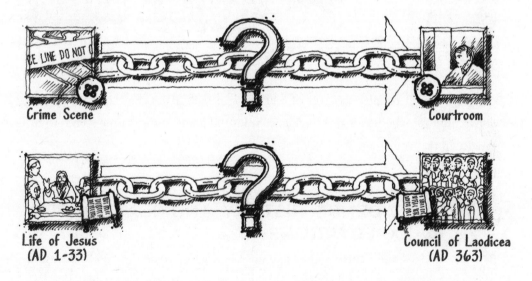

Crime Scene   Courtroom

Life of Jesus
(AD 1-33)   Council of Laodicea
(AD 363)

That's quite an expansive span of time between the "crime scene" and the "courtroom," don't you think? A lot could happen in 330 years. I thought it was tough to trace and track the evidence in my cases, and they were only decades old! Imagine tracking the evidence for ten times as many years. Skeptics consider this period of time and argue the eyewitness evidence of the Gospels was "planted." Like the defense attorney who argued the button was added to the collection of evidence sometime *after* the crime occurred, skeptics often argue the Gospels were written well after the life of Jesus. They are not true evidence; they were manufactured by conspirators who wanted to fool those who were not at the "crime scene."

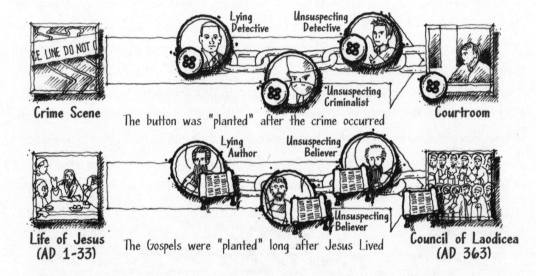

Crime Scene   The button was "planted" after the crime occurred   Courtroom

Life of Jesus   The Gospels were "planted" long after Jesus Lived   Council of Laodicea
(AD 1-33)   (AD 363)

The best way to counter this sort of a claim is to retrace the chain of custody to see if we can account for who handled the evidence from the point of the "crime scene" to its first appearance in the "courtroom."

EVIDENCE, HISTORY, AND REASONABLE EXPECTATIONS

While it may sound like an easy task to trace the chain of custody, it can be extremely difficult in older cases. This is often my dilemma as a cold-case detective. When I open a case from the past, the first thing I try to do is collect all the original documents written during the first investigation. That should be easy, right? Well, not always. While these cases were important to our agency, there are times when unexpected issues, unrelated to the investigation, can make this task difficult. Sometimes things are lost when a records database is upgraded as the result of new storage technology. Sometimes notes or other reports have simply deteriorated to the point they are no longer usable. Sometimes documents are accidentally destroyed or purged. The longer an event slips into the past, the more likely I may have a problem retrieving all the information I need to trace the chain of custody. Despite this, I have been able to assemble enough of the chain of custody to demonstrate a level of responsibility to the jury. Given the age of the case, jurors understand we simply cannot expect the same level of precise *record keeping* when outside forces cannot be controlled over long periods of time.

Something very similar happens when trying to trace the chain of custody for the gospel eyewitness accounts. Imagine trying to control outside forces for thousands of years instead of just a few decades. The "original reports" in the "Christian cold case" were written on papyrus, an excellent material if you are looking for something readily available in the first century, but a terrible material if you are looking for something that won't fall apart when handled frequently. As a result, we no longer have the original writings (sometimes called "autographs"). The first eyewitness accounts were copied repeatedly so they could be distributed throughout the church and retained despite the nature of the papyrus. It's now difficult to precisely retrace the movement of the Gospels over time and establish a *chain of custody.*

To have any success at all, we need to first identify the players who would be involved in such a chain. In cold-case homicide investigations, the *links* in the chain include the responding officers, the crime-scene investigators, the first detectives, the criminalists, and then the cold-case detectives, who ultimately bring the case to the prosecutor. But who would we expect to be involved in the gospel *chain of custody*?

Life of Jesus
(AD 1-33)

Council of Laodicea
(AD 350-363)

To trace the New Testament Gospels, we need to identify the original eyewitnesses and their immediate disciples, moving from one set of disciples to the next until we trace the Gospels from AD 33 to AD 363. The New Testament gospel chain of custody, if it exists, would provide us with confidence the accounts we have today are an accurate reflection of what was observed at the "crime scene." This *link-by-link* approach to the history of the accounts would also help us to respond to the objections of skeptics who claim the Gospels were planted late in history. We will examine this issue in much more detail in section 2, and we will identify the historical links in this important chain.

 *A TOOL FOR THE CALLOUT BAG, A TIP FOR THE CHECKLIST*

As a detective, I quickly learned the importance of the chain of custody, and I eventually pulled this principle from my callout bag as I investigated the reliability of the Gospels. Before I became a Christian, I seldom held the same level of skepticism for other ancient documents I held for the biblical accounts. I can remember having an intense interest in ancient history from the time I was in high school. I had an honors class with a wonderful, sage-like teacher, Mr. Schultz, who had the ability to bring the past to life using the ancient written histories of Herodotus and Thucydides, among others. He taught from these accounts as if they were reliable and true, and I accepted them without much question.

Mr. Schultz never talked about the fact the earliest copies we have for these ancient writers appear in history approximately five hundred years after the events they claim to describe. There is no clear chain of custody for these historical accounts during this period. We don't know whom Herodotus, for example, entrusted with his writings. We don't know how Herodotus's record was preserved or what happened to it during these five hundred years. This is, of course, the nature of most ancient historical accounts. Given that we accept these accounts as historically factual even though their history of transmission is missing for five centuries or more, wouldn't it be fair to reconsider our historical view of the gospel record if we discovered it has a verifiable chain of custody? We need to keep this question in mind as we get ready to examine the issue more thoroughly in section 2.

Of all the documents written by Christians in the first and second centuries, the texts we care about most are those in the canon of Scripture. Few of us are familiar with the *noncanonical* writings from the earliest period of Christian history. Many early Christian leaders wrote letters and documents rich with theological content and historical detail, even though they are not considered *canonical*. These *noncanonical* early-church documents can tell us much about the teaching of the original eyewitnesses. They will eventually become part of the chain of custody as we examine the transmission of the Gospels in the first three centuries. We would be wise to have at least some understanding of the identity of the students and disciples of the apostles and some mastery of their writings. Many of these men (like Polycarp, Ignatius, and Clement) became known as the "early-church fathers." They led the church following the deaths of the apostles, and their letters and writings are widely available online and in print form. The earliest works of these church fathers are often interesting and enriching. They are worth our time and effort, particularly as we make a case for the New Testament chain of custody and the reliability of the Gospels as eyewitness accounts.

KNOW WHEN "ENOUGH IS ENOUGH"

"I wasn't convinced," said Juror Number 8 as he looked across the table at the other jurors. Some of them laughed and shook their heads. Juror Number 8 stood his ground. "Hey, this is a big deal to me. I needed to be sure."

We sat together in the jury room, relaxing around a long table after the trial concluded and the verdict had been read. The jurors were assembled and eager to ask us questions. They looked exhausted but relieved. The trial took six weeks, and this jury conscientiously deliberated for another week before delivering a guilty verdict. I was nervous when the deliberation stretched beyond the first two days; I suspected one (or more) of the jurors was delaying the verdict and we might be headed toward a "hung jury." In California criminal trials, all twelve jurors must agree on the outcome. If there are any holdouts, no verdict will be reached, and the case must be retried if the prosecutor hopes to convict the defendant. The longer the deliberation, the more likely the jury is divided. I was beginning to fear the group was hung until the court clerk called us and told us we had a verdict.

In all honesty, I thought the decision would come back much sooner. This case was overwhelming. We had nearly forty pieces of evidence pointing to the defendant as the killer. In fact, he was caught trying to commit a very similar crime about ten days after he killed the victim in our town. He even had a knife matching our victim's injuries when he was caught in this second crime. The case was robust and clear; I thought the jury would come back with a decision in less than a day. I typically join the prosecutor and interview the jury following their work on one of our cases because I want to learn from their observations. What was evidentially powerful? What was relatively insignificant? What was it that finally "made the case" for them? Today I was eager to learn why it took them so long to render a verdict. They told me after reviewing the evidence and taking their first vote, Juror Number 8 was the sole holdout. While everyone else was convinced the defendant was guilty, Juror Number 8 was not so sure.

"I take that 'reasonable doubt' stuff seriously," he said. "I mean, my gut was telling me he was guilty, but I wasn't sure if we had enough evidence to reach the 'standard' the judge was talking about. I just needed to see the evidence one more time."

"What was it that finally convinced you?" I asked.

"The Band-Aid."

The Band-Aid? Really? I could hardly believe it. When the defendant committed the murder, he cut his finger. He went home and bandaged the injury and was wearing this Band-Aid when the detectives later interviewed him. He didn't want the detectives to notice the injury, so he slipped off the Band-Aid and left it in a corner of the interview room. The detectives only noticed and collected the bandage after the interview was completed. We later had the Band-Aid tested for DNA to demonstrate it did, in fact, belong to the defendant. But I never considered this bandage an important part of the case. In fact, the prosecutor almost didn't include it in the presentation to the jury. Now I was very glad he did.

WHERE'S THE TIPPING POINT?

You never know the impact a particular piece of evidence will have on those who are considering your case. Sometimes the things that don't matter much to you personally are the very things that matter the most to someone else.

I've been producing a podcast and hosting a website (ColdCaseChristianity.com) for many years now, and people email me with their questions and doubts related to the evidence for the Christian worldview. Skeptics sometimes write to inform me they simply don't believe there is enough evidence to prove God exists. Christians sometimes write to tell me they are struggling with doubt because they aren't sure if the evidence is *sufficient*. In many ways, all these folks are struggling with the same question. It's a question jurors face in every case. When is enough, enough? When is it reasonable to conclude something is true? When is the evidence *sufficient*?

In legal terms, the *line* that must be crossed before someone can conclude something is evidentially true is called the "standard of proof" (the "SOP"). The SOP varies depending on the kind of case under consideration. The most rigorous of these criteria is the "beyond a reasonable doubt" standard required at criminal trials. But how do we know when we have crossed the line and are "beyond a reasonable doubt"? The courts have considered this important issue and have provided us with a definition:

> Reasonable doubt is defined as follows: It is not a mere possible doubt; because everything relating to human affairs is open to some possible or imaginary doubt. It is that state of the case which, after the entire comparison and consideration of all the evidence, leaves the minds of the jurors in that condition that they cannot say they feel an abiding conviction of the truth of the charge.[1]

This definition is important because it recognizes the difference between *reasonable* and *possible* we discussed earlier. There are, according to the ruling of the court, "reasonable doubts," "possible doubts," and "imaginary doubts." The definition acknowledges something important: every case has unanswered questions. Jurors may have doubts as they ponder a decision. It's not possible to remove every potential uncertainty; that's why the standard is not "beyond any

The Escalating Standard of Proof

"Some Credible Evidence"

The lowest possible standard (used in some child protection hearings). This standard simply establishes there is enough evidence to begin an inquiry, investigation, or trial.

"Preponderance of the Evidence"

This is the next standard of proof (used in most civil trials). This standard is established if a proposition is more likely true than untrue (i.e., 51% more likely).

"Clear and Convincing Evidence"

This is an intermediate standard of proof (used in some civil and criminal proceedings). This standard is met when a proposition is significantly and substantially more likely true than untrue.

"Beyond a Reasonable Doubt"

This is the highest level of proof required by the law (usually reserved for criminal trials). This standard is met when there is no plausible reason to believe a proposition is untrue.

doubt." Being "beyond a reasonable doubt" simply requires us to separate our *possible* and *imaginary* doubts from those that are *reasonable*.

"SHUNNING" THE TRUTH

There are many reasons why people may deny (or "shun") the truth. Not all reasons are based on evidence. Jurors can reject a truth claim for "ra'shun'al," "emo'shun'al" or "voli'shun'al" reasons. Sometimes jurors have *rational* doubts based on the evidence. Perhaps the defense has convinced them an alternative explanation is better supported evidentially. Sometimes jurors have purely *emotional* doubts. I've been involved in cases where jurors had an emotional reaction to the prosecutor or defense attorney and struggled to overcome negative *feelings* so they could evaluate the case fairly. Sometimes jurors deny the truth for *volitional* reasons. They are willfully resistant and refuse to accept any position offered by the group. Attorneys on both sides do their best to identify *strong-willed* people such as these during the jury selection process to make sure the jury is comprised of people who will listen to the arguments of others. When making a decision based on evidence, it's important for us to understand the "shuns" we've described and limit our doubts to those that are rational and reasonable.

"Ra'SHUN'al"   "Emo'SHUN'al"   "Voli'SHUN'al"

This makes the decision-making process much easier. When assessing the case, we simply need to examine our doubts and separate those based on evidence (rational doubts) from those that are not (emotional or volitional doubts). If the doubts we still possess fall into the second category, we can be comfortable with our decision. Once we realize our doubts are not reasonable, we can deliver a verdict, even though we may still have unanswered questions.

YOU'LL NEVER KNOW ALL THERE IS TO KNOW

It's important to remember truth can be known even when some of the facts are missing. None of us has ever made a decision with *complete* knowledge of all the possible facts. There are always unanswered questions. I use a version of the puzzle illustration (from chapter 6) when trying to help jurors understand this truth. As we assemble a case pointing to any particular defendant, we begin to collect pieces of evidence slowly revealing the identity of the killer. We begin to assemble the puzzle (much like we did from the puzzle pieces in the family room drawer in chapter 6). While there might be a large amount of evidence in the prosecution's case, no criminal case possesses every possible piece of evidence. No prosecutor can answer every conceivable question.

Like this puzzle, every cold case I investigate has missing pieces. Some of these pieces are obvious and glaring. But notice their absence doesn't keep us from having certainty about the image (like the prior puzzle of Jesus); we recognize the picture even though some things are missing. We have certainty because the pieces we *do* have reveal the killer's identity (in this case, Al Capone, the famous Chicago gangster and crime syndicate leader of the 1920s). We have certainty because additional pieces, even if they are different from what we might imagine, would not significantly change the identity we see in the puzzle. We have confidence in concluding Al Capone is pictured here, even though there are unanswered questions about the puzzle.

For some, the idea of making a decision while there are still unanswered questions seems premature and even dangerous. What if there are outstanding facts yet unknown to us? What if new, additional information comes to light in a few years contradicting the evidence we have in front of us today? Wouldn't it be wiser for us to simply withhold judgment until every question can be answered (including those we haven't even thought of yet)? But juries understand the importance of acting on what they *do* know rather than fretting about what *could be* known. In courtrooms across America, jurors are asked to act (in the present) on the evidence available (from the past) to decide what ought to happen (in the future). They make these decisions because what they *do* know outweighs what might *possibly be known* if every question could be answered. The evidence is either sufficient today or it is not; jurors must assess what they have in front of them at the moment rather than speculate about what they might find out later.

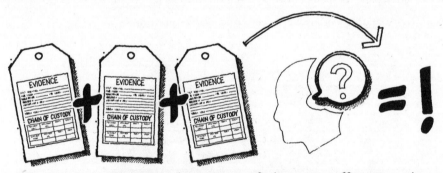

We step over unanswered questions if there is sufficient evidence

EVIDENTIAL SUFFICIENCY AND THE PROBLEM OF EVIL

A listener of the *Cold-Case Christianity Podcast* once sent me an email expressing his doubts in the existence of an all-powerful and all-loving God, given the presence of evil in the world. This is a classic objection to theism. If God does exist, why would He allow people to do evil things? This "God" is either unable to stop people from acting as they do (in which case He is not all-powerful), or He is unwilling to stop them (in which case He is not all-loving). The writer posed this question to me because he knew what I did for a living:

"I bet you see many terrible things people do to one another. How can you still believe in such a God?"

The problem of evil is perhaps the most difficult issue to address because it is emotionally loaded. It's at times like these I try to help people walk through the distinctions between *reasonable doubts* (grounded rationally) and *possible doubts* (grounded emotionally). Let me explain.

We need to start by recognizing there are many good reasons to believe God exists (we talked about some of them in chapter 3). These pieces of the puzzle are already in place before we start talking about the issue of evil. Yes, there are some unanswered questions related to the existence of evil, but we must begin our examination by recognizing the puzzle is well on its way to completion even though this piece may seem to be missing. Next, we must ask ourselves if the presence of evil truly represents a missing piece. Is it possible, instead, the existence of evil may actually be an *additional* piece helping to make the puzzle more certain?

Epicurus and the "Problem of Evil"

Ancient Greek philosopher Epicurus is credited with first posing the "Problem of Evil" as it relates to the existence of God:

"Either God wants to abolish evil, and cannot; or he can, but does not want to. If he wants to, but cannot, he is impotent. If he can, but does not want to, he is wicked. If God can abolish evil, and God really wants to do it, why is there evil in the world?" (According to Lactantius in *The Wrath of God*, ca. AD 313).

When someone complains there is evil in the world, they are not simply offering their *opinion*. They are instead claiming true, *objective* evil exists. They are complaining about evil behavior as though this behavior ought to be recognized by *all* of us, regardless of our personal likes, dislikes, or opinions about human conduct. If evil were a matter of opinion, we could eliminate it by simply changing our minds. People who complain about evil behavior must accept the premise that true objective "right" and "wrong" exists in the first place. They must accept some things are morally virtuous and some things are morally repulsive, no matter who you are, where you are located, or when you live in history. This kind of moral evil transcends all of us; if it doesn't, why complain in the first place? If evil is simply a matter of opinion, why doesn't the man who emailed me simply change his opinion?

You see, for true evil to exist (so the emailer has something legitimate to complain about), there must be a true barometer of right and wrong. For an act to be objectively "bad," there must be some standard of objective "good" by which to measure it. What might that standard be if not God? Can the standard come from some evolutionary process? Can it come from the slow development of cultural groups? If so, morals are simply a matter of opinion (albeit a largely held opinion), and there is nothing objectively evil to complain about. Remember, even the most heinous regimes of history identified their own behavior as morally virtuous. For true *evil* to exist, there must be a source of true *good* transcending any and all groups who might make a claim about the existence of evil. In other words, the existence of true evil necessitates the presence of God as a standard of true virtue. It turns out the existence of evil is another evidence *for* God's existence; another piece of the puzzle revealing God's image.

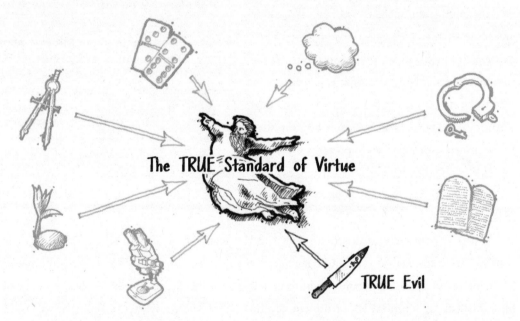

But let's return to the very real issue of evil behavior. Why would God allow people to kill each other if He loves us and is powerful enough to stop it? While this question has emotional power, we must ask ourselves if there might be a reasonable explanation. Are we thinking it through evidentially, or are we reacting emotionally? Are we rejecting the existence of God because there is no rational explanation for the existence of evil, or are we resisting volitionally because we stubbornly refuse to accept any explanation one might offer?

I can think of several very good reasons why God would allow people to behave immorally, even though He loves His creation and is certainly powerful enough to stop evil. Ask yourself the question: Which is more loving, a God who creates a world in which love is *possible* or a God who creates a world in which love is *impossible*? It seems reasonable a loving God would create a world where love is possible and can be experienced by creatures designed "in His image." But a world in which love is possible can be a dangerous place. Love requires freedom. True love requires humans to freely choose; love cannot be forced if it is to be heartfelt and real. The problem, of course, is people who have the freedom to love often choose to hate. That's why freedom of this nature is so costly. A world in which people have the freedom to love and perform great acts of kindness is also a world in which people have the freedom to hate and commit great acts of evil. You cannot have one without the other.

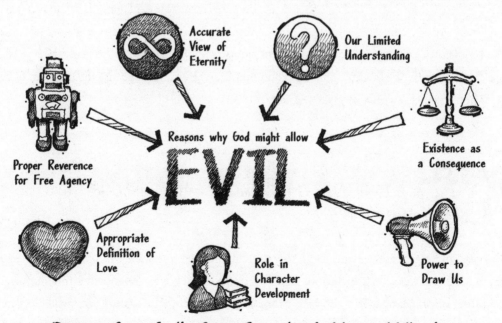

(Diagram from *God's Crime Scene* by J. Warner Wallace)

In addition to this, from a Christian perspective, we are all eternal creatures who will live beyond the grave. If this is true, then questions about why God might not stop evil are a bit premature. At best, we can only say God hasn't stopped evil *yet*. But God has all eternity to act in this regard. Our eternal life provides the context for God to deal justly with those who choose hate and perform acts of evil. God *is* powerful enough to stop evil completely, and He *does* care about justice. But as an eternal Being, He may choose to take care of it on an eternal timeline. Compared to eternity, this mortal existence is but a vapor, created by God to be a wonderful place where love is possible for those who choose it.

Theodicy

"The theological discipline that seeks to explain how the existence of evil in the world can be reconciled with the justice and goodness of God" (*Webster's New World College Dictionary*, Wiley Publishing Inc., Cleveland, 2010).

If there are good reasons why God might permit evil in this life (such as the preservation of free will and the ability to love genuinely), concerns about His failure to act are simply unreasonable. Doubts about God's existence based on the problem of evil may have emotional appeal, but they lack rational foundation because reasonable explanations do, in fact, exist. While one can imagine *possible doubts* related to the problem of evil, careful consideration of the nature of objective evil reveals these doubts are not *reasonable*. We ought to move beyond our reservations here because the problem of evil does not present us with a *reasonable doubt*.[2]

A TOOL FOR THE CALLOUT BAG, A TIP FOR THE CHECKLIST

In every investigation I've conducted, this principle related to *evidential sufficiency* has helped me to evaluate my own conclusions and determine if they were reasonable; this important tool from our *callout* bag can also help us assess the claims of Christianity. We make decisions every day with less than perfect knowledge and less than complete information. We act with certainty even though we don't know everything that could be known. We learn to trust our cars, even though we don't completely understand how they operate mechanically. We trust our mates and children, even though we don't know everything they are thinking or everything they are doing when we are away. We make a case for what we believe, and we accept the fact we can't know everything.

Criminal cases require the highest legal standard; they require jurors to come to a decision "beyond a reasonable doubt." The decisions jurors make are often a matter of life and death for the defendants involved. If this standard is appropriate for important cases involving *temporal* matters of life and death, it's appropriate for the case determining our eternal life or death. Jurors render verdicts beyond a reasonable doubt, even though there are still some unanswered questions. They do this because the reasonable evidence they possess is greater than the unanswered questions. Let's make sure our objections and doubts are less emotional or volitional than they are rational. When I was an atheist, I never took the time to categorize my doubts into "rational" versus "emotional" classifications. I also never took the time to see if theism (or Christianity) offered a reasonable response to my doubts. Looking back at it, many of my doubts were merely *possible doubts* based on an emotional or volitional response.

I often get frustrated when sharing what I believe about God with my skeptical friends, coworkers, and family members. Those of us who are interested in making a rational, evidential case for our Christian worldview sometimes find our efforts completely unfruitful. Try as we might, even when we make a cogent, articulate, reasonable case for our view, our efforts seem to have no impact on our listeners. It's tempting to get frustrated and begin to doubt our own evidence. In times like these, it's important to remember the "shuns" of denial. Many of the people we are trying to reach are willing to deny the truth of God's existence based on an emotional or volitional response, rather than good evidence. This is not to say all atheists are irrational, emotional, or willfully resistant. Many have taken the time to make a reasoned case of their own. It's our responsibility as Christians to know our friends and family well enough to understand the nature of their denial. When they are resisting based on evidence, let's examine the facts together and assess which explanations are the most reasonable. When they are resisting for other reasons, let's be sensitive enough to ask questions so we can understand where they are coming from before we overwhelm them with the evidence we are so eager to share. Don't expect someone to respond to your *reasoned* arguments when the *evidence* wasn't important to him or her in the first place.

Chapter 10

Principle #10:

PREPARE FOR AN ATTACK

My partner sent me a joke involving a defense attorney and a murder trial that has been circulating around our police agency for some time:

A defendant was on trial for a murder. There was overwhelming circumstantial evidence pointing to the defendant's guilt despite the fact the body of the victim was never recovered. After sitting through weeks of the trial, the defendant and his lawyer knew he would probably be convicted. In an act of desperation, the defense attorney resorted to a trick.

"Ladies and gentlemen of the jury, I have a surprise for you," the attorney proclaimed as he looked down at his watch. "Within sixty seconds, the person you thought had been murdered will walk into this courtroom."

He turned and looked toward the courtroom door. The jurors, surprised by the proclamation, turned and watched the door in anticipation. A minute passed. Nothing happened.

Finally, the defense attorney said, "I need to admit to you I lied about that last statement. But all of you turned with me and watched that door with eager anticipation. This demonstrates you have a reasonable doubt in this case as to whether anyone was killed in the first place! I, therefore, insist you return a verdict of not guilty."

The jury, openly rattled by the clever effort, retired to deliberate on the case. Moments later they returned and promptly delivered a verdict of guilty. The defense attorney was shocked.

"How could you return with a verdict so quickly?" he asked the jury. "You must have had some doubt; I saw all of you watch that door with expectation!"

The jury foreman replied, "Yes, we did look, but your client didn't."

I've been involved in several homicide trials over the years. Some of our cases were evidentially overwhelming, and others were more difficult to prove. In every case, the defendant was represented by an articulate, intelligent, and committed defense attorney who carefully crafted a defense for his or her client. Many of these attorneys appeared incredibly confident, despite the overwhelming evidence pointing to the guilt of their clients.

I'm never surprised by the enthusiasm and self-assurance of good defense attorneys. Many factors can motivate an attorney to perform confidently and aggressively on behalf of a defendant. I suspect some attorneys work diligently because they have a true belief in the innocence of their clients. Others probably work diligently because they have a true belief in the importance of fair and adequate representation in our criminal justice system, even if they don't personally believe their clients are innocent. Some attorneys may work diligently because they have a true belief in advancing their careers. One thing is for sure, defense attorneys present the best case they can, even when they may not believe they are defending the truth.

 ## THE GROWING ATTACK FROM SKEPTICS

I became a Christian in 1996. Until 2001, the Jim Wallace I knew prior to 1996 was the most sarcastic atheist I had ever known. I can remember some of my conversations with Christians prior to becoming a believer, and I am now embarrassed by the way I behaved; many of my coworkers continue to remind me of those days. But my own level of prior sarcasm was quickly eclipsed by the atheists who began to write and speak against religion following the attack on the World Trade Center in 2001. A new era in atheistic rhetoric began following that dreadful day, as prominent atheists responded to what they saw as evidence of the evil of "religious fundamentalism." Several books flooded the shelves of local bookstores. Sam Harris wrote *The End of Faith: Religion, Terror, and the Future of Reason* (2004) and *Letter to a Christian Nation* (2006). Richard Dawkins wrote *The God Delusion* (2006), and Christopher Hitchens wrote *God Is Not Great: How Religion Poisons Everything* (2007). The attack from atheists and skeptics grew and took on a new form of immediacy, aggression, and sarcasm.

Many Christians, especially those who had been believers for most of their lives, were caught off guard by the confidence and articulate opposition of these authors and those who shared their negative view of Christianity. The culture quickly seemed to embrace the winsome atheist criticisms; book sales for these three writers were phenomenal. The mere fact anyone could offer a thoughtful and engaging defense of atheism seemed to shake the confidence of many believers who may have taken their faith for granted. It wasn't as though these skeptics were offering anything new. Instead, they were presenting old arguments with new vigor, humor, cynicism, and urgency. They were much like the defense attorneys I had faced over the years.

I've discovered good defense attorneys typically bring out the best in prosecutors and detectives, so I've learned to embrace the work of defense lawyers who have caused me to make sure my case is sound and reasonable. The fact that there is a defender on the opposite side of the issue who is arguing vociferously against us is no reason to believe the defender possesses the truth. Defense attorneys operate that way even when they are defending what turns out to be a lie. The existence of a well-articulated defensive argument alone is no reason to surrender our position, but it ought to encourage us to know our case better than anyone else. Defense attorneys (just like those who oppose the claims of Christianity) ought to bring out the best in us.

THE DEFENSIVE STRATEGY

Defense attorneys approach each case differently, but I've noticed several general strategies lawyers have taken when trying to defeat my cold-case investigations. By examining these defensive strategies and comparing them to the approach often taken by those who oppose Christianity, we can assess the validity of these tactics.

DEFENSE ATTORNEYS CHALLENGE THE NATURE OF TRUTH

If all truth is simply a matter of perspective and subjective opinion, it's virtually impossible to convict someone of a crime. We live in a culture that is more and more pluralistic with each passing generation. Many of our young adults have been taught (in universities and colleges and through movies, television, and books) that objective truth does not exist or simply cannot be known. As a result, relativism is a common feature of our cultural worldview. People are less and less comfortable accepting the notion one particular version of the truth is exclusively correct. In fact, many believe such a view of truth is arrogant and narrow-minded. To make matters worse, a new cultural definition of "tolerance" has emerged. Tolerance used to be the attitude we took toward one another when we disagreed about an important issue; we would agree to treat each other with respect, even though we refused to embrace each other's view on a particular topic. Tolerance is now the act of recognizing *and embracing* all views as equally valuable and true, even though they often make opposite truth claims. According to this redefinition of tolerance, anything other than acceptance and approval is narrow-minded and bigoted. Defense attorneys are capitalizing on these evolving redefinitions of truth and tolerance. If a lawyer can convince a jury that no version of what happened is better than another (because all truth is simply a matter of personal perspective and opinion), the jury will have trouble convicting the defendant with any level of confidence. For this reason, some defense attorneys begin by attacking the nature of truth before they ever attack the nature of the prosecution's case.

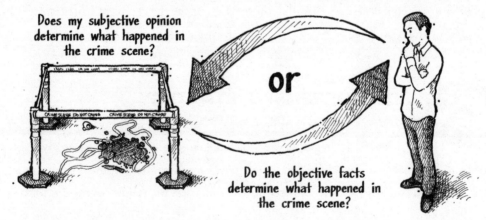

The erosion of the classic view of objective truth and tolerance is also taking its toll on those who hold a Christian worldview. The notion there might be only one way to God (or only one truth about the identity and nature of God) is offensive and intolerant to many skeptics and nonbelievers. Like prosecutors who face similar misunderstandings about the nature of truth, Christians may also have to expose the logical problems inherent to the new cultural definitions. While some may argue all religions are basically the same, this is simply untrue. The world's religions propose contrary claims related to the nature of God. Eastern religions propose the existence of an impersonal God, while the monotheistic religions of Judaism, Christianity, and Islam claim God is personal. Judaism refuses to recognize Jesus as anything other than a "rabbi" or spiritual teacher, while Christianity claims Jesus was God Himself. Islam denies Jesus died on the cross, while Christianity claims Jesus died at the crucifixion and rose from the dead, verifying His deity. All these claims about God and Jesus may be false, but they cannot all be true; they contradict one another by definition. The logical law of "non-contradiction" states contradictory statements cannot both be true at the same time. Those who are evaluating the claims of the world's religions, like jurors evaluating a criminal case, must decide which of the views is supported by the evidence, rather than surrender the decision to an errant view of truth.

"Objective Truth"

While many truths are certainly a matter of opinion, some truths are completely independent of anyone's personal view. My statement "Police cars are the coolest cars on the road" may be true for me (given I am often the one driving these cars), while completely untrue for you (especially when I pull you over for rolling through a stop sign). This statement is a matter of my "subjective" opinion; it is dependent on the "subject" who possesses it. The statement "Police cars are equipped to travel in excess of 100 mph" is not dependent on my opinion, however; this second statement is either true or false on the basis of the "object" itself. Police cars are equipped to travel this fast, and my "subjective" opinion has nothing to do with it.

In addition to this, those who are investigating Christianity may want to rethink the latest cultural definitions of truth and tolerance. Those who claim truth is a matter of perspective and opinion are proclaiming this as more than a matter of perspective and opinion. They would like us to believe this definition is objectively true, even as they deny the existence of objective truth. When a statement fails to meet its own standard for being true, it is said to be "self-refuting." The claim "objective truth does not exist" is self-refuting because it is, in fact, an objective claim about truth. The current redefinition of tolerance doesn't fare much better. Those who claim tolerance requires all ideas and perspectives to be embraced as equally true and valuable simultaneously deny the classic view of tolerance.

In other words, the new definition of tolerance is intolerant of the old definition. It cannot follow its own rules. It is just as self-refuting as the new redefinition of truth; we simply need to help people understand this is the case.

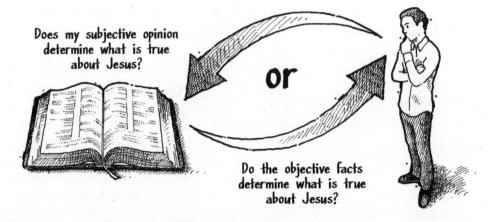

Does my subjective opinion determine what is true about Jesus?

or

Do the objective facts determine what is true about Jesus?

2. DEFENSE ATTORNEYS FOCUS ON THE BEST THE PROSECUTION HAS TO OFFER

While circumstantial cases are built on many pieces of evidence evaluated as a group, some pieces are better (and more important to the case) than others. For this reason, defense attorneys focus their attention on the heart of the prosecution's case, the prominent and most condemning pieces of evidence. If they can discredit or eliminate these key pieces of evidence, the foundation of the prosecution's case may begin to crumble. In fact, if I want to know what the defense thinks of my case (and what they consider the most devastating piece of evidence), I simply pay attention to what they are attacking with the most vigor. If my case is thin or weak, the defense will be comfortable attacking the one piece they believe to be critical. If my case is substantial and strong, the defense will find itself trying to attack a much larger number of issues in an effort to limit the cumulative impact of the evidence. I know where my case is strong when I see what the defense has chosen to attack.

Skeptics do something similar when they attack the claims of Christianity. The Christian worldview is built on the eyewitness testimony of the gospel writers. For this reason, many skeptics attack the reliability of the Gospels as their primary tactic in trying to defeat the case for Christianity. This focused attack on the Gospels reveals the strength of our case. Like defense attorneys, skeptics recognize our most valuable piece of evidence. As a result, some critics attempt to undermine the reliability of the gospel writers as eyewitnesses (we'll examine this more in section 2), while others seek to have this testimony "tossed out" as unreliable "hearsay" before it can even be evaluated. They argue the gospel accounts fail to meet the judicial standard we require of eyewitnesses in criminal cases. Witnesses must be present in court for their testimony to be considered in a criminal trial. This often presents a problem for me as a cold-case detective. I have a few unsolved cases because key witnesses died and are unavailable to testify in court. Though these witnesses may have described their observations to a friend or family member, I can't summon these "second level" witnesses into court, as their testimony would be considered "hearsay." The statements of friends or family members would be inadmissible because the original witness would not be available for cross-examination or evaluation. This exclusion of hearsay testimony from secondary witnesses is reasonable in criminal trials; as a society, we believe "it is better that ten guilty persons escape … than that one innocent suffer."[1] For this reason, we've created a rigorous (and sometimes difficult) legal standard for eyewitnesses.

But this standard is simply too much to require of historical eyewitness testimony. The vast majority of historical events must be evaluated despite the fact the eyewitnesses are now dead and cannot come into court to testify. The eyewitnesses who observed the crafting and signing of the Constitution of the United States are lost to us. Those who wit-

What Makes It "Hearsay"?

A "hearsay" statement is anything said outside of the courtroom that is then offered inside the courtroom (during a court proceeding) as evidence of the truth of the matter asserted. Since jurors must assess the credibility of a witness, courts generally require witnesses to be in the courtroom so (1) they can "swear" or promise their testimony is true, (2) they can be personally present at the proceeding so the jury can assess them visually, and (3) they can be cross-examined by the opposition.

nessed the life of Abraham Lincoln are also lost to us. It's one thing to require eyewitness cross-examination on a case that may condemn a defendant to the gas chamber; it's another thing to hold history up to such an unreasonable necessity. If we require this standard for historical accounts, be prepared to jettison everything you think you know about the past. Nothing can be known about history if live eyewitnesses are the only reliable witnesses we can consult. If this were the case, we could know nothing with certainty beyond two or three living generations, including two or three living generations of *your own family*.

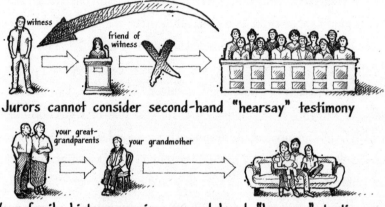

Jurors cannot consider second-hand "hearsay" testimony

Your family history *requires* second-hand "hearsay" testimony

Once the eyewitnesses die, history is lost. But we have great confidence about many historical events, despite the fact the eyewitnesses have long been in their graves. As we evaluate the writers of any historical account, we must simply do our best to assess them under the four criteria we discussed in chapter 4 (we'll apply these criteria in section 2). Our goals are the same as we have for living courtroom eyewitnesses, but our expectations are appropriate to the examination of history. This is reasonable, given the nature of events occurring in the distant past.

3 DEFENSE ATTORNEYS TARGET THE MICRO AND DISTRACT FROM THE MACRO

As we've already described, strong circumstantial cases are built on large collections of evidence; the more pieces of evidence pointing to the suspect, the stronger the case. For this reason, defense attorneys attempt to distract juries from the larger collection by focusing them on individual pieces. The last thing the defense attorney wants the jury to see is how the pieces come together as a group to complete the puzzle. Instead, a defense lawyer wants jurors to examine each piece of the puzzle in isolation from all the rest, hoping the item under consideration can be explained in some manner that won't implicate his or her client. If there is more than one reasonable way to interpret an individual piece of evidence, the law requires juries decide in favor of the defendant's innocence. Defense attorneys, therefore, spend time trying to take the jury's eyes off the larger collection and focus the jury on the minutiae. A single puzzle piece, when examined in isolation, is difficult to understand without seeing the larger puzzle. One little puzzle piece might be part of any number of puzzles; there's just no way to know until we see how it fits with the rest. It's the job of defense attorneys to keep jurors from seeing how the pieces fit together.

Those who challenge the claims of Christianity take a similar approach. Let's look at the case for Peter's influence on the gospel of Mark as an example. Skeptics have noticed Mark's account fails to include the fact Peter got out of the boat and nearly drowned when Jesus was walking on water (as we described earlier, compare Mark 6:45–52 with Matt. 14:22–33).

If this part of the puzzle is examined in isolation, it seems reasonable Peter had no influence on the gospel of Mark at all (as many skeptics claim). How could Mark leave out this detail if he truly had access to Peter? Skeptics have used this passage of Scripture to argue against the eyewitness authorship and reliability of the Bible. But when this individual passage is examined alongside all the other verses involving Peter in the gospel of Mark, the more reasonable explanation emerges. It's only when examining all these passages *collectively* we see Mark's consistent pattern of respect and stewardship toward Peter. It's in the larger context where we discover Mark consistently seeks to protect Peter's reputation and honor. When we combine this fact with the other pieces of the puzzle offered in chapter 5, the case for Peter's influence on Mark's gospel is substantial and reasonable. Like jurors in a criminal trial, we need to resist the effort of those who want us to focus on the individual puzzle pieces as though they are not part of a larger puzzle.

Focus on
the complete
puzzle,
rather than
one piece

DEFENSE ATTORNEYS ATTACK THE MESSENGER

Nearly every piece of courtroom evidence is submitted through the involvement of a human agent. Eyewitness testimony is one obvious example of this, but even forensic evidence is dependent on human participation: a detective who first observed it or a criminalist who later examined it. Defense attorneys sometimes attack the person presenting the evidence when they don't like what the evidence says about their client. This is why you often see a vigorous (and critical) cross-examination of key witnesses; defense attorneys typically vilify these witnesses, claiming some bias or highlighting potentially offensive behavior in the witness's professional or personal life. If the defense can get the jury to hate the witness, they may be able to get the jury to hate the evidence the witness has presented.

"Ad Hominem" Attacks

"Ad hominem" (Latin for "to the man") is an abbreviated form of "Argumentum ad hominem." It describes what is normally seen as a logical fallacy: the attempt to discredit the truth of a claim by pointing out some negative characteristic, behavior, or belief of the person who is making the claim. Dictionary.com describes "ad hominem" as "attacking an opponent's character rather than answering his argument."

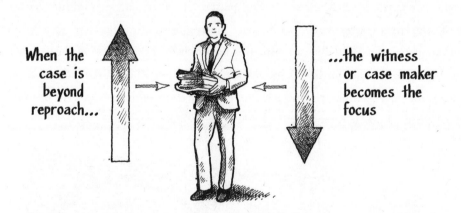

When the case is beyond reproach...

...the witness or case maker becomes the focus

This has become a prominent tactic of skeptics who deny the claims of Christianity. History is obviously replete with examples of people who claimed to be Christians, yet behaved poorly. In fact, many people have committed great violence in the name of Christianity, claiming their Christian worldview authorized or justified their actions, even though the teaching of Jesus clearly opposed their behavior. But a fair examination of history will also reveal Christians were not alone. Groups holding virtually every worldview, from theists to atheists, have been equally guilty of violent misbehavior. Atheists point to the Crusades and the Spanish Inquisition when making a case against Christians; theists point to the atheistic regimes of Joseph Stalin and Mao Zedong when making a case against atheists. Death statistics are debated in an effort to argue which groups were more violent, but all this seems to miss the point. The common denominator in this violent misbehavior was not worldview; it was the presence of humans.

If we intend to decide what's true based on how people behave, we're in big trouble, because every worldview suffers from examples of adherents who have behaved inconsistently and poorly. I expect news headlines will continue to feature the apparent hypocrisy of those who claim to be Christians. Jesus certainly predicted there would be counterfeit Christians ("weeds") living alongside those who were true followers of Christ ("wheat") in the "Parable of the Weeds" (Matt. 13:24–30). I also expect skeptics will continue to use incidents involving "counterfeit Christians" to their advantage, seeking to vilify these people to invalidate the evidence itself. Discourse and dialogue related to Christianity seem to become more vitriolic and demeaning with each passing year. Public debates are often less about substantive arguments than they are about ad hominem attacks. In the end, however, it will come down to the evidence. That's why prosecutors warn juries about the difference between personal attacks and reasoned explanations. Tactics relying on sarcasm and ridicule must not be allowed to replace arguments relying on evidence and reason.

 ## *DEFENSE ATTORNEYS WANT PERFECTION*

Every criminal investigation (and prosecution) is a serious matter, and juries understand this. Defense attorneys sometimes capitalize on the appropriately serious attitude of jurors by criticizing the fact the prosecution's case was something less than perfect. Given the grave importance of these kinds of cases, shouldn't the authorities have done everything conceivable to conduct a perfect, flawless investigation? Shouldn't every imaginable piece of evidence have been recovered? Shouldn't every possible witness have been located? By identifying the imperfections and limitations of the investigation, attorneys hope to reveal a lack of concern and accuracy to undermine the prosecution's case.

Something similar occurs when skeptics point to the allegedly "imperfect" or "incomplete" historical evidence supporting the claims of Christianity. Why, for example, don't we have a complete set of documents from all the apostles who wrote in the first century? Why don't we have some of the missing letters mentioned in the New Testament, like Paul's prior letter to the Corinthian church described in 1 Corinthians 5:9 or John's letter to Diotrephes's church cited in 3 John 1:9? Why isn't there more evidence from sources outside the biblical record corroborating the events described in the Bible (more on this in chapter 12)?

While expectations of perfection may assist defense attorneys as they attack the prosecution's case and skeptics as they attack the claims of Christianity, these kinds of expectations are unreasonable. I've never seen a "perfect" investigation, and I've certainly never conducted one. All inquiries and examinations of the truth (including historical investigations) have their unique deficiencies. Jurors understand they must work with what they have in front of them. The evidence is either sufficient or it is not. Jurors can't dwell on what "might have been" or what "could have been done," unless they have evidence and good reason to believe the truth was lost along the way. Juries cannot assume there is a better explanation (other than the one offered by the prosecution) simply because there were imperfections in the case; reasonable doubts must be established with evidence. In a similar way, skeptics cannot reject the reasonable inferences from the evidence we *do* have, simply because there may possibly be some evidence we *don't* have; skeptics also need to defend their doubt evidentially.

Working with All the Imperfections

Juries must understand there is no such thing as a "perfect" case. Jurors are told in advance, for example, that they will not have access to everything that could be known about a case. Judges instruct juries "neither side is required to call all witnesses who may have information about the case or to produce all physical evidence that might be relevant" (Section 300, Judicial Council of California Criminal Jury Instructions, 2006). Juries are not allowed to speculate about what is missing, but must focus instead on the reasonable inferences drawn from what is not.

DEFENSE ATTORNEYS PROVIDE ALTERNATIVE "POSSIBILITIES"

Defense attorneys do their best to prevent jurors from accepting the prosecution's version of events. Sometimes it's not enough to simply "poke holes" in the prosecution's case to distract the jury from the totality of the evidence. Defense attorneys will sometimes provide an alternative theory about what happened in a particular crime, building their own evidential case for a completely different explanation. More often than not, however, the defense will simply imply an alternative explanation by asking suggestive questions opening up a number of alternate "possibilities," even though these "possibilities" are not supported by any evidence. The goal here is to provide jurors with some way to assemble a narrative in which the defendant is *uninvolved*. Prosecutors must help jurors to assess the difference between "possible" and "reasonable" in times like this, and encourage jurors to limit their deliberations to reasonable inferences from the evidence rather than speculating on unsupported possibilities.

Those who deny the historicity of Jesus sometimes take an approach similar to defense attorneys. Some skeptics have denied the existence of Jesus altogether by proposing an alternative possibility. Citing the similarities between Jesus and other "savior mythologies" of antiquity, they've argued Jesus is simply another work of fiction, created by people who wanted to start a new religious tradition. Many of these critics point to the ancient deity Mithras as a prime example of the fictional borrowing they claim occurred in the formation of Christianity. They describe Mithras as a savior who appeared nearly four hundred years prior to the first Christians, and they point to the following similarities:

Mithras was born of a virgin.

Mithras was born in a cave, attended by shepherds.

Mithras had twelve companions or disciples.

Mithras was buried in a tomb and after three days rose again.

Mithras was called the "Good Shepherd."

Mithras was identified with both the lamb and the lion.

While these similarities are striking and seem to sustain an alternative theory related to the historicity of Jesus, a brief investigation quickly reveals they are unsupported by the evidence. There is no existing "Mithraic scripture" available to us today; all our speculations about the Mithras legend are dependent on Mithraic paintings and sculptures and on what was written about Mithras worshippers by the Christians who observed them

Alternative Explanations

Judges instruct juries to be wary of explanations that are not reasonably supported by the evidence. Judges advise jurors they "must be convinced that the only reasonable conclusion supported by the circumstantial evidence is that the defendant is guilty. If you can draw two or more reasonable conclusions from the circumstantial evidence, and one of those reasonable conclusions points to innocence and another to guilt, you must accept the one that points to innocence. However, when considering circumstantial evidence, you must accept only reasonable conclusions and reject any that are unreasonable" (Section 224, Judicial Council of California Criminal Jury Instructions, 2006).

between the first and third centuries. Even with what little we do know, it is clear Mithras was not born of a virgin in a cave. Mithras reportedly emerged from solid rock, leaving a cave in the side of a mountain. There is also no evidence Mithras had twelve companions or disciples; this similarity may be based on a mural placing the twelve personages of the Zodiac in a circle around Mithras. There is no evidence Mithras was ever called the "Good Shepherd," and although Mithras was a "sun god" and associated with Leo (the House of the Sun in Babylonian astrology), there is no evidence he was identified with the lion. There is also no evidence Mithras ever died, let alone rose again after three days. These claims of skeptics (like the "possibilities" offered by defense attorneys) are not supported by the evidence. It's important to remember a "possible" response is not necessarily a "plausible" refutation.

7   DEFENSE ATTORNEYS EMPLOY A CULTURALLY WINSOME ATTITUDE

Most defense lawyers understand the importance of "first impressions." I've been involved in several high-profile cases with prominent defense attorneys. These attorneys were brutally aggressive, sarcastic, and rancorous in the preliminary hearings, while personable, endearing, and charismatic in the jury trials. What's the difference? The presence of a jury; jurors are not present at preliminary hearings. Defense lawyers understand style is often as important as substance. How you deliver a claim is sometimes more important than the claim itself. For this reason, defense attorneys are often keen observers of the culture; they borrow mannerisms and language to effectively endear themselves to the jury they are trying to convince. The facts are sometimes of secondary importance.

The skeptics in our midst are equally savvy. Christians are not the only people who take an urgent, evangelical approach to their worldview. Many popular atheists are equally interested in proselytizing those around them. They are keenly aware of what is popular. As a part of the culture they are trying to reach, they understand what people are watching on television and on the Internet. They've seen the hit movies and purchased the bestselling music. They've mastered the language and are shaping the art, music, and literature of our society. They often portray Christians as antiquated, backward-thinking "dinosaurs" who are out of touch with progressive concepts and the current culture. They recognize and capitalize on the well-intentioned desire of many Christians to resist the things of the world in favor of the things of God (1 John 2:14–15). Skeptics often have an advantage in communicating their opposition and alternative theories simply because they are more aligned with the culture they are trying to influence.

This is often revealed most glaringly in televised debates between Christians and nonbelievers. The most effective skeptics are those who (like effective defense attorneys) make a winsome connection with the audience. They are endearing. They are entertaining. They understand and highlight the doubts and concerns people have about Christianity. They use persuasive rhetoric to make their points. I've seen a number of debates in which the Christian representative possessed the best arguments and mastery of the evidence, yet seemed less influential from the perspective of communication. In a culture where image is more important than information, style more important than substance, it is not enough to possess the truth. Case makers must also master the media.

A Presentation Is Not a Piece of Evidence

Jurors are also advised the words of the attorneys are not considered *evidence*: "Nothing that the attorneys say is evidence. In their opening statements and closing arguments, the attorneys will discuss the case, but their remarks are not evidence. Their questions are not evidence. Only the witnesses' answers are evidence. The attorneys' questions are significant only if they help you understand the witnesses' answers. Do not assume that something is true just because one of the attorneys asks a question that suggests it is true" (Section 104, Judicial Council of California Criminal Jury Instructions, 2006).

When the prosecution presents a case in the courtroom, the defense is left with three possible responses: they can declare, destroy, or distract. On rare occasions, the defense declares a robust alternative theory to explain what happened in a particular case. This is difficult, however, because it requires the defense to substantiate their alternative scenario with evidence. In essence, they've got to build their case the same way the prosecution has already built a case against their client. More often than not, defense attorneys take a different approach: they focus on destroying the prosecution's case by discrediting the evidence. If they can find legitimate shortcomings in the individual pieces of evidence, they can undermine the prosecution's case, piece by piece. A third tactic is often just as effective in circumstantial cases, however. Using the tactics we've discussed in this chapter, defense lawyers can distract the jury from the cumulative impact of the circumstantial evidence.

By attacking the nature of truth, targeting the foundation of the prosecution's case, focusing on the micro rather than the macro, disparaging the prosecution's witnesses, raising the expectation of perfection, offering unsupported possibilities, and delivering all of this in a winsome way, defense attorneys attempt to distract juries from the larger picture. They don't want the jury to see the forest through the trees. They don't want the jury to see the connected and reasonable nature of the cumulative circumstantial case.

Those who oppose the claims of Christianity often take a very similar approach. Like defense attorneys, they sometimes ignore the larger connected nature of the case for Christianity and focus on possibilities and claims either untrue or without detrimental impact.

A TOOL FOR THE CALLOUT BAG, A TIP FOR THE CHECKLIST

While the tactics of defense attorneys may not seem like tools appropriate for your investigative *callout* bag, think of them as *precautionary* principles for your *checklist*. If these tactics are inappropriate for defense attorneys, they're equally inappropriate for those of us who are presenting the claims of Christianity. Let's hold ourselves to a high standard, even as we require our opponents to recognize their own reasonable responsibilities. It's well known the "burden of proof" in criminal trials rests upon the prosecution. Defendants are presumed innocent until found guilty; they are under no obligation to mount any defense at all. But if, for example, a defendant in a murder trial wants the jury to believe he simply committed the homicide in self-defense, the burden to raise this doubt falls on the defense team. Skeptics have long claimed the burden of proof for the truth of the Christian worldview (e.g., the existence of God or the deity of Jesus) falls on Christians; naturalism is their assumed "default" position. The burden of proof *shifts*, however, once they declare an alternative possibility (e.g., Jesus is a re-creation of Mithras). *Possible alternatives are not reasonable refutations.* If they're not offering a declaration supported by evidence, they're probably attempting to *destroy* or *distract*. I hope my skeptical friends will see the deficiencies of these two approaches. Destruction tactics that try to disqualify the Gospels would also disqualify other historical texts. If skeptics applied an equal standard to other documents of antiquity, they would be hard-pressed to believe anything about the ancient past. In addition to this, any efforts to distract from the cumulative case for Christianity by redefining truth or vilifying Christians, while potentially effective, do nothing to demonstrate the truth of naturalism. I've known many defense attorneys who worked hard because they truly believed their client was innocent. I've known some who worked hard for other reasons. I have skeptical friends who are in a similar position. Some reject Christianity because they believe it is evidentially false, and they are prepared to declare (and argue) an alternative case. On the other hand, some reject Christianity for another reason (perhaps some past personal experience or a desire to live their life without religious restrictions). When this is the case, they often resort to *destroy* or *distract* tactics. Let's help our doubting friends to examine the character of their objections. All of us ought to be willing to argue the merits of our case without resorting to tactics unbecoming of our worldviews.

While I grew up as an atheist, many of my Christian friends either grew up in the church or lived in areas of the country where they met little or no opposition to their Christian worldview. As a result, some were shaken when they had their first encounter with someone who not only opposed them but did so tactically and winsomely. For some Christians, their first encounter with atheistic opposition occurs at the university level, either as a student or the parent of a student. The number of young Christians who reject Christianity in college is alarming, according to nearly every study done on the topic.[2] Part of this is a matter of preparation. While we are often willing to spend time reading the Bible, praying, or participating in church programs and services, few of us recognize the importance of becoming good Christian *case makers*. Prosecutors are successful when they master the facts of the case and then learn how to navigate and respond to the tactics of the defense team. Christians need to learn from that model as well. We need to master the facts and evidence supporting the claims of Christianity and anticipate the tactics of those who oppose us. This kind of preparation is a form of worship. When we devote ourselves to this rational preparation and study, we are worshipping God with our mind, the very thing He has called us to do (Matt. 22:37).

EXAMINE THE EVIDENCE

*Applying the principles of investigation to
the claims of the New Testament*

I was lying in bed, staring at the ceiling.

"I think it may be true," I said to my wife.

"What may be true?" she asked.

"Christianity." I'm sure she was weary of my growing obsession. For several weeks now, it was all I could think about, and I had already talked her ears off on several occasions. She knew I was more serious about this than I had ever been in the past, so she patiently tolerated my obsession and constant conversation. "The more I look at the Gospels, the more I think they look like real eyewitness accounts," I continued. "And the writers seem to have believed what they were writing about."

I knew I was standing on the edge of something profound; I started reading the Gospels to learn what Jesus taught about living a good life and found He taught much more about His identity as God and the nature of eternal life. I knew it would be hard to accept one dimension of His teaching while rejecting the others. If I had good reasons to believe the Gospels were reliable eyewitness accounts, it was time to confront much of what I resisted as a skeptic. What about all the miracles wedged between the remarkable words of Jesus? How would I separate the miraculous from the remarkable? And why was I continuing to resist the miraculous elements in the first place?

The initial step in my journey toward Christianity was an evaluation of the Gospels. I spent weeks and weeks examining the gospel accounts as I would any eyewitness account in a criminal case. I used many of the tools I've already described to make a decision that changed my life forever. I'd like to share some of that investigation with you.

Chapter 11

WERE THEY PRESENT?

"Why was the tomb supposedly empty? I say supposedly because, frankly, I don't know that it was. Our very first reference to Jesus' tomb being empty is in the Gospel of Mark, written forty years later by someone living in a different country who had heard that it was empty. How would he know?"[1]

Bart Ehrman, New Testament scholar, professor of religious
studies, and author of *Jesus Interrupted*

"The so-called Gospel of John is something special and reflects … the highly evolved theology of a Christian writer who lived three generations after Jesus."[2]

Geza Vermes, scholar, historian, and author of *The Changing Faces of Jesus*

"No work of art of any kind has ever been discovered, no painting, or engraving, no sculpture, or other relic of antiquity, which may be looked upon as furnishing additional evidence of the existence of these gospels, and which was executed earlier than the latter part of the second century."[3]

Charles Burlingame Waite, historian and author of *History of
the Christian Religion to the Year Two Hundred*

 ## IF THE GOSPELS ARE LATE, THEY'RE A LIE

When I was a nonbeliever, I eagerly accepted the skeptical claims of people like Ehrman, Vermes, and Waite. In fact, I often made similar statements (although mine were much less articulate) as I argued with Christian friends and coworkers at the police department. Like the skeptics quoted here, I was inclined to reject the Gospels as late works of fiction. I considered them mythological accounts written well after all the true eyewitnesses were dead. They were late, and they were a lie.

I worked in our Gang Detail in the early 1990s and investigated a variety of gang-related assaults. One of them involved a stabbing between members of two rival gangs; both parties were armed with knives. It was hard to determine which of the two gang members was actually the victim, as both were pretty seriously injured, and no eyewitnesses were willing to come forward to testify about what really happened. About a year after the case was assigned to me, I got a telephone call from a woman who told me she witnessed the entire crime and was willing to tell me how it occurred. She said she had been deployed as a member of the army for the past year, and, for this reason, she was unaware the case was still unresolved. After a little digging, I discovered this "eyewitness" was a *cousin* of one of the gang members. After a lengthy interview, she finally admitted to being in another state at the time of the stabbing. She didn't even hear about it until about a week before she contacted me. She was lying to try to implicate the member of the rival gang and protect her cousin. Clearly, her story was a late piece of fiction, created long after the original event for the express purpose of achieving her goal. She wasn't even available or present at the crime to begin with, and for this reason, she was worthless to me as a *witness*.

As a skeptic, I believed the Gospels were penned in the second century and were similarly worthless. If they were written *that* late, they were not eyewitness accounts. It's really as simple as that; true eyewitnesses to the life of Jesus would have lived (and written) in the first century. The first criterion of eyewitness reliability requires us to answer the question: "Were the alleged eyewitnesses present in the first place?" Like the unbelieving scholars, I answered this question by arguing the Gospels were written in the second or third centuries, much closer to the establishment of Christianity in the Roman Empire than to the alleged life of Jesus:

Before I could ever take the Gospels seriously as eyewitness accounts, I needed to decide where they fell on this timeline. If the writers first appeared toward the right (closer to the various church councils and the formal establishment of the Catholic Church), there was good reason to doubt they were true witnesses to the sufferings of Christ (1 Pet. 5:1) and good reasons to doubt they saw Jesus with their own eyes (1 John 1:1–3). If, on the other hand, they appeared to the left of the timeline, I could at least begin to consider them earnestly. The closer they appeared to the life and ministry of Jesus, the more seriously I could consider their claims.

INCHING BACK ON THE TIMELINE

There are many pieces of circumstantial evidence forming a compelling case for the early dating of the Gospels. There are several good reasons to believe the gospel writers are standing on the left side of the timeline. The more I examined this evidence, the more I came to believe the Gospels were written early enough in history to be taken seriously as eyewitness accounts. Let's look at this evidence before we locate each piece on the timeline.

THE NEW TESTAMENT FAILS TO DESCRIBE THE DESTRUCTION OF THE TEMPLE

We begin with perhaps the most significant Jewish historical event of the first century: the destruction of the Jerusalem temple in AD 70. Rome dispatched an army to Jerusalem in response to the Jewish rebellion of AD 66. The Roman army (under the leadership of Titus) ultimately destroyed the temple in AD 70,[4] just as Jesus had predicted in the Gospels (in Matt. 24:1–3). You might think this important detail would be included in the New Testament record, especially since this fact would corroborate Jesus's prediction. But no gospel account records the destruction of the temple. In fact, no New Testament document mentions it at all, even though there are many occasions when a description of the temple's destruction might have assisted in establishing a theological or historical point.

THE NEW TESTAMENT FAILS TO DESCRIBE THE SIEGE OF JERUSALEM

Even before the temple was destroyed, the city of Jerusalem was under assault. Titus surrounded the city with four large groups of soldiers and eventually broke through the city's "Third Wall" with a battering ram. After lengthy battles and skirmishes, the Roman soldiers eventually set fire to the city's walls and the temple was destroyed as a result.[5] No aspect of this three-year siege is described in any New Testament document, despite the fact the gospel writers could certainly have pointed to the anguish resulting from the siege as a powerful point of reference for the many passages of Scripture extensively addressing the issue of *suffering*.

LUKE SAID NOTHING ABOUT THE DEATHS OF PAUL AND PETER

Years before the siege of Jerusalem and the destruction of the temple, another pair of events occurred, both significant to the Christian community. The apostle Paul was martyred in the city of Rome in AD 64, and Peter was martyred shortly afterward in AD 65.[6] While Luke wrote extensively about Paul and Peter in the book of Acts and featured them prominently, he said nothing about their deaths. In fact, Paul was still alive (under house arrest in Rome) at the end of the book of Acts.

LUKE SAID NOTHING ABOUT THE DEATH OF JAMES

Luke featured another important figure from Christian history in the book of Acts. James (the brother of Jesus) became the leader of the Jerusalem church and was described in a position of prominence in Acts 15. James was martyred in the city of

Jerusalem in AD 62,[7] but like the deaths of Paul and Peter, the execution of James is absent from the biblical account, even though Luke described the deaths of Stephen (Acts 7:54–60) and James the brother of John (Acts 12:1–2).

Life of Jesus
(AD 1-33)

Deaths of James,   Siege of   Temple
Peter, and Paul   Jerusalem   Destroyed
AD 61-65   AD 67-70   AD 70

LUKE'S GOSPEL PREDATES THE BOOK OF ACTS

Luke wrote both the book of Acts and the gospel of Luke. These two texts contain introductions tying them together in history. In the introduction to the book of Acts, Luke wrote:

> *The first account I composed, Theophilus, about all that Jesus began to do and teach, until the day when He was taken up to heaven, after He had by the Holy Spirit given orders to the apostles whom He had chosen. (Acts 1:1–2)*

It's clear Luke's gospel (his "former book") was written prior to the book of Acts.

PAUL QUOTED LUKE'S GOSPEL IN HIS LETTER TO TIMOTHY

Paul appeared to be aware of Luke's gospel and wrote as though it was common knowledge in about AD 63–64, when Paul penned his first letter to Timothy. Note the following passage:

> *The elders who direct the affairs of the church well are worthy of double honor, especially those whose work is preaching and teaching. For the Scripture says, "Do not muzzle the ox while it is treading out the grain," and "The worker deserves his wages." (1 Tim. 5:17–18)*

Paul quoted two passages as "scripture" here—one in the Old Testament and one in the New Testament. "Do not muzzle the ox while it is treading out the grain" refers to Deuteronomy 25:4, and "The worker deserves his wages" refers to Luke 10:7. It's clear Luke's gospel was already common knowledge and accepted as Scripture by the time this letter was written. To be fair, several critics (like Bart Ehrman) have argued Paul was not actually the author of 1 Timothy. They maintain this letter was written much later in history. Most scholars, however, recognize the earliest leaders of the church were familiar with 1 Timothy at a very early date.[8]

PAUL ECHOED THE CLAIMS OF THE GOSPEL WRITERS

While some modern critics challenge the authorship of Paul's pastoral letters, even the most skeptical scholars agree Paul is the author of the letters written to the Romans, the Corinthians, and the Galatians. These letters are dated between AD 48 and AD 60. The letter to the Romans (typically dated at AD 50) reveals something important. Paul began the letter by proclaiming Jesus is the resurrected "Son of God." Throughout the letter, Paul accepted the view of Jesus the gospel eyewitnesses described in their own accounts. Just seventeen years after the resurrection, Jesus was described as divine. He is God incarnate, just as the gospel eyewitnesses described in their own accounts. In fact, Paul's outline of Jesus's life matches that of the Gospels. In 1 Corinthians 15 (written from AD 53–57), Paul summarized the gospel message and reinforced the eyewitness accounts as they were described to him:

> For I delivered to you as of first importance what I also received, that Christ died for our sins according to the Scriptures, and that He was buried, and that He was raised on the third day according to the Scriptures, and that He appeared to Cephas, then to the twelve. After that He appeared to more than five hundred brethren at one time, most of whom remain until now, but some have fallen asleep; then He appeared to James, then to all the apostles; and last of all, as to one untimely born, He appeared to me also. (1 Cor. 15:3–8)

In his letter to the Galatians (also written in the mid-50s), Paul described his interaction with these apostles (Peter and James) and said their meeting occurred at least fourteen years prior to the writing of his letter:

But when God, who had set me apart even from my mother's womb and called me through His grace, was pleased to reveal His Son in me so that I might preach Him among the Gentiles, I did not immediately consult with flesh and blood, nor did I go up to Jerusalem to those who were apostles before me; but I went away to Arabia, and returned once more to Damascus. Then three years later I went up to Jerusalem to become acquainted with Cephas, and stayed with him fifteen days. But I did not see any other of the apostles except James, the Lord's brother. (Gal. 1:15–19)

Then after an interval of fourteen years I went up again to Jerusalem with Barnabas, taking Titus along also. (Gal. 2:1)

This means Paul saw the risen Christ and learned about the gospel accounts from the eyewitnesses (Peter and James) within five years of the crucifixion (most scholars place Paul's conversion from AD 33–36, and he visited Peter and James within three years of his conversion, according to Galatians 1:19). This is why Paul was able to tell the Corinthians there were still "more than five hundred brethren" who could confirm the resurrection accounts (in 1 Cor. 15:6). That's a gutsy claim to make in AD 53–57, when his readers could easily have accepted his challenge and called him out as a liar if the claim was untrue.

| Jesus appears to Paul | Paul confers with James and Peter | Paul confers with John, Peter, and James in front of Barnabas and Titus | Paul first tells Corinth about Jesus | Paul writes 1 Corinthians |

Life of Jesus (AD 1-33) — AD 34-35 Acts 9:1-19 — AD 37-38 Galatians 1:15-19 — AD 48-50 Galatians 2:1-2 — AD 51 — AD 55 1 Corinthians 15:3-7

PAUL QUOTED LUKE'S GOSPEL IN HIS LETTER TO THE CORINTHIANS

Paul also seems to have been familiar with the gospel of Luke when he wrote to the Corinthian church (nearly ten years earlier than his letter to Timothy). Notice the similarity between Paul's description of the Lord's Supper and Luke's gospel:

For I received from the Lord that which I also delivered to you, that the Lord Jesus in the night in which He was betrayed took bread; and when He had given thanks, He broke it and said, "This is My body, which is for you; do this in remembrance of Me." In the same way He took the cup also after supper, saying, "This cup is the new covenant in My blood." (1 Cor. 11:23–25)

And when He had taken some bread and given thanks, He broke it and gave it to them, saying, "This is My body which is given for you; do this in remembrance of Me." And in the same way He took the cup after they had eaten, saying, "This cup which is poured out for you is the new covenant in My blood." (Luke 22:19–20)

Paul appears to be quoting Luke's gospel—the only gospel in which Jesus says the disciples are to "do this in remembrance of me." If Paul is trying to use a description of the meal already well known at the time, this account must have been circulating for a period prior to Paul's letter.

Life of Jesus
(AD 1-33)

Paul quotes Luke	Luke writes Acts	Deaths of James, Peter, and Paul	Siege of Jerusalem	Temple Destroyed
AD 53-57	AD 57-60	AD 61-65	AD 67-70	AD 70

LUKE QUOTED MARK (AND MATTHEW) REPEATEDLY

Luke, when writing his own gospel, readily admitted he was not an eyewitness to the life and ministry of Jesus. Instead, Luke described himself as a historian, collecting the statements from the eyewitnesses who were present at the time:

Many have undertaken to draw up an account of the things that have been fulfilled among us, just as they were handed down to us by those who from the first were eyewitnesses and servants of the word. Therefore, since I myself have carefully

*investigated everything from the beginning, it seemed good also to me to write
an orderly account for you, most excellent Theophilus, so that you may know the
certainty of the things you have been taught. (Luke 1:1–4)*

As a result, Luke often repeated or quoted entire passages offered previously by either Mark (350 verses from Mark appear in Luke's gospel) or Matthew (250 verses from Matthew appear in Luke's account).[9] These passages were inserted into Luke's gospel as though they were simply copied over from the other accounts. It's reasonable, therefore, to concluded Mark's account was already recognized, accepted, and available to Luke prior to his authorship of the gospel.

Life of Jesus
(AD 1-33)

| Luke writes his Gospel AD 50-53 | Paul quotes Luke AD 53-57 | Luke writes Acts AD 57-60 | Deaths of James, Peter, and Paul AD 61-65 | Siege of Jerusalem AD 67-70 | Temple Destroyed AD 70 |

MARK'S GOSPEL APPEARS TO BE AN EARLY "CRIME BROADCAST"

Mark's gospel bears a striking resemblance to a "crime broadcast." When first-responding officers arrive at the scene of a crime, they quickly gather the details related to the crime and the description of the suspect, then "clear the air" with the radio dispatchers so they can broadcast these details to other officers who may be in the area. This first *crime broadcast* is brief and focused on the essential elements. There will be time later to add additional details, sort out the order of events, and write lengthy reports. This first broadcast is driven by the immediacy of the moment; we've got to get the essentials out to our partners because the suspects in this case may still be trying to flee the area. There is a sense of urgency in the first broadcast because officers are trying to catch the bad guys before they get away.

Although Mark's gospel contains the important details of Jesus's life and ministry, it is brief, less ordered than the other gospels, and filled with "action" verbs and adjectives. There is a sense of urgency about it. This is what we might expect, if it was, in fact, an early account of Jesus's ministry. It is clear the eyewitnesses felt this urgency and believed Jesus would return very soon. Paul wrote "salvation is nearer now than when we first believed" (Rom. 13:11), and James said "the Lord's coming is near" (James 5:8). Peter, Mark's mentor and companion, agreed "the end of all things is near" (1 Pet. 4:7). Surely Mark wrote with this same sense of urgency as he penned Peter's experiences in his own gospel. Mark's account takes on the role of "crime broadcast," delivering the essential details without regard for composition or stylistic prose. Papias confirmed this in his statement about Mark's efforts:

> Mark, having become the interpreter of Peter, wrote down accurately, though not indeed in order, whatsoever he remembered of the things said or done by Christ. For he neither heard the Lord nor followed him, but afterward, as I said, he followed Peter, who adapted his teaching to the needs of his hearers, but with no intention of giving a connected account of the Lord's discourses, so that Mark committed no error while he thus wrote some things as he remembered them. For he was careful of one thing, not to omit any of the things which he had heard, and not to state any of them falsely.[10]

The accuracy of the account was more important to Mark than anything else; for all Mark knew, Jesus would return before there would be any need to write an ordered *biography* of sorts. Mark was in charge of the essential *crime broadcast*. As the years passed and the eyewitnesses aged, others made a more deliberate effort to place the narrative in its correct order. Papias seems to indicate this was Matthew's intent:

> Therefore Matthew put the *logia* in an ordered arrangement in the Hebrew language, but each person interpreted them as best he could.[11]

Luke also seems to be doing something similar according to the introduction of his own gospel:

> *Therefore, since I myself have carefully investigated everything from the beginning, it seemed good also to me to write an orderly account for you. (Luke 1:3)*

Both Matthew and Luke appear to be writing with a much different intent than Mark. Their accounts are more robust and ordered. While Mark provides us with the initial "crime broadcast," Matthew and Luke are more concerned about the "final report."

Life of Jesus (AD 1-33) | Mark writes his Gospel AD 45-50 | Luke writes his Gospel AD 50-53 | Paul quotes Luke AD 53-57 | Luke writes Acts AD 57-60 | Deaths of James, Peter, and Paul AD 61-65 | Siege of Jerusalem AD 67-70 | Temple Destroyed AD 70

MARK APPEARS TO BE PROTECTING KEY PLAYERS

We've already talked about how important it is to "hang on every word." In my years as an investigator, there were many times when a witness carefully chose his or her words to avoid dragging someone else into the case. This was particularly true when working gang cases. There were a number of times when a witness had the courage to come forward with information, but was less than forthcoming about the identity of others who might have seen something similar. Driven by the fear these additional witnesses might be in a position of jeopardy, the witness would mention them in his or her account but refuse to specifically identify them. Most of the time the witnesses were simply trying to protect someone they thought was defenseless and vulnerable.

I experienced just the opposite in some of my cold-case investigations. When re-interviewing witnesses who spoke to investigators years earlier, I found they were now willing to provide me with the identities of people they previously refused to identify. Sometimes this was because they developed some animosity toward these people over the years; this was especially true when boyfriends and girlfriends broke up and were eventually willing to talk about each other. Sometimes it was a matter of diminishing fear; when the suspect in a case died, it wasn't unusual to have people come forward and identify themselves simply because they were no longer afraid to do so.

Many careful readers of Mark's gospel have observed there are several unidentified people described in his account. These *anonymous* characters are often in key positions in the narrative, yet Mark chose to leave them unnamed. For example, Mark's description of the activity in the garden of Gethsemane includes the report that, during the arrest of Jesus, "one of those who stood by drew his sword, and struck the slave of the high priest and cut off his ear" (Mark 14:47). Mark chose to leave both the attacker and the man attacked unnamed in his description, even though John identified both (Peter as the attacker and Malchus as the person being attacked) in his gospel account. Similarly, Mark failed to identify the woman who anointed Jesus at the home of Simon the leper (Mark 14:3–9), even though John told us it was Mary (the sister of Martha) who poured the perfume on Jesus's head.[12] While skeptics have offered a number of explanations for these variations (arguing, for example, they may simply be late embellishments in an effort to craft the growing mythology of the Gospels), something much simpler might be at work. If Mark, like some of the witnesses in my gang cases, was interested in protecting the identity of Peter (as Malchus's attacker) and Mary (whose anointing may have been interpreted as a proclamation of Jesus's kingly position as the Messiah), it makes sense he might leave them unnamed so the Jewish leadership would not be able to easily target them. In fact, Mark never even described Jesus's raising of Mary's brother, Lazarus. This also makes sense if Mark was trying to protect Lazarus's identity in the earliest years of the Christian movement, given the resurrection of Lazarus was of critical concern to the Jewish leadership and prompted them to search for Jesus in their plot to kill him. If Mark wrote his gospel early, while Mary, Lazarus, Peter, and Malchus were still alive, it is reasonable Mark might have wanted to leave them unnamed or simply omit the accounts including them in the first place.

Scholars generally acknowledge John's gospel as the final addition to the New Testament collection of gospel accounts. It was most likely written at a time when Peter, Malchus, and Mary were already dead. John, like some of the witnesses in my cold cases, had the liberty to identify these important people; they were no longer in harm's way.

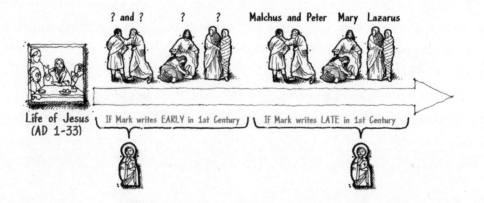

THEY WERE EARLY ON THE TIMELINE

Given these eleven pieces of circumstantial evidence, what reasonable inference can be drawn about the dating of the Gospels? First, we must account for the suspicious absence of several key historical events in the New Testament record: the destruction of the temple, the siege of Jerusalem, and the deaths of Peter, Paul, and James. These omissions can be reasonably explained if the book of Acts (the biblical text most likely to describe these events) was written prior to AD 61–62. These events are missing from the accounts because they hadn't happened yet.

We know from the introductory lines of the book of Acts that Luke's gospel was written prior to Acts, but we must use the remaining circumstantial evidence to try to determine *how* much prior. The fact that Paul echoed the description of Jesus offered by the gospel writers is certainly consistent with the fact he was aware of the claims of the Gospels, and his quotations from Luke's gospel in 1 Timothy and 1 Corinthians reasonably confirm the early existence of Luke's account, placing it well before AD 53–57. Paul was able to quote Luke's gospel and refer to it as Scripture because it was already written, circulating at this time, and broadly accepted. Paul's readers recognized this was true as they read Paul's letters.

Luke told us he was gathering data from "those who from the first were eyewitnesses and servants of the word" (Luke 1:2). As a result, he either referred to (or quoted directly from) over 500 verses found in either the gospel of Mark or the gospel of Matthew. It is reasonable to infer these accounts were in existence prior to Luke's investigation. If this is the case, Mark's gospel would date much earlier than Luke's and can be sensibly placed in either the late 40s or very early 50s. This then explains some of the characteristics we see in Mark's gospel. There appears to be a sense of urgency in the gospel, similar to the *crime broadcasts* made by responding officers, and Mark appears to be protecting key players in the account as if they were still alive at the time of his writing.

Let's place the evidence on the timeline to see where the gospel accounts are located relative to the life of Jesus:

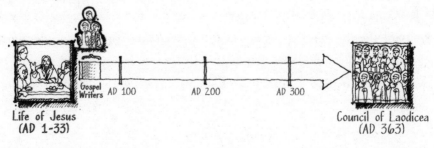

Gospel Writers   AD 100   AD 200   AD 300

Life of Jesus
(AD 1-33)

Council of Laodicea
(AD 363)

The reasonable inference from the circumstantial evidence is the Gospels were written very early in history, at a time when the original eyewitnesses and gospel writers were still alive and could testify to what they had seen. This is why Mark was careful not to identify key players and Paul could reasonably point to five hundred living eyewitnesses who could still testify to their observations of Jesus's resurrection. While skeptics claim the Gospels were written well after the alleged life of the apostles and much closer to the councils affirming them, the evidence indicates something quite different.

The circumstantial evidence supports an early dating for the Gospels. The gospel writers appear in history right where we would expect them to appear if they were, in fact, eyewitnesses. This early placement alone does not assure the Gospels are reliable accounts, but it keeps them "in the running" and becomes an important piece of circumstantial evidence, in and of itself, as we determine the reliability of the gospel writers.

SO, WHY DO SOME CONTINUE TO DENY IT?

Some are still skeptical of the early dating of the Gospels, despite the circumstantial evidence supporting such a conclusion. Many skeptics are quick to embrace alternative explanations placing the Gospels so late in history they simply could not have been written by eyewitnesses. As with any process of *abductive reasoning*, we need to examine the alternative *possibilities* to see if any of them are *reasonable* (based on evidence). Let's examine some of the reasons why skeptics like Ehrman, Vermes, and Waite claim the Gospels were written either "forty years later," "three generations after Jesus," or in "the latter part of the second century."

THE AUTHORS OF THE GOSPELS ARE ANONYMOUS

Some have argued the Gospels are late due to the fact none of the authors specifically identify themselves in the accounts. This lack of identification is seen as evidence the accounts were not actually written by anyone in the first century, but were falsely attributed to these authors much later in an effort to legitimize the forgeries.

BUT ...

The Gospels are not the only ancient documents failing to identify the author within the text of the manuscripts. Tacitus (the Roman senator and historian who lived from AD 56 to AD 117) wrote a history of the Roman Empire from the reign of Augustus Caesar to Nero entitled *Annals*. Tacitus was, in fact, present during much of this period, but failed to include himself in any of his descriptions or identify himself as the author. Like the Gospels, the *Annals* are written *anonymously* yet are attributed to Tacitus without reservation by historical scholars. Why? Because, like the Gospels, Tacitus's authorship is supported by external evidence (such as the claims of other early writers who credited Tacitus with the work). The Gospels were also attributed to their traditional authors quite early in history (Papias, living in the late first century and early second century, is one such example).

In fact, no one in antiquity ever attributed the Gospels to anyone other than the four traditionally accepted authors. That's a powerful statement, in and of itself, especially considering the fact early Christians consistently recognized, identified, and condemned the false writings of forgers who tried to credit false gospels to the apostolic eyewitnesses. *The Traditions of Matthias* (AD 110–160), for example, was identified as a forgery by early Christians and was eventually included in a list with other forgeries (including the gospels of Thomas and Peter) by Eusebius, the "Father of Church History."

One might also wonder why, if these gospel accounts were falsely attributed to the authors we accept today, the second- or third-century forgers would not have picked better *pseudonyms* (false attributions) than the people who were ultimately credited with the writings. Why would they pick Mark or Luke when they could easily have chosen Peter, Andrew, or James? Mark and Luke appear nowhere in the gospel records as eyewitnesses, so why would early forgers choose these two men around which to build their lies when there were clearly better candidates available to legitimize their work?

It's not as if the Gospels of Mark, Matthew, Luke, or John have been discovered in some ancient collection under someone else's name. The only copies we possess of these Gospels, regardless of antiquity or geographic location, are attributed to one of the four traditional authors. No early-church leader has ever attributed these Gospels to anyone other than Mark, Matthew, Luke, or John. There is no alternative ancient tradition claiming, for example, the gospel of Mark is written by anyone other than Mark.

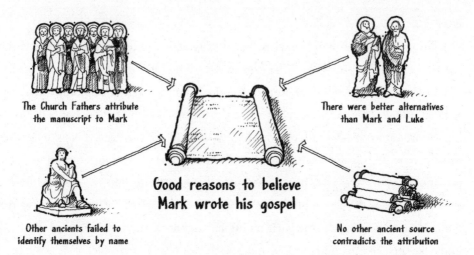

The Church Fathers attribute
the manuscript to Mark

There were better alternatives
than Mark and Luke

Good reasons to believe
Mark wrote his gospel

Other ancients failed to
identify themselves by name

No other ancient source
contradicts the attribution

While it is *possible* the Gospels were not written by the traditional first-century authors and were only given these attributions much later in history, it is not evidentially *reasonable*. If skeptics were willing to give the Gospels the same "benefit of the doubt" they are willing to give other ancient documents, the Gospels would easily pass the test of authorship.

THE TEMPLE DESTRUCTION IS PREDICTED

While the absence of any description of the temple's destruction can reasonably be interpreted as a piece of circumstantial evidence supporting the early dating of the New Testament accounts, skeptics sometimes use this fact to make just the opposite case. Many have proposed Jesus's prediction related to the destruction was inserted to legitimize the text and make it appear he had some prophetic power. If this were the case, the Gospels would clearly date to *after* the event (post AD 70), as the writers already knew the outcome before they cleverly inserted the prediction.

BUT ...

This sort of skepticism is clearly rooted in the presupposition we described in chapter 1. If we begin from a position of philosophical naturalism (the presumption only natural laws and forces—as opposed to supernatural ones—operate in the universe), we have no choice but to describe the supernatural elements we find in the Gospels as lies. From a naturalistic perspective, prophetic claims are impossible. The skeptic, therefore, must find another explanation for Jesus's prediction related to the temple; critics typically move the date of authorship beyond the date when the prophecy was fulfilled to avoid the appearance of supernatural confirmation. But as we described earlier, a fair examination of the evidence supporting supernaturalism must at least allow for the possibility of supernaturalism in the first place. The naturalistic bias of these critics prevents them from accepting any dating preceding the destruction of the temple in AD 70 and forces them to ignore all the circumstantial evidence supporting the early dating.

When explaining why the destruction of the temple itself was not included in the gospel record, skeptics argue the gospel writers intentionally omitted the fulfillment to make the accounts look like they were written early. But if this was the case, why were the gospel writers unafraid to describe the fulfillment of prophecy in other passages in the Gospels? We repeatedly see the fulfillment of Old Testament messianic prophecies attributed to Jesus in one manner or another. In addition to this, on several occasions Jesus predicted His own resurrection. The gospel writers readily described the fulfillment of these predications in the resurrection accounts. Why would they be willing to describe this aspect of fulfilled prophecy, but shy away from discussing the destruction of the temple?

In addition, Luke freely admitted he was not an eyewitness to the events in his gospel. He told us from the outset he was writing at some point well after the events actually occurred, working as a careful historian. Why not include the siege of Jerusalem and the destruction of the temple? There was no reason to be shy here. Other Old Testament authors wrote from a perspective following the events they described and were unafraid to say so. Moses, Joshua, and Samuel, for example, repeatedly reported on events taking place well before their written account; they often wrote the conditions they were describing continued from the point of the event "to this day" (indicating the late point at which they were writing). Why wouldn't Luke take a similar approach to the destruction of the temple, especially given he made no pretense about writing as a historian?

While it is certainly *possible* the Gospels were all written after the destruction of the temple, it is not evidentially *reasonable*. In fact, the primary motivation for denying the early authorship of the Gospels is simply the bias against supernaturalism, leading skeptics to redate the Scriptures to some point following the fulfillment of Jesus's prophecy.

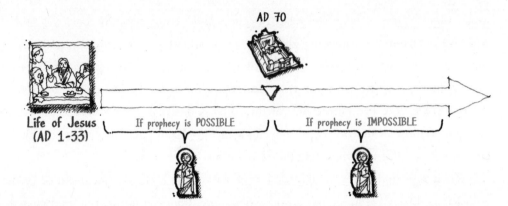

THE ACCOUNTS ARE REPLETE WITH MIRACULOUS EVENTS

Many critics have also pointed to the presence of the miraculous to make a case for late dating. Surely the miracles are works of fiction. If the gospel accounts were written early, eyewitnesses to the life of Jesus would have exposed these miracles as fictitious, right? Much of this critical analysis comes from a literary discipline known as "form criticism." Form critics attempt to classify portions of Scripture on the basis of their literary "type," "pattern," or "form." Once these pieces are isolated within the larger narrative, form critics attempt to explain their origin. In the case of the Gospels, form critics have argued the supernatural elements are different from those parts of the narrative trusted as accurate history. They explain the "paradigms,"[13] "sayings,"[14] "miracle stories,"[15] and "legends"[16] as late additions inserted by local Christian communities to make a particular theological case or to present Jesus as something more than He was.

BUT ...

By now you probably recognize the presupposition of naturalism (and the bias against supernaturalism) is once again the impetus behind this criticism. The *form critics* of history (a movement most popular in the mid-twentieth century) simply rejected the possibility any description of a miracle could be factually true. It turns out it was the miraculous "content" of these passages, rather than their common literary *style* or *form*, that caused critics to identify the verses they thought should be removed or handled with suspicion. In fact, they often selected passages differing from one another stylistically. Sometimes they identified passages failing to fit neatly into one of their categories (or appearing to be a blend of more than one literary form), and they often disagreed with one another about the identity of particular types of literary *forms* and passages. They did agree on one thing, however: passages containing miraculous events were not to be taken seriously as part of the original narrative.

These skeptics evaluate the gospel accounts with the assumption (based on the presence of the miraculous) they must have been written in the second or third centuries by authors who were unafraid their lies would be detected by those living in the first century. This assumption ignores, of course, all the evidence supporting an early dating for the New Testament documents. It also assumes the gospel accounts are false until proven true. This is just the opposite approach we take with witness testimony when it is presented in court. We ought to presume witnesses are telling us the truth until we discover otherwise, and the presence of the miraculous alone should not cause us to believe the gospel eyewitnesses were lying.

Remember also, most philosophical naturalists critical of the miracle accounts in the Gospels simultaneously accept the notion our universe came into existence *from nothing*. As described in chapter 3, this kind of finite universe requires a cause outside of space, time, and matter; an extra-natural, "supernatural" cause, *by definition*. To date the Gospels based on the rejection of relatively minor supernatural elements while embracing the existence of a "supernatural" causal force for the universe reveals a logical contradiction.

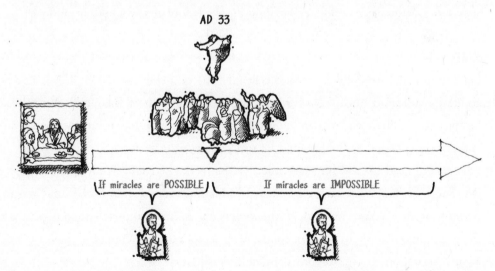

There is no evidence, aside from the existence of supernatural elements within the gospel accounts, to support the assumption of late dating critics have proposed. While the insertion of miraculous elements late in history might be *possible*, it is not evidentially *reasonable*. Once again, the primary motivation for denying the early authorship of the Gospels is simply the bias against supernaturalism.

THERE WAS A SECOND-CENTURY BISHOP IN ANTIOCH NAMED "THEOPHILUS"

Some have tried to argue the "Theophilus" described by Luke in the introduction to his gospel and the book of Acts was Theophilus, the bishop of Antioch (who served from approximately AD 169–183). They support this claim by citing some ancient authorities who maintained Luke originally came from this city, and the fact Theophilus of Antioch wrote a defense of Christianity mentioning the canon of the New Testament (which, of course, would have included the gospel of Luke). Skeptics who argue for this identification of Theophilus also point to the opening sentence of Luke's gospel, where Luke wrote, "Many have undertaken to draw up an account of the things that have been fulfilled among us." Isn't it reasonable Luke was referring to the many late-second-century heretical, false gospels (like the gospel of the Egyptians) that caused Theophilus of Antioch to write his own defense in the first place? If this is true, Luke's gospel ought to be dated in the second century, after the appearance of these heretical gospels and during the tenure of Theophilus of Antioch.

BUT ...

Luke addressed Theophilus as "most excellent" in his gospel introduction. This is a title of authority, indicating Theophilus held a position of leadership. If Theophilus were already in a position of lifetime Christian leadership (governing the church of Antioch as a bishop and deserving of Luke's title), would he really know so little about the life of Jesus that Luke would need to send him "an orderly account" so he could "know the certainty of the things [he had] been taught"? Luke's introduction makes it sound as if Luke was in a position of greater knowledge than Theophilus and seems completely inconsistent with the possibility Theophilus was someone already knowledgeable enough to have ascended to such an important position of Christian leadership.

It does appear, however, Theophilus was in some position of leadership, given the way Luke addressed him. Are there any reasonable first-century explanations consistent with the other pieces of circumstantial evidence placing the gospel in the first century? Yes, in fact, there are. Paul used the same "most excellent" title when addressing Felix (in Acts 24:3) and Festus (in Acts 26:25), both of whom were Roman officials. Theophilus may, therefore, have been a Roman official of some sort. It's interesting to note Luke did not use this title when addressing Theophilus in the book of Acts. This may reflect the fact Theophilus was serving a short-term position in the Roman government (rather than a lifetime position as a bishop in Antioch). Perhaps Theophilus began to serve his term of office during the time when Luke was writing the gospel. Such positions of leadership were certainly available in the first-century government of the Roman Empire.

Roman officials of the first century aren't the only reasonable candidates for Theophilus's identity. There were several Jewish leaders in the first century who possessed the name, including Theophilus ben Ananus (the Roman-appointed high priest of the Jerusalem temple between AD 37–41).[17] If this was, in fact, the Theophilus whom Luke was addressing, it might explain why Luke began his gospel with a description of another priest, Zechariah, and his activity in the temple. This might also explain why Luke alone spent so much time writing about the way Joseph and Mary took Jesus to the temple following His days of purification and

Who Is "Theophilus"?

Many people have tried to identify "Theophilus." While no one knows the answer for sure, there are many reasonable possibilities:

He's Every "Friend of God"

Some scholars have observed the word "Theophilus" is Greek for "Friend of God." For this reason, they propose Luke wrote his works for all those who were friends of God and interested in the claims of Jesus.

He's a Roman Official

Since Paul only used the expression "most excellent" when addressing Roman officials, and Luke 1:3 uses it for Theophilus, many believe Theophilus must have held some similar Roman position. Paul Maier, in his novel *The Flames of Rome* (Kregel, 1995), makes a case for Titus Flavius Sabinus II as the person to whom Luke is writing.

He's a Jewish High Priest

Others have identified a pair of Jewish high priests who lived in the 1st century (Theophilus ben Ananus or Mattathias ben Theophilus), arguing Luke's focus on the temple and Jewish customs related to the Sadducees could best be explained if one of these two priests were his intended audience.

then again when He was twelve years old. It might also explain why, interestingly, Luke failed to mention Caiaphas's role in the crucifixion of Jesus (Caiaphas was Theophilus ben Ananus's brother-in-law).

While it is *possible* Luke was writing to Theophilus of Antioch late in the second century, it is not evidentially *reasonable*. Even if we don't have enough evidence to identify the *true* Theophilus with precision, there are some reasonable first-century explanations available, and the way Luke described Theophilus in Luke 1 is inconsistent with Theophilus of Antioch.

LUKE AGREED WITH MUCH OF WHAT JOSEPHUS REPORTED

Some skeptics have examined the writings of Titus Flavius Josephus, the first-century Roman-Jewish historian who lived from AD 37 to approximately AD 100 and wrote about life in the area of Palestine, including the siege of Jerusalem and the destruction of the temple. Josephus wrote *Antiquities of the Jews* in the early 90s (AD 93–94). Critics cite several similarities between Luke and Josephus and argue Luke actually used Josephus as a source for his own work. This, of course, would place the date of Luke's work sometime after the early 90s, perhaps even as late as the early second century.

BUT ...

The fact Josephus mentioned historical details also described by Luke (e.g., the census taken under Quirinius, the death of Herod Agrippa, the identity of the tetrarch Lysanias, and the famine during the reign of Claudius) does not necessarily mean Luke was using Josephus as his source. Josephus may, in fact, be referencing Luke's work; both may be referencing the work of someone who preceded them; or each may simply be citing the facts of history independently. In any case, the dual citations we see here ought to give us confidence Luke's record is historically accurate.

Luke and Josephus do not agree on every historical detail, however. Some critics have even pointed to these disagreements in an effort to discredit Luke's account. If Luke is merely copying Josephus in the early second century, why wouldn't he agree *entirely* with Josephus?

Finally, if Luke was using Josephus as a source (in a manner similar to his use of Mark or Matthew), why didn't he quote Josephus? This would certainly be consistent with his introductory proclamation in which he claimed to reference other sources to compile his history. Luke readily quoted Mark and inserted many parallel accounts also found in Matthew's record; why not quote or mirror Josephus in a similar way? Luke never did this, however, and his work demonstrates no similarity with Josephus's literary style.

While it is certainly *possible* Luke was borrowing from Josephus, it is not evidentially *reasonable*. There are several unrelated pieces of circumstantial evidence pointing to an early date for Luke's gospel, nearly forty years prior to the work of Josephus. All the alleged evidence supporting the claim Luke referenced Josephus can also be used to defend the claim Josephus referenced Luke. The cumulative circumstantial case for early dating can help us to determine which of these possibilities is the most reasonable.

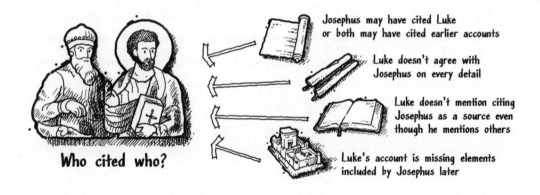

Josephus may have cited Luke or both may have cited earlier accounts

Luke doesn't agree with Josephus on every detail

Luke doesn't mention citing Josephus as a source even though he mentions others

Luke's account is missing elements included by Josephus later

Who cited who?

THE MOST REASONABLE CONCLUSION

We can now employ some *abductive reasoning* as we try to determine which explanation related to dating is the most sensible. Like our dead-body scene described in chapter 2, we begin by listing all the evidence we've examined so far, including the evidence identified by skeptics. Next, we list the two possible explanations accounting for this evidence:

The New Testament Fails to Describe the Temple Destruction
The New Testament Fails to Describe the Siege of Jerusalem
Luke Says Nothing About the Death of Paul, Peter or James
Luke's Gospel Pre-Dates the Book of Acts
Paul Quotes Luke's Gospel in His Letter to Timothy
Paul Echoes the Claims of the Gospel Writers
Paul Quotes Luke's Gospel in His Letter to the Corinthians
Luke Quotes Mark (and Matthew) Repeatedly
Mark's Gospel Appears to Be An Early "Crime Broadcast"
Mark Appears to Be Protecting Key Players
The Authors of the Gospels Are Anonymous
The Temple Destruction is Predicted
The Accounts Are Replete with Miraculous Events
There Was A 2nd Century Bishop Named "Theophilus"
Luke Agrees With Much of What Josephus Reported

The Gospels were written in the 1st Century during the lifetime of the eyewitnesses

The Gospels were written in the 2nd Century after the deaths of the eyewitnesses

Using the lifetime of the alleged eyewitnesses (the gospel writers) and the destruction of the temple as a point of differentiation, the evidence allows for two possible inferences: the Gospels were either written prior to the destruction of the temple (and during the span of time in which the alleged eyewitnesses were alive), or the Gospels were written well after the destruction of the temple and after the alleged eyewitnesses would have been long in the grave. If we accept the first explanation, we can integrate and embrace all the evidence without any contradiction or friction between pieces. The second explanation may explain the last five pieces of evidence, but has great difficulty (at best) explaining the first eleven. The inference the Gospels were written in the first century, prior to the destruction of the temple (and during the lifetime of those who claimed to see Jesus), is the best explanation. The explanation is *feasible*, *straightforward*, and *logical*. It *exhausts* all the evidence we have assembled and it is *superior* to the alternative explanation. It meets the five criteria we established for abductive reasoning; we can have confidence we've arrived at the most reasonable explanation.

THE GOSPELS PASS THE FIRST TEST

Juries are encouraged to evaluate eyewitnesses in the four categories we described in chapter 4. They begin by making sure witnesses were truly present at the time of the crime. When evaluating the gospel writers, the most reasonable inference from the evidence is an early date of authorship. Does this mean they are reliable? Not yet; there's much more to consider. But the Gospels have passed the first test; their testimony appears early enough in history to confirm they were actually present to see what they said they saw.

Chapter 12

WERE THEY CORROBORATED?

"The word god is for me nothing more than the expression and product of human weaknesses, the Bible a collection of honourable, but still primitive legends which are nevertheless pretty childish. No interpretation no matter how subtle can (for me) change this."[1]

Albert Einstein, father of modern physics

"Is there an intelligent man or woman now in the world who believes in the Garden of Eden story? If there is, strike here (tapping his forehead) and you will hear an echo. Something is for rent."[2]

Robert Green Ingersoll, the nineteenth-century American
political leader known as "The Great Agnostic"

"I think that the people who think God wrote a book called The Bible are just childish."

Bill Maher, comedian, television host, and political commentator

THERE OUGHT TO BE SOME SUPPORT

Christian Scripture is not merely a collection of proverbs or commandments related to moral living, although the New Testament certainly contains these elements. The Bible is a claim about history. Like other eyewitness accounts, the Bible describes events occurring in the past in a particular way, at a particular time, with a particular result. If the accounts are true, they are not merely "legends" or "childish" stories, even though they may contain miraculous elements difficult for skeptics to accept. It's not surprising those who reject the supernatural would doubt those who claimed to see something miraculous. It's also not surprising these skeptics would want miraculous claims to be corroborated.

While there are times when an eyewitness is the only piece of evidence I have at my disposal, most of my cases are buttressed by other pieces of evidence corroborating the eyewitness. I once had a case from 1982 in which a witness (Aimee Thompson) claimed to see a murder suspect (Danny Herrin) standing in the front yard of the victim's house just minutes before the murder took place. At the time of the original investigation, Aimee identified Danny from a "six-pack photo lineup," a series of six photographs of men (complete strangers to Aimee), arranged in two rows in a photo folder. Aimee did not know Danny personally, but she recognized his face in the photo. She remembered he was wearing a popular concert T-shirt with a logo from the musical band Journey, promoting their tour in support of their *Escape* album. In addition to this, she told me the man she observed stood in a peculiar way, hunched over just slightly as if he had some sort of physical injury. I knew Danny also had this unusual posture and fit her description. Given this identification, I traveled out to the city where Danny lived for an interview. When I spoke with Danny, he denied he was anywhere near the victim's house. In fact, he claimed he wasn't even in the same city as the victim on the day in question. While it would have been nice to find some forensic evidence at the scene corroborating Aimee's observations, this was unfortunately not the case. The original investigators did, however, find a gas receipt in Danny's car issued from a gas station on the day of the murder, just a quarter mile from the victim's house. In addition to this, I later interviewed Danny's sister; she told me Danny mentioned stopping by to see the victim on the day of the murder.

Now it's true the gas receipt and his sister's statement alone would not prove Danny murdered the victim, but these two additional facts did corroborate Aimee's claims; if nothing else, her assertions were made more reasonable by her observations of Danny's unusual stance and these additional supporting facts. There were two forms of corroboration working here. First, there was corroboration *internal* to Aimee's statement. She described something true about the suspect (his stance) that could not have been known by Aimee unless she was present as she claimed. In addition to this internal evidence, there was also *external* evidence corroborating her claim. The gas receipt and Danny's sister's statement were independent of Aimee, but still supported her assertions. Together, the internal and external evidence *agreed* with Aimee's primary claims as an eyewitness.

CORROBORATION FROM THE "INSIDE OUT"

As it turns out, there is similar corroboration available to us when we examine the claims of the gospel accounts. Some of this corroboration is *internal* (evidence from within the gospel documents consistent with the claims of the text) and some is *external* (evidences independent of the gospel documents yet verifying the claims of the text). Much has been written about the internal evidence supporting the reliability of the New Testament authors; scholars have studied the use of language and Greek idioms to try to discover if the writing styles of each author corroborate the New Testament claims related to the authors. Is John's use of language consistent with that of a first-century fisherman? Is Luke's language consistent with that of a first-century doctor? While these exercises are interesting from a scholarly perspective, they did not pique my investigative curiosity as a detective. Two areas of internal evidence, however, did interest me as someone who has interviewed hundreds of witnesses.

THE GOSPEL WRITERS PROVIDED UNINTENTIONAL EYEWITNESS SUPPORT

As we discussed in chapter 4, one of the most important tasks for a detective is to listen carefully when multiple eyewitnesses provide a statement about what they observed at the scene of a crime. It's my job to assemble the complete "picture" of what happened at the scene. No single witness is likely to have seen every detail, so I must piece together the accounts, allowing the observations of one eyewitness to *fill in the gaps* existing in the observations of another eyewitness. That's why it's so important for eyewitnesses to be separated before they are interviewed. True, reliable eyewitness accounts are never completely parallel and identical. Instead, they are different pieces of the same puzzle, unintentionally supporting and complementing each other to provide all the details related to what really happened.

When I first read through the Gospels forensically, comparing those places where two or more gospel writers were describing the same event, I was immediately struck by the inadvertent support each writer provided for the other. The accounts *puzzled together* just the way one would expect from independent eyewitnesses. When one gospel eyewitness described an event and left out a detail raising a question, this question was unintentionally answered by another gospel writer (who, by the way, often left out a detail provided by the first gospel writer). This interdependence between the accounts could be explained in one of two ways. Maybe the writers worked together, writing at precisely the same time and location, to craft a clever lie so subtle very few people would even notice it at all. The second possibility is the Gospels were written by different eyewitnesses who witnessed the event and included these unplanned supporting details; they were simply describing *true events.*

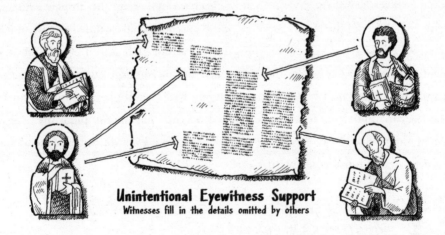

Unintentional Eyewitness Support
Witnesses fill in the details omitted by others

As someone who was new to the Bible, I began to investigate whether anyone else had observed this phenomenon, and I found that a professor of divinity named J. J. Blunt wrote a book in 1847 entitled *Undesigned Coincidences in the Writings of the Old and New Testament, an Argument of Their Veracity; with an Appendix, Containing Undesigned Coincidences between the Gospels and Acts, and Josephus.* This was one of the first books about the Bible I ever purchased. In his section related to the Gospels and the book of Acts, Blunt identified the very same inadvertent parallel passages I discovered when examining the Gospels forensically. Blunt described the phenomenon as a series of "undesigned coincidences" and identified over forty locations in the New Testament where this feature of unintentional eyewitness support could be seen on the pages of Scripture. Let me give you a few examples of what we are talking about here.

THE CALLING OF THE DISCIPLES
As someone unfamiliar with the Bible, the calling of Peter, Andrew, James, and John seemed odd to me when I first read it in the gospel of Matthew:

> *Now as Jesus was walking by the Sea of Galilee, He saw two brothers, Simon who was called Peter, and Andrew his brother, casting a net into the sea; for they were fishermen. And He said to them, "Follow Me, and I will make you fishers of men." Immediately they left their nets and followed Him. Going on from there He saw two other brothers, James the son of Zebedee, and John his brother, in the boat with Zebedee their father, mending their nets; and He called them. Immediately they left the boat and their father, and followed Him. (Matt. 4:18–22)*

That's it? Jesus walked up and said, "Follow Me," and they dropped everything "immediately"? Who would do that? How did they even know who Jesus was or if anything about Him was worthy of dedication? If Matthew's account was the only testimony available to us (and for many communities in the ancient world, it *was* the only testimony available for many years), this would remain a mystery. I do believe there is a clue in Matthew's version of events (the mending of the nets), but the questions raised by Matthew aren't answered for us until we hear from Luke:

> *Now it happened that while the crowd was pressing around Him and listening to the word of God, He was standing by the lake of Gennesaret; and He saw two boats lying at the edge of the lake; but the fishermen had gotten out of them and were washing their nets. And He got into one of the boats, which was Simon's, and*

asked him to put out a little way from the land. And He sat down and began teaching the people from the boat. When He had finished speaking, He said to Simon, "Put out into the deep water and let down your nets for a catch." Simon answered and said, "Master, we worked hard all night and caught nothing, but I will do as You say and let down the nets." When they had done this, they enclosed a great quantity of fish, and their nets began to break; so they signaled to their partners in the other boat for them to come and help them. And they came and filled both of the boats, so that they began to sink. But when Simon Peter saw that, he fell down at Jesus' feet, saying, "Go away from me Lord, for I am a sinful man!" For amazement had seized him and all his companions because of the catch of fish which they had taken; and so also were James and John, sons of Zebedee, who were partners with Simon. And Jesus said to Simon, "Do not fear, from now on you will be catching men." When they had brought their boats to land, they left everything and followed Him. (Luke 5:1–11)

More "Unintentional Support"

There are many examples of "undesigned coincidences" in the gospel eyewitness accounts. Here are two more:

Question: Matthew 8:16:

Why did they wait until evening to bring those who needed healing?

Answer: Mark 1:21, Luke 4:31:

Because it was the Sabbath.

Question: Matthew 14:1–2:

Why did Herod tell his *servants* he thought Jesus was John the Baptist, raised from the dead?

Answer: Luke 8:3, Acts 13:1:

Several of Jesus's followers were from Herod's household.

The disciples didn't just *jump in* with Jesus on a whim after all. Matthew was interested in describing how the disciples were called, but Luke was interested in providing a bit more detail. When the testimony of all the witnesses is considered in unison, we get the complete picture. The disciples heard Jesus preach and saw the miracle of the abundant catch of fish. This harvest of fish was so impressive and large it broke their nets. Only after returning to the shore (and while James and John were mending their torn nets) did Jesus call them to follow Him. They left their lives as fishermen based on the things Jesus taught and the miracle Jesus performed.

THE STRIKING OF JESUS

In the next example, let's examine the description of Jesus's beating offered by Matthew in chapter 26 of his gospel. In this scene, describing Jesus's examination before Caiaphas, Matthew told us the chief priests and the members of the council struck Jesus and slapped Him when He "blasphemed" by identifying Himself as the "Son of Man":

> *Then they spat in His face and beat Him with their fists; and others slapped Him, and said, "Prophesy to us, You Christ; who is the one who hit You?" (Matt. 26:67–68)*

This question posed by members of the council seems odd. Jesus's attackers were standing right in front of Him; why would they ask Him, "Who is the one who hit You?" It doesn't seem like much of a challenge, given Jesus could look at His attackers and identify them easily. Luke told us more, however:

> *Now the men who were holding Jesus in custody were mocking Him and beating Him, and they blindfolded Him and were asking Him, saying, "Prophesy, who is the one who hit You?" And they were saying many other things against Him, blaspheming. (Luke 22:63–65)*

Once again, one gospel eyewitness unintentionally supported the other in what J. J. Blunt called an "undesigned coincidence." Matthew's narrative makes sense once we read what Luke has to say about Jesus being blindfolded. Imagine for a moment you are one of the earliest converts to Christianity, at a time and place in history where the gospel of Matthew was the only available account. This passage would be puzzling; it would raise a question that might never be answered unless you had access to the other eyewitness accounts. As a cold-case detective, I've experienced something similar to this a number of times. Often, questions an eyewitness raises at the time of the crime are left unanswered until we locate an additional witness years later. This is a common characteristic of true, reliable eyewitness accounts.

THE FEEDING OF THE FIVE THOUSAND

Perhaps the finest example of *unintentional support* is found in an episode described in all four gospels: the miracle of the "feeding of five thousand." Mark's account of this miracle raises a question when considered without input from the other gospel writers. Just prior to this event (according to Mark), Jesus sent out the disciples to preach repentance in the local towns and villages. When they returned, they found themselves surrounded by a multitude of people:

> *The apostles gathered together with Jesus; and they reported to Him all that they had done and taught. And He said to them, "Come away by yourselves to a secluded place and rest a while." (For there were many people coming and going, and they did not even have time to eat.) They went away in the boat to a secluded place by themselves. The people saw them going, and many recognized them and ran there together on foot from all the cities, and got there ahead of them. When Jesus went ashore, He saw a large crowd, and He felt compassion for them because they were like sheep without a shepherd; and He began to teach them many things. When it was already quite late, His disciples came to Him and said, "This place is desolate and it is already quite late; send them away so that they may go into the surrounding countryside and villages and buy themselves something to eat." But He answered them, "You give them something to eat!" And they said to Him, "Shall we go and spend two hundred denarii on bread and give them something to eat?" And He said to them, "How many loaves do you have? Go look!" And when they found out, they said, "Five, and two fish." And He commanded them all to sit down by groups on the green grass. They sat down in groups of hundreds and of fifties. And He took the five loaves and the two fish, and looking up toward heaven, He blessed the food and broke the loaves and He kept giving them to the disciples to set before them; and He divided up the two fish among them all. They all ate and were satisfied, and they picked up twelve full baskets of the broken pieces, and also of the fish. There were five thousand men who ate the loaves. (Mark 6:30–44)*

According to Mark, many people were coming and going in the area, even before Jesus and His disciples became the focal point of this crowd. Why was this crowd in the area in the first place? Mark never said. The question Mark's account raised isn't answered until we hear John's testimony:

After these things Jesus went away to the other side of the Sea of Galilee (or Tiberias). A large crowd followed Him, because they saw the signs which He was performing on those who were sick. Then Jesus went up on the mountain, and there He sat down with His disciples. Now the Passover, the feast of the Jews, was near. Therefore Jesus, lifting up His eyes and seeing that a large crowd was coming to Him, said to Philip, "Where are we to buy bread, so that these may eat?" This He was saying to test him, for He Himself knew what He was intending to do. Philip answered Him, "Two hundred denarii worth of bread is not sufficient for them, for everyone to receive a little." One of His disciples, Andrew, Simon Peter's brother, said to Him, "There is a lad here who has five barley loaves and two fish, but what are these for so many people?" Jesus said, "Have the people sit down." Now there was much grass in the place. So the men sat down, in number about five thousand. Jesus then took the loaves, and having given thanks, He distributed to those who were seated; likewise also of the fish as much as they wanted. When they were

More "Unintentional Support"

Here are a few more "undesigned coincidences" in the gospel eyewitness accounts.:

Question: Luke 23:1–4:

Why didn't Pilate find a charge against Jesus even though Jesus claimed to be a king?

Answer: John 18:33–38:

Jesus told Pilate His kingdom was not of this world.

Question: Matthew 26:71:

Why did the maid notice Peter?

Answer: John 18:16:

A disciple spoke with her when he brought Peter inside.

Question: Mark 15:43:

Why did Mark say Joseph of Arimathea acted "boldly"?

Answer: John 19:38:

Joseph was previously a secret disciple who was in fear of the Jews.

filled, He said to His disciples, "Gather up the leftover fragments so that noth-
ing will be lost." So they gathered them up, and filled twelve baskets with
fragments from the five barley loaves which were left over by those who had
eaten. (John 6:1–13)

John answered the question raised by Mark. The large crowd was the result of two circumstances: First, John alone reported the people searched for Jesus because they knew He had been performing miraculous healings. Second, John alone said it was nearly Passover, the holy Jewish holiday causing thousands to travel through this area to arrive at Jerusalem for the celebration. While Mark mentioned the crowd, only John told us why they were there in the first place. But in unintentionally answering the question raised by Mark, John raised an unanswered question of his own. John's account mentioned Philip and Andrew specifically. This stood out to me, only because the use of pronouns and proper names is an important focus of forensic statement analysis. Andrew and Philip are not major characters in the Gospels; the gospel writers seldom mention them, especially when compared with Peter, John, and James. For this reason, their appearance here raises a couple of questions. Why did Jesus ask Philip where they ought to go to buy bread? Why did Andrew get involved in the answer? In addition to this, John also mentioned a detail not found in Mark's briefer account. John said the disciples fed the crowd "barley loaves." John also repeated Mark's testimony describing "much grass" in the area. To make sense of the questions raised by John and the role of the grass and the barley, let's finish with an examination of Luke's account:

"Harmonization" or "Interpolation"?

When two or more eyewitness accounts are considered by an investigator, it's the duty of the detective to "harmonize" the accounts. The details from each account must be assembled without modifying the statements or adding details foreign to the observations of the witnesses. In the end, the final "harmony" will provide a version of events in which the eyewitnesses can be heard clearly and distinctly, even though they may be providing different details. Detectives must avoid "interpolation," the insertion of additional or extraneous material into the eyewitness record.

When the apostles returned, they gave an account to Him of all that they had done. Taking them with Him, He withdrew by Himself to a city called Bethsaida. But the crowds were aware of this and followed Him; and welcoming them, He began speaking to them about the kingdom of God and curing those who had need of healing. Now the day was ending, and the twelve came and said to Him, "Send the crowd away, that they may go into the surrounding villages and countryside and find lodging and get something to eat; for here we are in a desolate place." But He said to them, "You give them something to eat!" And they said, "We have no more than five loaves and two fish, unless perhaps we go and buy food for all these people." (For there were about five thousand men.) And He said to His disciples, "Have them sit down to eat in groups of about fifty each." They did so, and had them all sit down. Then He took the five loaves and the two fish, and looking up to heaven, He blessed them, and broke them, and kept giving them to the disciples to set before the people. And they all ate and were satisfied; and the broken pieces which they had left over were picked up, twelve baskets full. (Luke 9:10–17)

Luke is the only one reporting this event as occurring when Jesus withdrew to the city of Bethsaida. This revelation unlocks the mystery of Philip and Andrew's prominence in John's testimony; they were both from Bethsaida (according to John 1:44). We learned this detail not from Luke (who described the miracle occurring in Bethsaida) but from John (who mentioned it without any connection to the miracle). Jesus asked Philip about sources for the bread because He knew Philip was from this part of the country. Philip and Andrew naturally tried their best to respond, given they were uniquely qualified to answer Jesus's question.

What about the grass and barley? Why were these details included in the narrative? Are they consistent with what eyewitnesses might have seen or experienced? As it turns out, the Passover occurred at a time (in April) following five of the rainiest months for the area of Bethsaida. In addition to this, the Passover occurred at the end of the barley harvest.[3] These insignificant particulars are just what I would expect to hear from eyewitnesses who were simply describing what they saw, including relatively meaningless details in the larger narrative.

Unintentional Eyewitness Support
Witnesses fill in the details omitted by others

The gospel writers provide unintentional eyewitness support for one another just like many of the eyewitnesses I've interviewed over the years. Their accounts support and complement one another as they describe the details related to what really happened.

THE GOSPEL WRITERS REFERENCED NAMES CORRECTLY

When I interview eyewitnesses, I listen carefully to their descriptions of the suspect and the environment in which the crime took place. Their observations of the scene, if they are genuine, should reflect the true nature of the time and location of the crime. When Aimee told me about her observations of the suspect in 1982, she described a Journey concert shirt promoting an album (*Escape*) released in 1981. The description of the shirt was consistent with the time frame of the murder. If Aimee had described a shirt unavailable until 1990, for example, I would have been concerned her statement was either inadvertently inaccurate or deliberately false.

Something similar can be observed in the gospel accounts. The gospel writers are believed to have written from several geographic locations. Mark probably wrote from Rome, Matthew may have written from Judea, Luke from either Antioch or Rome, and John from Ephesus.[4] Skeptics have argued these accounts were not written by people who had firsthand knowledge of the life and ministry of Jesus but were simply inventions written generations later by people who weren't all that familiar with the locations they were describing. The gospel writers described many people as they wrote out their testimonies, and often identified these individuals by name. As it turns out, these names provide us with important clues to help us determine if the writers of the Gospels were familiar with life in first-century Palestine.

Richard Bauckham[5] examined the work of Tal Ilan[6] and used Ilan's data when investigating the biblical use of names. Ilan assembled a lexicon of all the recorded names used by the Jews of Palestine between 330 BC and AD 200. She examined the writings of Josephus, the texts of the New Testament, documents from the Judean desert and Masada, and the earliest rabbinic works of the period. She even examined ossuary (funeral-tomb) inscriptions from Jerusalem. Ilan included the New Testament writings in her study as well. She discovered the most popular men's names in Palestine (in the timespan encompassing the gospel accounts) were Simon and Joseph. The most popular women's names were Mary and Salome. You may recognize these names from the gospel accounts. As it turns out, when Bauckham examined all the names discovered by Ilan, he found the New Testament narratives reflect nearly the same percentages found in all the documents Ilan examined:

The Corroboration of Language

The gospel writers do more than correctly cite the popular names of 1st-century Palestinian Jews. They also appear to have written in a style similar to those who lived at that time. Nonbiblical scraps of papyrus and pottery from the 1st century provide us with samples of the form of Greek popular in the ancient Middle East. The Greek used by the gospel writers is very similar to the vernacular "common" Greek used by others who lived in this region at this time in history. (Refer to *The New Testament Documents: Are They Reliable?* by F. F. Bruce [Wilder, 2010].)

Popularity of Names Cited in Palestinian Literature of the Time	Popularity of Names Cited by the New Testament Authors
15.6% of the men had the name Simon or Joseph	18.2% of the men had the name Simon or Joseph
41.5% of the men had one of the nine most popular names	40.3% of the men had one of the nine most popular names
7.9% of the men had a name no one else had	3.9% of the men had a name no one else had
28.6% of the women had the name Mary or Salome	38.9% of the women had the name Mary or Salome
49.7% of the women had one of the nine most popular names	61.1% of the women had one of the nine most popular names
9.6% of the women had a name no one else had	2.5% of the women had a name no one else had[7]

The most popular names found in the Gospels just happen to be the most popular names found in Palestine in the first century. This is even more striking when you compare the ancient popular Palestinian Jewish names with the ancient popular Egyptian Jewish names:

Top Jewish Men's Names in Palestine	Top Jewish Men's Names in Egypt
Simon	Eleazar
Joseph	Sabbataius
Eleazar	Joseph
Judah	Dositheus
Yohanan	Pappus
Joshua	Ptolemaius

If the gospel writers were simply guessing about the names they were using in their accounts, they happened to guess with remarkable accuracy. Many of the popular Jewish names in Palestine were different from the popular names in Egypt, Syria, or Rome. The use of these names by the gospel writers is consistent with their claim they were writing based on true eyewitness familiarity.

When names are very common, people find themselves having to make a distinction by adding an extra piece of information. My name is Jim Wallace, but I am often confused with Jim Wallis, the founder and editor of *Sojourners* magazine. For this reason, I will sometimes add the additional descriptor "of ColdCaseChristianity.com" when describing myself. I am Jim Wallace "of ColdCaseChristianity.com" (as opposed to Jim Wallis "of *Sojourners*"). When you see the addition of a descriptor, you can be sure the name being amended is probably common to the region or time in history. We see this throughout the gospel accounts. The gospel writers introduce us to Simon "Peter," Simon "the Zealot," Simon "the Tanner," Simon "the Leper," and Simon "of Cyrene." The name Simon was so common to the area of Palestine in the first century that the gospel writers had to add descriptors to differentiate one Simon from another. This is something we would expect to see if the gospel writers were truly present in Palestine in the first century and familiar with the common names of the region (and the need to better describe those who possessed these popular names).

Jesus (Hebrew: Joshua) was one of these popular first-century names in Palestine, ranking sixth among men's names. For this reason, Jesus was one of those names often requiring an additional descriptor for clarity's sake. Interestingly, the gospel writers themselves (when acting as narrators) didn't use additional descriptors for Jesus, even though they quoted characters within the narrative who did. Matthew, for example, repeatedly referred to Jesus as simply "Jesus" when describing what Jesus did or said. But when quoting others who used Jesus's name, Matthew quoted them identifying Jesus as "Jesus from Nazareth in Galilee," "Jesus the Galilean," "Jesus of Nazareth," "Jesus who was called Christ," "Jesus who was crucified." Why the difference? Matthew, as the narrator of history, simply called Jesus by His first name over the course of many chapters. His readers were already familiar with the person of Jesus Matthew introduced early in his account. But Matthew accurately

The Corroboration of Location

The gospel writers were evidently extremely familiar with the locations they wrote about. While late noncanonical forgeries written from outside the area of Palestine seldom mention any city other than Jerusalem (the one famous city everyone knew was in Israel), the gospel writers alone include the specific names of lesser-known 1st-century towns and villages. The gospel writers mention or describe Aenon, Arimathea, Bethphage, Caesarea Philippi, Cana, Chorazin, Dalmanutha, Emmaus, Ephraim, Magadan, Nain, Salim, and Sychar. Some of these villages are so obscure only people familiar with the area would even know they existed.

recorded the way we would expect people to identify Jesus in the context of the first century. Matthew appears to be acting merely as an eyewitness *recorder of facts*, limiting himself to "Jesus" when he is doing the talking, but accurately reporting the way he heard others refer to Jesus.

The way the gospel writers described details (unintentionally supporting one another) and the approach the gospel writers took when they referred to people (using the names and descriptors we would expect in first-century Palestine) corroborate their testimonies *internally*. The gospel accounts appear authentic from the "inside out." The words of the Gospels themselves are consistent with what we would expect from eyewitnesses.

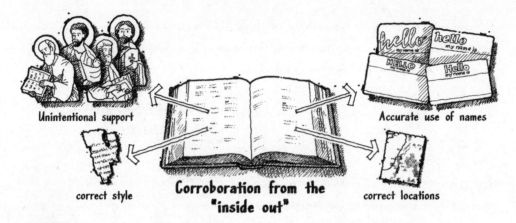

Unintentional support

correct style

Corroboration from the "inside out"

Accurate use of names

correct locations

CORROBORATION FROM THE "OUTSIDE IN"

If the Gospels are true, we should also expect them to be corroborated *externally*. Aimee's testimony, for example, was corroborated by two additional pieces of evidence (the discovery of the gas receipt and the testimony of Danny's sister). The Gospels are similarly corroborated from the "outside in" by the testimony of ancient "reporting parties" who described what they knew to be true, even though they were not Christians and did not necessarily believe the testimony of the gospel writers. These non-Christians were often hostile to the growing Christian movement and critical of the claims of the Gospels. Despite this, they affirmed many of the details reported by the gospel writers.

As a cold-case detective, I've encountered this sort of thing many times. I once had a case with a victim who was killed in her condominium. The primary suspect in her murder originally denied ever being in her home. I interviewed him a second time and told him we discovered his DNA was in the house, in the very room where the victim was murdered. He changed his story and told me he remembered the victim called him and asked him to come over to the house to help move some boxes from this room to her garage. The suspect said he came over on the day of the murder and was in the victim's room for a very short time to help her move these boxes. He still denied being involved in her murder, however. Although he continued to deny his involvement in the crime, his new statement included two *reluctant admissions*. The suspect now admitted he was in the room where the murder occurred, on the very day when the victim was killed. While he still denied committing the crime, he *reluctantly admitted* important facts that would eventually be assembled with other pieces of circumstantial evidence to form the case against him.

3 NONBIBLICAL EYEWITNESSES CORROBORATED THE GOSPELS

In a similar way, ancient observers and writers who were hostile to Christianity *reluctantly admitted* several key facts corroborating the claims of the Christian eyewitnesses, even though they denied Jesus was who He claimed to be. Let's examine some of these *reluctant admissions* and reconstruct the picture they offer of Jesus.

JOSEPHUS (AD 37–101) DESCRIBED JESUS

Josephus described the Christians in three separate citations in his *Antiquities of the Jews*. In one of these passages, Josephus described the death of John the Baptist, in another he mentioned the execution of James (the brother of Jesus), and in a third passage he described Jesus as a "wise man." There is controversy about Josephus's writing because early Christians appear to have altered some copies of his work in an effort to *amplify* the references to Jesus. For this reason, as we examine Josephus's passage related to Jesus, we will rely on a text scholars believe escaped such alteration. In 1971, Shlomo Pines, scholar of ancient languages and distinguished professor at the Hebrew University of Jerusalem, published a long-lost tenth-century Arabic text written by a Melkite bishop of Hierapolis named Agapius. This Arabic leader quoted Josephus and did so in the Arabic language, unlike the Greek used by other authors from antiquity. Overtly Christian references seen in other ancient versions of Josephus's account are also missing from Agapius's quote, and as a result, scholars believe this version best reflects Josephus's original text:

> At this time there was a wise man who was called Jesus. And his conduct was good, and [he] was known to be virtuous. And many people from among the Jews and the other nations became his disciples. Pilate condemned him to be crucified and to die. And those who had become his disciples did not abandon his discipleship. They reported that he had appeared to them three days after his crucifixion and that he was alive; accordingly, he was perhaps the

Messiah concerning whom the prophets have recounted wonders. (Agapius, Kitâb al-ʿunwân 2:15–16)[8]

There are many other ancient versions of Josephus's citation more explicit about the nature of Jesus's miracles, His life, resurrection, and status as "the Christ," but this brief and conservative version of Josephus's text reluctantly admits several key facts about Jesus. From this text, we can conclude Jesus lived, was a wise and virtuous teacher who reportedly demonstrated wondrous power, was condemned and crucified under Pilate, had followers who reported He appeared to them after His death on the cross, and was believed to be the Messiah.

THALLUS (CA. AD 5-60) DESCRIBED JESUS

Thallus was a Samaritan historian who wrote an expansive (three-volume) account of the history of the Mediterranean area in the middle of the first century, only twenty years after Jesus's crucifixion. Like the writings of many ancient historians, much of his work is now lost to us. Another historian, Sextus Julius Africanus, wrote a text entitled *History of the World* in AD 221, however, and Africanus quoted an important passage from Thallus's original account. Thallus chronicled the alleged crucifixion of Jesus and offered an explanation for the darkness observed at the time of Jesus's death. Africanus briefly described Thallus's explanation:

On the whole world there pressed a most fearful darkness; and the rocks were rent by an earthquake, and many places in Judea and other districts were thrown down. This darkness Thallus, in the third book of his *History*, calls, as appears to me without reason, an eclipse of the sun.[9]

We don't have the complete account and explanation from Thallus, but in explaining the darkness, Thallus reluctantly admitted important details corroborating portions of the Gospels. Even though Thallus denied the darkness at the point of the crucifixion was caused supernaturally, he inadvertently corroborated Jesus was indeed crucified and darkness covered the land when He died on the cross.

TACITUS (AD 56–117) DESCRIBED JESUS

Cornelius Tacitus was known for his analysis and examination of historical documents and is among the most trusted of ancient historians. He was a senator under Emperor Vespasian and was also proconsul of Asia. In his *Annals* of AD 116, he described Emperor Nero's response to the great fire in Rome and Nero's claim the Christians were to blame:

Consequently, to get rid of the report, Nero fastened the guilt and inflicted the most exquisite tortures on a class hated for their abominations, called Christians by the populace. Christus, from whom the name had its origin, suffered the extreme penalty during the reign of Tiberius at the hands of one of our procurators, Pontius Pilatus, and a most mischievous superstition, thus checked for the moment, again broke out not only in Judaea, the first source of the evil, but even in Rome, where all things hideous and shameful from every part of the world find their centre and become popular.[10] (*Annals*, 15:44)

Ancient Jewish Corroboration

The Jewish Talmud (the writings and discussions of ancient rabbis) dates to the 5th century, but is thought to contain the ancient teachings from the early Tannaitic period from the 1st and 2nd centuries. Many of the Talmudic writings reference Jesus:

"Jesus practiced magic and led Israel astray" (b. Sanhedrin 43a; cf. t. Shabbat 11.15; b. Shabbat 104b).

"Rabbi Jeremiah bar Abba said, 'What is that which is written, "No evil will befall you, nor shall any plague come near your house"'? (Psalm 91:10) … 'No evil will befall you' (means) that evil dreams and evil thoughts will not tempt you; 'nor shall any plague come near your house' (means) that you will not have a son or a disciple who burns his food like Jesus of Nazareth" (b. Sanhedrin 103a; cf. b. Berakhot 17b).

"It was taught: On the day before the Passover they hanged Jesus. A herald went before him for forty days (proclaiming), 'He will be stoned, because he practiced magic and enticed Israel to go astray. Let anyone who knows anything in his favor come forward and plead for him.' But nothing was found in his favor, and they hanged him on the day before the Passover" (b. Sanhedrin 43a).

From just these passages mentioning Jesus by name, we can conclude Jesus had magical powers, led the Jews away from their beliefs, and was executed on the day before the Passover.

Tacitus, in describing Nero's actions and the presence of the Christians in Rome, *reluctantly admitted* several key facts related to the life of Jesus. Tacitus corroborated Jesus lived in Judea, was crucified under Pontius Pilate, and had followers who were persecuted for their faith in Him.

MARA BAR-SERAPION (AD 70–UNK.) DESCRIBED JESUS

Sometime after AD 70, a Syrian philosopher named Mara Bar-Serapion, writing to encourage his son, compared the life and persecution of Jesus with that of other philosophers who were persecuted for their ideas. The fact that Mara Bar-Serapion described Jesus as a real person with this kind of influence is important:

> What advantage did the Athenians gain from putting Socrates to death? Famine and plague came upon them as a judgment for their crime. What advantage did the men of Samos gain from burning Pythagoras? In a moment their land was covered with sand. What advantage did the Jews gain from executing their wise King? It was just after that that their kingdom was abolished. God justly avenged these three wise men: the Athenians died of hunger; the Samians were overwhelmed by the sea; the Jews, ruined and driven from their land, live in complete dispersion. But Socrates did not die for good; he lived on in the teaching of Plato. Pythagoras did not die for good; he lived on in the statue of Hera. Nor did the wise King die for good; he lived on in the teaching which he had given.[11]

Although Mara Bar-Serapion does not seem to place Jesus in a position of pre-eminence (he simply lists Him alongside other historic teachers like Socrates and Pythagoras), Mara Bar-Serapion does admit several key facts. At the very least, we can conclude Jesus was a wise and influential man who died for His beliefs. We can also conclude the Jews played a role in Jesus's death and Jesus's followers adopted and lived lives reflecting His beliefs.

PHLEGON (AD 80-140) DESCRIBED JESUS

In a manner similar to his citation of Thallus, Sextus Julius Africanus also wrote about a historian named Phlegon who penned a record of history in approximately AD 140. In his historical account, Phlegon also mentioned the darkness surrounding the crucifixion:

Phlegon records that, in the time of Tiberius Caesar, at full moon, there was a full eclipse of the sun from the sixth hour to the ninth.[12]

Origen, the Alexandrian-born, early-church theologian and scholar, also cited Phlegon several times in a book he wrote in response to the criticism of a Greek writer named Celsus:

Now Phlegon, in the thirteenth or fourteenth book, I think, of his Chronicles, not only ascribed to Jesus a knowledge of future events (although falling into confusion about some things which refer to Peter, as if they referred to Jesus), but also testified that the result corresponded to His predictions. So that he also, by these very admissions regarding foreknowledge, as if against his will, expressed his opinion that the doctrines taught by the fathers of our system were not devoid of divine power.

And with regard to the eclipse in the time of Tiberius Caesar, in whose reign Jesus appears to have been crucified, and the great earthquakes which then took place, Phlegon too, I think, has written in the thirteenth or fourteenth book of his Chronicles.

He imagines also that both the earthquake and the darkness were an invention; but regarding these, we have in the preceding pages made our defence, according to our ability, adducing the testimony of Phlegon, who relates that these events took place at the time when our Saviour suffered.[13]

Although Phlegon was not a follower of Jesus and denied many of the claims of the gospel writers, his statements did *reluctantly admit* Jesus had the ability to accurately predict the future and was crucified under the reign of Tiberius Caesar.

These late first-century and early second-century writers were not friends of Christianity. In fact, they were largely indifferent to the fledgling Christian movement. Despite this, they all provided important corroborating details of Jesus's life, even if they did so *reluctantly*. If all the Christian documents had been destroyed, we would still be able to reconstruct a modest description of Jesus from these writers.

The ancient (and reluctant) nonbiblical description of Jesus would include the fact Jesus was a true historical person and a virtuous, wise man who worked wonders, accurately predicted the future, and taught His disciples. His teaching drew a large following of both Jews and Gentiles; He was identified as the "Christ," believed to be the Messiah, and widely known as the "Wise King" of the Jews. His disciples were eventually called Christians. His devoted followers became a threat to the Jewish leadership, and as a result, these leaders presented accusations to the Roman authorities. Pontius Pilate condemned Jesus to crucifixion during the reign of Tiberius Caesar. A great darkness descended over the land when Jesus was crucified, and an earthquake shook a large region surrounding the execution. Following His execution, a "mischievous superstition" spread about Him from Palestine to Rome.

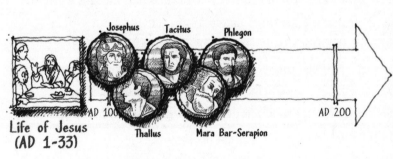

This description of Jesus, although incomplete, is remarkably similar to the description offered by the gospel writers. Early, external, non-Christian sources corroborate the testimony of the New Testament authors (for much more on the early confirmation of details related to the life and ministry of Jesus found in literature, art, music, education, science, and non-Christian religious worldviews, refer to my book *Person of Interest: Why Jesus Still Matters in a World That Rejects the Bible*).

ARCHAEOLOGY CONTINUES TO CORROBORATE THE GOSPELS

Because Christianity makes historical claims, archaeology is a tool we can use to determine if these claims are true. In fact, archaeology has repeatedly corroborated many claims of the New Testament, particularly related to historical figures, geographic locations, events, and conditions of the time. Educator and archaeologist Dr. Joseph P. Free notes, "Archaeology has confirmed countless passages which had been rejected by critics as unhistorical or contrary to known facts."[14] The archaeological efforts of the past two centuries have confirmed several details skeptics used to highlight as areas of weakness in the case for Christianity. There are many biblical passages now corroborated by both ancient non-Christian witnesses and archaeological evidence. Here are just a few.

NEW TESTAMENT HISTORICAL FIGURES CORROBORATED BY ARCHAEOLOGY:

PONTIUS PILATE

For many years, the only corroboration we had for the existence of Pontius Pilate (the governor of Judea who authorized the crucifixion of Jesus) was a very brief citation by Tacitus (described in the previous section). In 1961, however, a piece of limestone was discovered bearing an inscription with Pilate's name.[15] The inscription was discovered in Caesarea, a provincial capital during Pilate's term (AD 26–36), and it describes a building dedication from Pilate to Tiberius Caesar. This single discovery corroborates what the gospel writers said about Pilate's existence in history, his position within the government, and his relationship to Tiberius Caesar.

CAIAPHAS

Caiaphas was the high priest who presided over the trial of Jesus as recorded in the gospels of Matthew, Luke, and John (the earliest primary sources mentioning him). While Josephus also acknowledges Caiaphas's existence,[16] archaeology appears to further confirm his presence in history. In the early 1990s, twelve ossuaries (funeral boxes) were discovered in a family tomb south of Jerusalem. Most scholars now believe one of these ossuaries contains the remains of the Caiaphas described in the Gospels.[17]

SERGIUS PAULUS

In Acts 13, Luke identified Sergius Paulus, a proconsul in Paphos. Skeptics doubted the existence of this man and claimed any leader of this area would be a "propraetor" rather than a proconsul. But an inscription discovered at Soli in Cyprus acknowledges Paulus and identifies him as a proconsul. Another inscription discovered in Rome describes Lucius Sergius Paulus's role under the Emperor Claudius, and an inscription naming "L. Sergius Paulus" was also uncovered near Pisidian Antioch.[18]

LYSANIAS

Luke also described a tetrarch named Lysanias and described this man reigning over Abilene when John the Baptist began his ministry (Luke 3:1). Josephus also recorded the existence of a man named Lysanias[19] but this man was a king who ruled over the region from 40–36 BC (long before the birth of John the Baptist). Skeptics once again used this apparent discrepancy to cast doubt on Luke's account. As before, archaeology appears to have resolved the issue and corroborated Luke's claim. Two inscriptions have been discovered mentioning Lysanias by name. One of these, dated from AD 14–37, identifies Lysanias as the tetrarch in Abila near Damascus.[20] This inscription confirms the reasonable existence of two men named Lysanias, one who ruled prior to the birth of Jesus, and a tetrarch who reigned in the precise period described by Luke.[21]

GALLIO

Skeptics also thought the designation of "proconsul" given to Gallio (Lucius Junius Gallio Annaeanus) in Acts 18:12–17 was doubtful[22] until the discovery of what is now called the Gallio Inscription (also identified as the Delphi Inscription). Nine fragments from Emperor Claudius were discovered at Delphi, Greece, in which Junius Gallio is described as "my friend and proconsul." Archaeologists are now able to date the proconsulship of Gallio from May 1, AD 51, to end of April AD 52, helping to establish the chronology of the apostle Paul's mission journey.[23]

ERASTUS

In Romans 16:23, Paul wrote, "Erastus the city treasurer greets you." For many years, scholars were unsure if Paul was using the Greek word for "treasurer" (*oikonomos*) as an official title for Erastus, or as merely a description of his role (*oikonomos* can also be translated as "manager" or "steward"). Archaeologists in Corinth uncovered a large pavement stone bearing an inscription from the mid-first century: "Erastus, in return for his *aedileship*, laid (this pavement) at his own expense." *Aediles* were Roman magistrates accountable for the maintenance of public buildings, the administration of public games, and the supply of grain. It appears Luke rightly used the term *oikonomos* to describe the role Erastus played as an *aedile*.[24]

QUIRINIUS

Luke wrote Joseph and Mary returned to Bethlehem because a Syrian governor named Quirinius was conducting a census (Luke 2:1–3). Josephus confirmed the existence of this governor, but Josephus recorded Quirinius's governorship from AD 5 to AD 6.[25] This period is too late, however, as Matthew wrote Jesus was born during the reign of Herod the Great (who died nine years prior to Quirinius's governorship as recorded by Josephus). For many years, skeptics pointed to this discrepancy as evidence Luke's gospel was written late in history by someone who was unfamiliar with the chronology of leaders. Archaeological discoveries in the nineteenth century have provided additional information to remedy this apparent contradiction, revealing Quirinius (or someone with the same name) was also a proconsul of Syria and Cilicia from 11 BC to the death of Herod. Quirinius's name was discovered on a coin from this period,[26] and on the base of a statue erected in Pisidian Antioch.[27] Archaeology now corroborates the early existence of Quirinius as a governor at the time of the census recorded by Luke.

POLITARCHS

For many centuries, Luke was the only ancient writer known to use the word "politarchs" to describe "rulers of the city" (as he did in Acts 17:6, 8). Skeptics doubted it was a legitimate Greek term[28] until inscriptions were discovered by archaeologists. A marble building block from a Roman gateway at Thessalonica included an inscription listing six politarchs, a treasurer, and a director of higher education. Importantly, these inscriptions were discovered in the very city in which Luke was claiming to have heard the term.[29]

NEW TESTAMENT CITIES AND LOCATIONS CORROBORATED BY ARCHAEOLOGY:

BETHLEHEM

According to Luke, Jesus was born in the town of Bethlehem, even though there was no place for Joseph and Mary in the "inn." Many readers have speculated about the nature of the "manger" described by Luke. Church writers in the second and third century, for example, described the birthplace of Jesus as a "cave."[30] Is it reasonable to believe there might have been a "stable" or "manger" in a cave in Bethlehem in the first century? Archaeologists have uncovered the remains of the ancient village of Bethlehem, and we now have evidence that caves (or "stone pens") were used to house animals, making sense of both the biblical account and earliest church references.[31]

NAZARETH

Much skepticism also surrounded the first-century existence of Nazareth. The small town isn't referenced in any Jewish literature until long after the time of Jesus, nor is it ever mentioned by Josephus or the apostle Paul. But archaeologists uncovered an ancient mosaic in Caesarea Maritima confirming the existence of Nazareth,[32] and the discovery of an ancient house near the Church of the Annunciation confirms the existence of this small town during the time of Jesus.[33]

CAPERNAUM

The city of Capernaum was repeatedly mentioned by the gospel authors, and archaeologists have now confirmed much of what the New Testament authors described. Several one-story homes with flat thatch roofs have been discovered, matching the kind of house described in Mark 2:1–4 (when the paralytic was lowered through a roof to be healed by Jesus).[34] Many archaeologists believe we have also discovered Peter's home in Capernaum. A visitor to the city in AD 380 described an ancient church as having been built on the site of the "house of the prince of the Apostles,"[35] and scholars believe graffiti at the original site confirms its identity.[36] Peter's profession as a fisherman has also been supported by archaeological discoveries, as excavations in the city have uncovered artifacts demonstrating Capernaum was a fishing town.[37] Finally, the gospel authors described a synagogue in the city[38] built by a Roman centurion.[39] The foundations of a synagogue dating to the same period have been discovered under a fourth-century structure.[40] Several Roman-style buildings have also been discovered in Capernaum, confirming the presence of soldiers like the centurion mentioned by Luke.[41]

BETHSAIDA

The gospel authors describe the city of Bethsaida as a fishing town associated with Andrew, Peter, and Philip. Archaeologists believe the excavations at modern-day Et-Tel have uncovered this ancient New Testament city, and several fishing artifacts have been uncovered, consistent with the biblical descriptions of this town.[42]

ICONIUM

Luke described Iconium as a city in Phyrigia (Acts 14:1–6), but other ancient writers (like Cicero) described it as a city located in Lycaonia. Skeptics, therefore, doubted the reliability of Luke's account. But archaeologist William Ramsay discovered several ancient manuscripts confirming Iconium as a Phyrigian city.[43]

THE POOL OF BETHESDA

John wrote about the existence of a "pool of Bethesda" (John 5:1–9) and said it was located in the region of Jerusalem, near the Sheep Gate, surrounded by five porticos. For many years, there was no evidence for such a place outside of John's gospel; skeptics again pointed to this passage of Scripture and argued John's gospel was written late in history by someone who was unfamiliar with the features of the city. The twentieth-century discovery of the Dead Sea Scrolls, however, provided us with ancient confirmation of the pool's existence. The Copper Scroll (written between AD 25 and 68) described a list of locations in Jerusalem, including a pool called "Beth Eshdathayin" located near a porch.[44] In 1888, archaeologists began excavating the area near St. Anne's Church in Jerusalem and discovered the remains of the pool, complete with steps leading down from one side and five shallow porticos on another side.[45] Once again, the claims of a gospel writer were corroborated by archaeology.

THE POOL OF SILOAM

John also wrote about the "Pool of Siloam" (John 9:1–12) and described it as a place of ceremonial cleansing. Although the pool is also mentioned in the Old Testament (in Isaiah 8:6 and 22:9), John is the only other ancient author to ever describe its existence. Scholars were unable to locate the pool with any certainty until its discovery in the City of David region of Jerusalem in 2004. Archaeologists Ronny Reich and Eli Shukrun excavated the pool and dated it from 100 BC to AD 100 (based on the features of the pool and coins found in the plaster).[46] This discovery corroborated the reliability of Christian Scripture and the testimony of John.

THE TOMB OF LAZARUS

The village of el-Azariah (known in Arabic as "the place of Lazarus") has long been identified as the ancient town of Bethany where Jesus engaged Mary and Martha and raised Lazarus from the grave (in John 11:1–6). Many tombs have been excavated from the city bearing the names used by these three siblings (at least demonstrating the popularity of the names in this region), and one tomb was identified as the tomb of Lazarus. Archaeologists recognized it as a first-century tomb based on its shape and construction, and early Christians identified it as such.[47] In fact, an early Christian church was established near the tomb to commemorate the location.

NEW TESTAMENT CUSTOMS, EVENTS, AND CONDITIONS CORROBORATED BY ARCHAEOLOGY:

THE CUSTOM OF CRUCIFIXION

The gospel writers described the Roman custom of crucifixion, and Josephus, in his description of the destruction of Jerusalem, also described the practice.[48] But while thousands of condemned criminals and war prisoners were reported to have been executed in this manner, none had been discovered in any archaeological site for over 1,900 years following the execution of Jesus. Some skeptical scholars suggested crucified criminals were not afforded decent burials but were instead thrown into common graves along with other similarly executed prisoners. The gospel writers, however, claim Jesus was given a proper burial. Skeptics doubted this was true because they lacked evidence a victim of crucifixion had ever been buried in this way. In 1968, however, Vassilios Tzaferis found the first remains of a crucifixion victim, Yohanan Ben Ha'galgol, buried in a proper Jewish "kôkhîm-type" tomb.[49] Yohanan's remains revealed he had a spike driven into both feet and nails driven between the lower bones of the arms. A second similar skeletal remain was discovered in December of 2021 in a cemetery from the Roman period in the Cambridgeshire village of Fenstanton,[50] confirming some criminals were, in fact, crucified and given burials like the one described by the gospel writers.

THE EXISTENCE OF SYNAGOGUES

The gospel authors mentioned several synagogues when describing the activity of Jesus,[51] but many scholars were skeptical of the existence of early first-century synagogues in the region, believing religiously focused facilities such as these existed only after the destruction of the Jerusalem temple in AD 70. But now two synagogues have been discovered by archaeologists (one in 2009[52] and one in 2021[53]) in the ancient city of Magdala. These early first-century synagogues are important for two reasons. First, they demonstrate the existence of synagogues in the very region described by the gospel authors: near the road leading from Nazareth to Capernaum and in the hometown associated with Mary Magdalene. Second, evidence from the excavations indicates the facilities were used as community centers and included religious activities, again matching the description of the gospel authors.

THE BEHAVIOR OF GOVERNMENT

Luke accurately described the government existing in first-century Palestine under Roman rule. His account demonstrates he was writing at the time and place he claimed. For example, Luke correctly described two paths to Roman citizenship in Acts 22:28. He accurately described the process by which accused criminals were brought to trial in Acts 24:1–9. He rightly described the way a citizen could invoke their Roman citizenship with the legal formula "de quibus cognoscere volebam" in Acts 25:18. Finally, Luke correctly described the way prisoners were held by Roman soldiers and the conditions they experienced when imprisoned at one's own expense in Acts 28:16 and Acts 28:30–31.[54]

THE NATURE OF FISHING BOATS

The gospel authors also describe first-century fishing boats, including the famous episode in which Jesus falls asleep on a boat large enough to hold his "followers."[55] But were such boats even available to fishermen in the region this early in history? Following a drought in 1986, a portion of the Sea of Galilee was explored by two local amateur archaeologists. They recovered a fishing boat next to the ancient village of Magdala, the home of Mary Magdalene. Professional archaeologists recovered the first-century boat, which measured 26½ feet in length, 7½ feet in width, and 4½ feet in height. It was large enough to hold fifteen people, demonstrating these types of fishing boats existed just as the gospel authors reported.[56]

THE PREVALENCE OF LEPROSY

Gospel descriptions of leprosy were also doubted by skeptics who questioned the existence of this disease in the Middle East during the time of Jesus. But recent archaeological discoveries put the issue to rest.[57] A first-century tomb was discovered in Jerusalem in 2000. It contained a body and burial shroud later tested in 2009 by medical researchers at University College London. They discovered ancient DNA confirming the presence of leprosy (Hansen's disease), settling any debate about the existence of the disease in the region.

Many other gospel details have been corroborated by archaeology; such discoveries continue to validate the claims of the gospel writers from the "outside in." Even when the written accounts of ancient nonbiblical writers seem to contradict the testimony of the gospel authors, archaeological findings continue to resolve the apparent contradictions by confirming the claims of the New Testament.

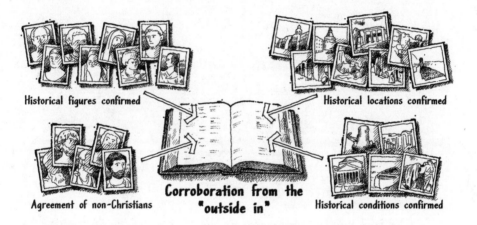

Historical figures confirmed

Historical locations confirmed

Agreement of non-Christians

Corroboration from the "outside in"

Historical conditions confirmed

BROAD STROKES AND MINOR DETAILS

The *internal* and *external* evidences corroborate the gospel narratives and capture an image of Jesus's life and ministry. The broad and general elements of the Gospels are *imaged* for us by the ancient, nonbiblical authors of the first and early second century, and they are confirmed by the archaeological record. This part of the picture is minimal and less focused, but the image is clear enough to recognize. It matches (in broad strokes) the testimony of the gospel writers found in the New Testament. Beyond this general corroboration, however, many of the specific details of the gospel accounts are made clear for us from the internal evidence of the Gospels themselves.

The more we identify instances of *unintentional support* occurring between the gospel writers (what J. J. Blunt referred to as "undesigned coincidences"), correct identification of proper names and locations, and the appropriate Greek language of the region and time, the more confidence we can have these accounts are providing details consistent with first-century Palestine.

Our picture of Jesus is made clearer by the corroboration of the *internal* evidence as it authenticates the *external* evidence and validates the claims of the gospel writers themselves.

The Broad Strokes Corroborated by the "External Evidence" of Ancient Nonbiblical Witnesses and Archaeology

The Fine Details Corroborated by the "Internal Evidence" of Names, Locations, Language, and "Unintentional Support"

SO, WHY DO SOME CONTINUE TO DENY IT?

Some critics of the Gospels are unimpressed with the internal and external evidences we've discussed so far, in spite of the fact these evidences are diverse and consistent with one another. Many skeptics argue there are still passages within the Gospels yet to be understood or supported by extrabiblical evidence. Let's look at the objections of skeptics related to these areas of internal and external evidence to see why some (like Albert Einstein) have described the Gospels as an "expression and product of human weaknesses."

5 SOME ORIGINAL WRITINGS OF ANCIENT AUTHORS ARE MISSING

Many critics have rejected some of the *external* corroboration we've described from ancient non-Christian authors like Thallus and Phlegon. They've argued the original texts from these two ancient historians are unavailable to us. Instead, we have been examining quotes from these writers as they were cited by Christian authors (Sextus Julius Africanus and Origen) who wrote much later in history. How do we know these ancient Christian apologists didn't distort or misquote Thallus and Phlegon? Skeptics argue we cannot trust the quotes we have today because we don't have access to the copies of Thallus's or Phlegon's complete texts.

BUT ...

Both Africanus and Origen cite the work of Thallus and Phlegon from a position of skepticism, not agreement. Africanus said Thallus proposed an eclipse to explain the darkness at Jesus's crucifixion, but Africanus clearly did not agree with this conclusion; he said Thallus made this claim "without reason." In a similar way, Origen argued Phlegon was mistaken about many aspects of his account ("falling into confusion about some things which refer to Peter"), even as Phlegon reluctantly admitted Jesus could predict the future. Neither Africanus nor Origen sterilized the accounts they cited, removing the details contradicting their case. Instead, Africanus and Origen quoted the work of Thallus and Phlegon even though they didn't always agree with their conclusions. The best inference from the evidence is Africanus and Origen were correctly and honestly citing their sources, especially since we have no other competing ancient citations of Thallus and Phlegon contradicting what Africanus and Origen reported.

6 SOME GOSPEL TERMS ARE STILL "TROUBLESOME"

Some critics identify terms in the text and claim they were used incorrectly by the gospel writers. They argue these "mistaken references" either expose the gospel writers were unfamiliar with the time and region they were describing, or that the Gospels were written much later than some would claim. As an example, skeptics have pointed to the Sermon on the Mount and argued that Jesus's remarks about praying in public, as the hypocrites did (Matt. 6:5), are out of place. Some Jewish scholars contend ancient Jews of Jesus's day did not pray in the synagogues and this practice only began after the temple was destroyed in AD 70.[58] If this were the case, the gospel of Matthew contains a claim curiously out of sequence. There are a handful of other similar examples offered by critics who claim there are terms either suspiciously unique to the gospel writers or appearing to be used in a way unparalleled in other ancient writings of the time.

BUT ...

Objections like these presume we have perfect knowledge of the first-century environment in Palestine. In this specific objection, for example, there is no archaeological or ancient-document evidence contradicting the claims of the gospel writers. Instead, critics have argued against the Gospels because they have not yet found external support for the biblical claims. But we've already seen several examples of other previously uncorroborated gospel claims (the pool of Bethesda, for example) or claims appearing contradictory (the identities of Quirinius or Lysanias, for example) but ultimately corroborated by archaeology. Much of the skepticism leveled at the biblical historical account is based on the presumption that, even without evidential support, the account is false unless corroborated. In essence, the gospel writers are guilty until proven innocent. There is no presumption of innocence for the authors of the New Testament. Unlike other ancient historical witnesses, the writers of the Gospels are not afforded the luxury of presumed credibility when there is silence on a particular claim from other ancient sources.

Much of this skepticism is due to the presupposition of philosophical naturalism I described in chapter 1. The Gospels contain descriptions of the supernatural: healings, prophetic utterances, and miracles. Because critics deny the possibility of such things, they reject the biblical accounts and look for ways to describe them as fallacious. It is this presupposition driving many skeptics to claim the Gospels were written late in history, far from the region where the miraculous events reportedly occurred. How else could the gospel writers have fooled so many people with these stories about the supernatural? Certainly they couldn't have written these accounts at a time or place in which the true eyewitnesses could expose their fabrications, could they? The evidence we have from archaeology and ancient sources does not support the claim for late or distant authorship, however, and Paul argued there were many eyewitnesses still available to corroborate the miracles of

Jesus (particularly His resurrection) at the time of Paul's letter to the Corinthians in AD 53–57 (1 Cor. 15:6). If we can overcome our bias against descriptions of the supernatural, the claims of the gospel accounts are convincingly corroborated.

7 ARCHAEOLOGY CANNOT CONFIRM EVERY GOSPEL DETAIL

Some skeptics argue archaeology simply cannot satisfactorily corroborate the claims of any historical author or ancient eyewitness. There are many portions of the gospel accounts unsupported by the current finds of archaeology, and (as we've demonstrated) there have been several biblical claims that seemed to contradict other ancient accounts and were unanswered by archaeology for many centuries. If archaeology is as limited as it appears to be, how can we trust it to completely corroborate the claims of the gospel writers? In addition, what kind of archaeological evidence could ever corroborate the miracles described in the Bible? Even if we believed miracles were reasonable, what kind of archaeological evidence could, for example, corroborate Jesus's healing of the blind man? For these skeptics, archaeology, while interesting, seems too limited to be of much assistance.

BUT ...

The archaeological evidences we've discussed in this chapter are only one category of evidence in the cumulative circumstantial case we are presenting for the corroboration of the Gospels. Like all circumstantial cases, each piece of evidence is incapable of proving the case entirely on its own. Circumstantial cases are built on the strength of multiple lines of evidence pointing to the same conclusion. The archaeological support we have for the gospel accounts (like the archaeological support for any ancient event) is limited and incomplete. That shouldn't surprise us. Dr. Edwin Yamauchi, historian and professor emeritus at Miami University, has rightly described archaeological evidence is a matter of "fractions." Only a fraction of the world's archaeological evidence still survives in the ground. In addition, only a fraction of the possible archaeological sites have been discovered. Of these, only a fraction have been excavated, and those only partially. To make matters more difficult, only a fraction of those partial excavations have been thoroughly examined and published. Finally, only a fraction of what has been examined and published has anything to do with the claims of the Bible![59] In spite of these limits, we shouldn't hesitate to use what we do know archaeologically in combination with other lines of evidence. Archaeology may not be able to tell us everything, but it can help us *fill in* the circumstantial case as we corroborate the gospel record.

It's also important to remember that many of the objections leveled by skeptics trade on the assumption the Gospels are written late, well after the lives of anyone who could testify to what really happened. The evidence from chapter 11, however, leaves little doubt the Gospels emerged within the lifetime of eyewitnesses. If Luke's gospel was written as early as the evidence suggests, then any claim that Luke errantly cited a particular governorship or errantly described a sequence of leaders is unreasonable. If this were the case, the early readers of Luke's gospel, reading it in the first century with a memory of what truly happened, would have caught Luke's error from the very beginning. If nothing else, we would expect to see some early scribe try to alter the narrative to correct the mistaken history. No alteration of this sort ever took place, and the early readers of Luke's gospel did not challenge Luke's account. The gospel was delivered to them early, while they still knew the correct order of governors and kings. Thousands of years later, we may initially doubt Luke, only to find archaeology eventually corroborates his account. If the evidence supporting the early dating of Luke's gospel is correct, however, we really shouldn't be surprised Luke will ultimately be vindicated.

 ## THE CASE FOR CORROBORATION

This circumstantial case can be examined with some *abductive reasoning* as we try to determine if the Gospels have been reasonably corroborated. Let's once again list all the evidence we've examined so far, including the claims of skeptics. Is it reasonable to infer the Gospels are sufficiently corroborated?

Even when considering the limits of archaeology and the limits of *internal* literary analysis, the most reasonable inference from the evidence is the Gospels are incredibly reliable, especially considering the nature of such accounts. Few ancient records have been as critically examined as the New Testament Gospels. Few other documents from antiquity have been as heavily challenged and scrutinized. This prolonged scrutiny has given us a robust and detailed set of evidences we can examine with abductive reasoning.

The Gospel Writers Provided Unintentional Eyewitness Support
The Gospel Writers Referenced Names Correctly
The Gospel Writers Used Appropriate Language
The Gospel Writers Identified the Correct Locations
Nonbiblical Eyewitnesses Corroborated the Gospels
Ancient Jewish Writers Corroborated the Gospels
Archaeology Corroborates the Gospels
Some Original Writings of Ancient Authors Are Missing
Some Gospel Terms Are Still Troublesome
Archaeology Cannot Confirm Every Gospel Detail

The Gospels are a reliable account, consistent with the claims of other contemporary evidences

The Gospels are not consistent with other contemporary evidences

If we accept the first explanation (the Gospels are reliable and trustworthy), we can integrate and embrace all the evidence without any contradiction or friction between pieces. The second explanation may exploit the last three claims but cannot account for the first seven truths. The best inference is the Gospels are reliable and consistent with other contemporary evidences. This explanation is *feasible, straightforward,* and *logical.* It is *superior* to the alternative explanation. Once again, it meets the criteria we established for abductive reasoning; we can have confidence we've arrived at the most reasonable explanation.

THE GOSPELS PASS THE SECOND TEST

So far, we've examined two areas juries consider when evaluating eyewitnesses. The evidence supports the fact the gospel writers were present in the first century, and their claims are consistent with many pieces of corroborative evidence. Does this mean they are reliable? Not yet, but we are halfway there. The Gospels have passed the first two tests: their testimony appears early enough in history, and their claims can be corroborated. Now we must make sure they haven't been corrupted over time. We've got to make sure the accounts we have today are an accurate reflection of what was originally recorded by the eyewitnesses.

Chapter 13

WERE THEY ACCURATE OVER TIME?

"The characters and events depicted in the damn bible are fictitious. Any similarity to actual persons, living or dead, is purely coincidental."[1]
Comedians and magicians Penn and Teller

"How do we know that our holy books are free from error? Because the books themselves say so. Epistemological black holes of this sort are fast draining the light from our world."[2]
Sam Harris, neuroscientist, speaker, and author of *The End of Faith: Religion, Terror, and the Future of Reason*

TIME, DOCUMENTATION, AND LIES

People who claim the biblical narratives are mere fiction and filled with error presume the authors of the Bible wrote the Gospels long after the reported events allegedly occurred and far from the locations they described. False, fictional elements can be inserted into an account if they are inserted well after any living eyewitnesses are alive to identify them as lies. In addition, if the true historical record has not been preserved well, or guarded to prevent corruption, errors can slip in without much notice. If this occurred with the

Gospels, they are untrustworthy. Even if they are corroborated at several points by archaeology or internal evidences, they may still be inaccurate about any number of episodes they describe.

Cold-case investigators understand the relationship between time and reliability. We must evaluate the prior statements of witnesses and suspects and do our best to figure out if these statements are true or fictional. Sometimes the passage of time provides an advantage to cold-case investigators previously unavailable to the detectives who originally investigated the case. Time often exposes the inaccuracy of eyewitnesses and the lies of suspects. I've taken advantage of this over the years.

I once had a case where the suspect (Jassen) provided an alibi at the time he was originally investigated in 1988. Jassen said he was driving to a friend's house at the time of the murder, although he never made it there because he had a flat tire. When he said this to the original detectives, they wrote it in their notes. They overlooked Jassen's statement, however, when they wrote their final report. They never found enough evidence to arrest Jassen, and as a result, they didn't write an arrest report; their closing reports were far less complete than they would have been if anyone had been arrested for this crime.

Years later, I reopened the case and examined the original reports and notes of the first detectives. They had been carefully preserved in our department's records division, where they were originally copied and stored on microfiche. I saw Jassen's original statement in the first detective's notes and asked this investigator to meet with me. He told me about his interview with Jassen, and without prompting from his notes, he recalled the details of what Jassen said with great accuracy. When I showed him the copy of his notes, he recognized them without hesitation.

I next arranged an impromptu interview with Jassen. While the original detective was careful to take notes during the interview he conducted in 1988, Jassen made no such record. With the passage of time, Jassen forgot what he first told the detective. The story he now gave was completely different from the story he first provided detectives. He no longer claimed he was driving to a friend's house. He no longer claimed he suffered a flat tire. Jassen now said he was changing the oil in his garage at the time of the murder. When I presented him with the original story, he not only failed to recognize it as his own; he adamantly denied ever making such a statement. Jassen couldn't remember (or repeat) his original lie. The more I talked to him, the more he exposed the fact the original story was *fiction*. Once he knew he had been caught in a lie, his alibi and confidence began to crumble.

Jassen was ultimately convicted of first-degree murder. The jury was convinced the original notes from the detective were authentic and well preserved. They were convinced the notes contained an accurate description of Jassen's first statement. They were also convinced Jassen's latest statement was untrue.

WHAT DID THEY SAY AND HOW WELL WAS IT PRESERVED?

How can we be sure the biblical documents we have today are accurate and reliable? How do we know they haven't been corrupted over time and contain little more than fiction? Like our cold-case investigations, we need certainty in two important areas of investigation. First, we need to make sure we know what the Gospels said in the first place. Second, we need to know if there is good reason to believe these documents were preserved well over time. Jassen's statement in 1988 was well documented and preserved. We were later able to make a case for the accuracy of his statement in front of the jury. Can a case be made for the accuracy of the Gospels? To find out if this is possible, we'll investigate what the gospel writers first said and then study the way these statements were preserved over time.

One way to be certain about the content and nature of the early eyewitness statements is to examine the evidence related to the *transmission* of the New Testament. In chapter 8 we talked about the importance of identifying the original eyewitnesses and their immediate disciples to establish a New Testament chain of custody. If we can examine what these first eyewitnesses said to their students, we can reasonably trace the content of the Gospels from their alleged date of creation to the earliest existing copies. The oldest complete, surviving copy of the New Testament we have (Codex Sinaiticus) was discovered in the Monastery of Saint Catherine, Mount Sinai. Constantine Tischendorf observed it and published the discovery in the nineteenth century; scholars believe it was produced sometime close to AD 350.[3] The text of Codex Sinaiticus provides us with a picture of what the New Testament said in the fourth century, and scholars have used it to inform and confirm the content of Bible translations for many years now. Our examination of the New Testament chain of custody will attempt to link the claims of the original authors to this fourth-century picture of Jesus's life and ministry.

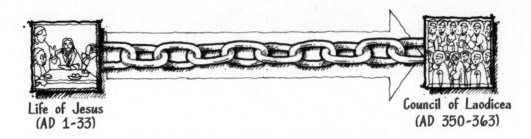

Life of Jesus
(AD 1-33)

Council of Laodicea
(AD 350-363)

When I first began to examine the "chain," I searched the historical record to identify the first students of the apostles. After all, the apostles claimed to have seen Jesus and experienced life with Him; I wanted to know what, exactly, they said to their students. While the apostles had several pupils, not every one of these *second-generation* Christians became a leader in his own right or was identified by history. Not every apostolic student had occasion to lead a group or author a letter revealing what the original disciples taught him. While many of the apostles' students may have written about the content of their teachers' testimony, only a few of these documents have survived. That shouldn't surprise us, given the antiquity of the events we are examining. Despite all this, I was able to identify several *chains of custody* revealing what the apostles observed and taught. In fact, I bet we could comfortably reconstruct an accurate image of Jesus from just the letters of the students of the apostles, even if all of Scripture was lost to us. Let's look at the evidence from the New Testament "chains of custody":

1. JOHN'S STUDENTS CONFIRMED THE ACCURACY OF THE GOSPELS

The apostle John (ca. AD 6–100) was the youngest of Jesus's disciples. He was the son of Zebedee and Salome and the brother of James. Unlike all the other apostles (who died violently as martyrs), it appears John lived to approximately ninety-four years of age and died a natural death. John taught two important students and passed his gospel into their trusted hands.

JOHN TAUGHT IGNATIUS

Ignatius (ca. AD 35–117) also called himself "Theophorus" (which means "God Bearer"). Not much is known about his early life, although early-church records describe Ignatius as one of the children Jesus blessed in the gospel accounts. We do know, however, Ignatius was a student of John and eventually became bishop at Antioch (Turkey), following the apostle Peter. He wrote several important letters to the early church, and seven authentic letters from Ignatius survive to this day (six to local church groups and one to Polycarp).[4] Some of these letters were corrupted in later centuries and amended with additional passages. We do, however, possess copies of the shorter, genuine versions of each epistle, and these brief writings reveal the influence of John (and other apostles) on Ignatius. It's important to remember it was not Ignatius's desire to retell the gospel narratives; his writings presume these Gospels were already available to his readers. It was Ignatius's goal to encourage and admonish local church groups. Along the way, he did, however, refer to the New Testament documents and the nature of Jesus, even though this was not his primary goal. It's clear from Ignatius's letters he knew many of the apostles, as he mentioned them frequently and spoke of them as though many of his older readers also knew them. Scholars have pored over the letters (written from AD 105 to AD 115) and have observed Ignatius quoted (or alluded to) seven to sixteen New Testament books (including the gospels of Matthew, John, and Luke, and several, if not all, of Paul's letters). While this confirms New Testament concepts and documents existed very early in history, Ignatius's letters also provide us with a picture of Jesus and a glimpse of how the apostle John (as an eyewitness) described Him. As I read through Ignatius's letters, I found the following portrayal of Jesus:

The prophets predicted and waited for Jesus.[5]

Jesus was in the line of King David.[6]

He was (and is) the "Son of God."[7]

He was conceived by the Holy Spirit.[8]

A star announced His birth.[9]

He came forth from God the Father.[10]

He was born of the virgin Mary.[11]

He was baptized by John the Baptist.[12]

He was the "perfect" man.[13]

He manifested the will and knowledge of God the Father.[14]

He taught and had a "ministry" on earth.[15]

He was the source of wisdom and taught many commandments.[16]

He spoke the words of God.[17]

Ointment was poured on Jesus's head.[18]

He was unjustly treated and condemned by men.[19]

He suffered and was crucified.[20]

He died on the cross.[21]

Jesus sacrificed Himself for us as an offering to God the Father.[22]

This all took place under the government of Pontius Pilate.[23]

Herod the Tetrarch was king.[24]

Jesus was resurrected.[25]

He had a physical resurrection body.[26]

He appeared to Peter and the others after the resurrection.[27]

He encouraged the disciples to touch Him after the resurrection.[28]

He ate with the disciples after the resurrection.[29]

The disciples were convinced by the resurrection appearances.[30]

The disciples were fearless after seeing the risen Christ.[31]

Jesus returned to God the Father.[32]

Jesus now lives in us.[33]

We live forever because of our faith in Christ.[34]

He has the power to transform us.[35]

Jesus is the manifestation of God the Father.[36]

He is united to God the Father.[37]

He is our only Master[38] and the Son of God.[39]

He is the "Door,"[40] the "Bread of Life,"[41] and the "Eternal Word."[42]

He is our High Priest.[43]

Jesus is "Lord."[44]

Jesus is "God."[45]

He is "our Savior"[46] and the way to "true life."[47]

His sacrifice glorifies us.[48]

Faith in Christ's work on the cross saves us.[49]

This salvation and forgiveness are gifts of grace from God.[50]

Jesus loves the church.[51]

We (as the church) celebrate the Lord's Supper in Jesus's honor.[52]

The letters of Ignatius demonstrate New Testament claims and writings existed early in history; Ignatius appears very familiar with many passages from the Gospels and the letters of Paul. In addition, Ignatius echoed John's description of Jesus.

JOHN TAUGHT POLYCARP

Polycarp (AD 69–155) was a friend of Ignatius and a fellow student of John. Irenaeus (we'll talk about him more in a moment) later testified he once heard Polycarp talk about his conversations with John, and Polycarp was known to have been converted to Christianity by the eyewitness apostles themselves. Polycarp eventually became the bishop of Smyrna[53] (now Izmir in Turkey) and wrote a letter to the church in Philippi, in response to their letter to him. The content of Polycarp's letter (an ancient document written from AD 100–150 and well attested in history) refers to Ignatius personally and is completely consistent with the content of Ignatius's letters. Polycarp also appears familiar with the other living apostles and eyewitnesses to the life of Jesus. He wrote about Paul, recognizing Paul's relationship with the church at Philippi and confirming the nature of Paul's life as an apostle. Polycarp's letter is focused on encouraging the Philippians and reminding them of their duty to live in response to the New Testament teaching with which they were clearly familiar. In fact, Polycarp confirmed the Philippians were well trained by the "sacred Scriptures," and he quoted Paul's letter to the Ephesians as an example of these Scriptures. Polycarp quoted or referenced fourteen to sixteen New Testament books (including Matthew, Luke, John, Acts, Romans, 1 Corinthians, Galatians, Ephesians, Philippians, 1 Thessalonians, 2 Thessalonians, 1 Timothy, 1 Peter, and 1 John, with some scholars observing additional references to 2 Timothy and 2 Corinthians). Along the way, Polycarp also presented the image of Jesus he gleaned from his teacher, the apostle John, describing Jesus in the following ways:

Jesus was sinless.[54]

He taught commandments.[55]

He taught the Sermon on the Mount.[56]

He suffered and died on a cross.[57]

He died for our sins.[58]

His death on the cross saves us.[59]

Our faith in Jesus's work on the cross saves us.[60]

We are saved by grace.[61]

Jesus was raised from the dead.[62]

His resurrection assures we will also be raised.[63]

Jesus ascended to heaven and is seated at God's right hand.[64]

All things are subject to Jesus.[65]

He will judge the living and the dead.[66]

Jesus is our "Savior."[67]

Jesus is "Lord."[68]

Like the writings of Ignatius, Polycarp's letters affirm the early appearance of the New Testament canon and echo the teachings of John related to the nature and ministry of Jesus. Ignatius and Polycarp are an important link in the New Testament chain of custody, connecting John's eyewitness testimony to the next generation of Christian "evidence custodians." We have a picture from the "crime scene" taken by the apostle John (recorded in his own gospel); this image was carefully handed to Ignatius and Polycarp who, in turn, treasured it as sacred evidence and transferred it carefully to those who followed them.

IGNATIUS AND POLYCARP TAUGHT IRENAEUS

Irenaeus (AD 120–202) was born in Smyrna, the city where Polycarp served as bishop. He was raised in a Christian family and was a "hearer" (someone who listened to the teaching) of Polycarp; he later recalled Polycarp talking about his conversations with the apostle John. He eventually became the bishop of Lugdunum in Gaul (now Lyon, France).[69] Irenaeus matured into a theologian and guardian of Christianity and wrote an important work called *Against Heresies*. This refined defense of Christianity provided Irenaeus with the opportunity to address the issue of scriptural authority, and he specifically identified as many as twenty-four New Testament books as Scripture (including Matthew, Mark, Luke, John, Acts, Romans, 1 Corinthians, 2 Corinthians, Galatians, Ephesians, Philippians, Colossians, 1 Thessalonians, 2 Thessalonians, 1 Timothy, 2 Timothy, Titus, 1 Peter, 1 John, 2 John, and Revelation). Irenaeus provided us with another link in the chain of custody, affirming the established eyewitness accounts and faithfully preserving them for the next generation as he connected the students of the apostles to the generations following him.

IRENAEUS TAUGHT HIPPOLYTUS

One of these "next-generation" Christians was a courageous man named Hippolytus (AD 170–236). Hippolytus was born in Rome and was a student and disciple of Irenaeus.[70] As he grew into a position of leadership, he opposed Roman bishops who modified their beliefs to accommodate the large number of "pagans" who were coming to faith in the city. In taking a stand for orthodoxy, Hippolytus became known as the first "antipope" or "rival pope" in Christian history. He was an accomplished speaker of great learning, influencing a number of important Christian leaders such as Origen of Alexandria. Hippolytus wrote a huge ten-volume treatise called *Refutation of All Heresies*. In this expansive work, Hippolytus identified as many as twenty-four New Testament books as Scripture (including Matthew, Mark, Luke, John, Acts, Romans, 1 Corinthians, 2 Corinthians, Galatians, Ephesians, Philippians, Colossians, 1 Thessalonians, 2 Thessalonians, 1 Timothy, 2 Timothy, Titus, Philemon, 1 Peter, 1 John, 2 John, and Revelation). Unfortunately, Hippolytus was persecuted under Emperor Maximus Thrax and exiled to Sardinia, where he most likely died in the mines. The writings of Hippolytus (like the writings of Irenaeus before him) confirm the existence of the New Testament accounts were established in the earliest years of the Christian movement.

As a result of Hippolytus's exile and martyrdom, this chain of custody ends without a clear *next link*, although Hippolytus likely had many important students who preserved the Scripture with the same passion he had as a student of Irenaeus. Although Origen of Alexandria once heard Hippolytus give a discourse in honor of Jesus (while in Rome in AD 212), we have no concrete evidence Origen was a *pupil* of Hippolytus. To be safe, we simply must acknowledge history has not yet revealed the certain identity of Hippolytus's students. One thing we know for sure: the truth about the life and ministry of Jesus (and the *canon of Scripture*) was established in the first century. The eyewitness account of John (along with the other New Testament documents) was recorded and handed down to his disciples.

John's students recorded this teaching and identified the sources for later generations. Long before the Codex Sinaiticus was first penned or the Council of Laodicea formalized the canon, the New Testament was established as a reliable eyewitness account.

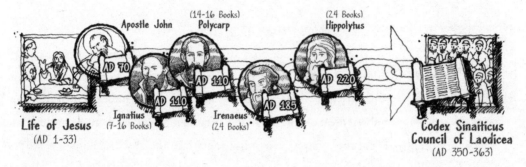

2 PAUL'S STUDENTS CONFIRMED THE ACCURACY OF THE GOSPELS

The apostle Paul (ca. AD 5–67) wrote the largest portion of the New Testament and was closely associated with several key apostles, historians, and eyewitnesses who helped to document and guard the Scripture we have today. Paul's friend Luke, for example, was a meticulous historian with access to the eyewitnesses and a personal involvement in the history of the New Testament church. As described in chapter 11, Paul quoted Luke's version of the gospel in 1 Timothy 5:17–18 and 1 Corinthians 11:23–26. Those who knew Paul were probably familiar with the writings of Luke. Paul had several key students and disciples who protected and transmitted his writings (along with the emerging writings of other eyewitnesses, including Luke) to the next generation of Christian leaders. Paul's chain of custody is much harder to trace than that of John, but we can follow Paul's influence through the early leadership in Rome to places as far away as Syria.

PAUL TAUGHT LINUS AND CLEMENT OF ROME

Paul spent his last years in Rome under house arrest awaiting trial. During this time, he had free access to other believers and taught many men who would eventually lead the church. We know two of these men specifically. Irenaeus described a man named Linus as one of Paul's coworkers (Paul identifies a coworker named Linus specifically in 2 Timothy 4:21, along with Eubulus, Pudens, and Claudia). History tells us Linus was born in Tuscany to Herculanus and Claudia and became the pope of Rome following the deaths of Peter and Paul.

History is unclear on the precise order of popes in these first years, and some early records indicate Clement of Rome may have preceded Linus.[71] Clement was also a coworker of Paul (mentioned specifically in Philippians 4:3), and he became an important assistant to Paul and Peter in the first years in Rome.[72] In fact, Peter appears to have elevated both Linus and Clement to positions of leadership so he could focus on prayer and preaching. Clement wrote several letters, and one of these letters (the First Epistle of Clement to the Corinthians) survives as the earliest Christian document outside the New Testament. Clement's letter (written in AD 80–140) was written to encourage the Corinthian church and call them to holy living. Clement referenced several examples from the Old Testament and also referred to the life and teaching of Jesus as it was passed on to him from Paul and Peter.

In fact, Clement talked about the chain of custody from the apostolic eyewitnesses to his own *second-generation* readers. Clement told the Corinthian believers "the Apostles for our sakes received the gospel from the Lord Jesus Christ; Jesus Christ was sent from God. Christ then is from God, and the Apostles from Christ. Both therefore came in due order from the will of God."[73] Clement understood the "appointed order" of the eyewitness "chain of custody." When examining the letter carefully, scholars observe Clement quoting or alluding to seven New Testament books (Mark, Matthew, John, Romans, Galatians, Ephesians, and Philippians) as he penned his work. Clement also described the person and work of Jesus, echoing the description of Jesus first communicated by the eyewitnesses. Clement's description of Jesus was very similar to the description offered by Ignatius and Polycarp:

The prophets predicted the life and ministry of Jesus.[74]

Jesus provided His disciples with important instruction.[75]

He taught principles as described by Mark and Luke.[76]

He was humble and unassuming.[77]

He was whipped.[78]

He suffered and died for our salvation.[79]

He died as a payment for our sin.[80]

He was resurrected from the dead.[81]

He is alive and reigning with God.[82]

His resurrection makes our resurrection certain.[83]

We are saved by the "grace" of God[84] through faith in Jesus.[85]

He is "Lord"[86] and the Son of God.[87]

He possesses eternal glory and majesty.[88]

All creation belongs to Him.[89]

He is our "refuge"[90] and our "High Priest."[91]

He is our "defender" and "helper."[92]

The church belongs to Him.[93]

While it is clear Clement presumed his readers already understood the truth about Jesus from the gospels he quoted, Clement still referenced many attributes of Jesus consistent with the picture painted by Peter, Paul, and the gospel writers. Clement certainly wrote much more than this single letter and may have affirmed an even larger number of texts. His surviving letter to the Corinthians provides us with another link in the chain of custody, acknowledging the delivery of the eyewitness accounts from the original eyewitnesses to the next generation of believers.

 *CLEMENT PASSED THE TRUTH FROM EVARISTUS TO PIUS I*
Linus and Clement of Rome established the lineage of bishops who followed Paul (and Peter) at Rome.[94] They taught, discussed, and passed the eyewitness Scripture along to their successors, from Evaristus (AD ?–109) to Alexander I (AD ?–115) to Sixtus I (AD ?–125) to Telesphorus (AD ?–136) to Hyginus (AD ?–140) to Pius I (AD 90–154). Ignatius, Polycarp, and Clement are examples of second-generation Christian leaders who already considered the writings of the eyewitnesses to be precious Scripture. It's reasonable to conclude the papal leaders who followed Clement were raised to appreciate and honor the primacy of the eyewitness accounts as well; they understood the importance of guarding these accounts for future generations.

PIUS I AND JUSTIN MARTYR GUARDED THE ACCOUNTS

In the early years of the Christian church, the city of Rome was filled with people who either came to faith there (under the preaching of the apostles or their disciples) or who traveled there after coming to faith somewhere else in the Roman Empire. One such person, Justin of Caesarea (AD 103–165), became an important philosopher and contributor to the history of Christianity. Justin Martyr, as he came to be known, was one of the earliest Christian apologists.[95] He was born in Flavia Neapolis (now Nablus, Palestine) to Greek parents. He was raised as a pagan and called himself a Samaritan, but he studied philosophy and eventually converted to Christianity. He taught Christian doctrine in Rome when Pius I was leading the Christian community. He wrote several voluminous and important works, including the *First Apology*, *Second Apology*, and *Dialogue with Trypho*. In these early Christian texts, Justin Martyr quoted or alluded to Matthew, Mark, Luke, John, and Revelation. While we don't have surviving writings from some of the earliest bishops and popes of Rome (including Pius I), Justin Martyr provided us with a contemporary glimpse of how these men viewed the eyewitness accounts and guarded them for the future.

JUSTIN TAUGHT TATIAN

Not everyone who played a role in the scriptural chain of custody had orthodox beliefs. Many recognized (and wrote about) the eyewitness accounts, while misinterpreting them for themselves and their followers. Tatian the Assyrian (AD 120–180) was one such example.[96]

Tatian was born (and probably died) in Assyria. He came to Rome, however, and studied the Old Testament. He met and became a student of Justin Martyr and converted to Christianity. He studied in Rome with Justin for many years and eventually opened a Christian school there. Over time, he developed a strict form of Christianity forbidding marriage and the eating of meat. When Justin died, Tatian was driven from the church in Rome. He traveled to Syria and eventually wrote his most famous contribution, the *Diatessaron*, a biblical paraphrase, or *harmony*, which recognized the existence of the four eyewitness accounts of the Gospels, even as it sought to combine them into one document. The earliest church records in Syria (traced back to Tatian) identified an early canon including the *Diatessaron*, the letters of Paul, and the book of Acts. Tatian's work, combined with this ancient canonical list, acknowledges the early formation of the canon in the chain of custody from Paul to the late second century.

History does not provide us with precise information about the next link in this chain of custody. In any case, this custodial sequence from Paul acknowledges the existence of the eyewitness accounts and the fact they were treated as sacred Scripture early in history and were handed down with care from one generation to another. All of this happened many years before any council determined what would officially become the New Testament record.

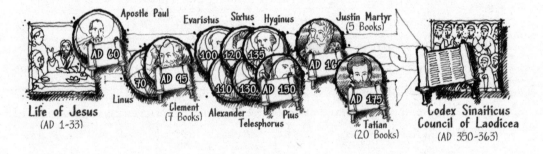

3 PETER'S STUDENTS CONFIRMED THE ACCURACY OF THE GOSPELS

The apostle Peter (ca. 1 BC–AD 67) was perhaps the oldest of Jesus's disciples. He was also known as Simon Cephas (from the Aramaic version of his name). He was the son of Jonah (John) and was raised in Bethsaida (in Galilee). He was a fisherman (along with his brother Andrew) when he first met Jesus and quickly became a disciple. His story is well known, replete with human failures and triumphs. After the ascension, Peter established the church in Antioch and served there as its bishop for seven years. He eventually traveled to Rome and became bishop there as well. In chapter 5 we discussed the evidence supporting Mark's authorship of Peter's eyewitness account in the gospel of Mark. This gospel (like the gospel of John) is a critical piece of evidence from the "crime scene," and Peter carefully handed it down (along with other eyewitness texts emerging in the first century) to his own students and disciples:

PETER COMMUNICATED THROUGH MARK

John Mark was the cousin of Barnabas, and his childhood home was well known to Peter (Col. 4:10; Acts 12:12–14). Peter loved Mark and described him as "my son" (1 Pet. 5:13). Peter preserved his eyewitness testimony through his primary disciple and student, who then passed it on to the next generation in what we now recognize as the "gospel of Mark."

MARK TAUGHT ANIANUS, AVILIUS, KEDRON, PRIMUS, AND JUSTUS

Mark established the church in Alexandria and immediately started preaching and baptizing new believers. History records the fact he had at least five disciples, and these men eventually became church leaders in North Africa.[97] Mark discipled and taught Anianus (AD ?–82), Avilius (AD ?–95), Kedron (AD ?–106), Primus (ca. AD 40–118), and Justus (AD ?–135), passing on his gospel along with the other early New Testament accounts from apostolic eyewitnesses. These five men eventually became bishops of Alexandria (one after the other) following Mark's death. They faithfully preserved the eyewitness accounts and passed them on, one generation to another.

JUSTUS PASSED THE TRUTH TO PANTAENUS

While Mark was still alive, he appointed his disciple Justus as the director of the Catechetical School of Alexandria. This important school became an esteemed place of learning where the eyewitness accounts and Scriptures were collected and guarded. A key figure in the early development of this school was an ex-Stoic philosopher who converted to Christianity. His name was Pantaenus.[98] He became an important teacher and missionary, traveling east of Alexandria (perhaps as far as India), reporting believers were already established in the east and were using the gospel of Matthew written in Hebrew letters. In any event, Pantaenus provided another important link in the chain of custody because the writing of one of his students survives to this day, chronicling and identifying the books of the New Testament already considered sacred.

PANTAENUS TAUGHT CLEMENT OF ALEXANDRIA

Titus Flavius Clemens (ca. AD 150–215) was also known as Clement of Alexandria.[99] He was a student of Pantaenus and eventually became the leader of the Catechetical School of Alexandria. Clement was very familiar with the pagan literature of his time and wrote extensively. Three important volumes (the *Protrepticus*, the *Paedagogus*, and the *Stromata*) address Christian morality and conduct. Most importantly, Clement discussed the existing Scripture of the time (as it was handed down to him by Pantaenus) and quoted or alluded to all the New Testament books except for Philemon, James, 2 Peter, 2 John, and 3 John. Clement appears to have received and accepted the same New Testament documents known to his predecessors in the "chain of custody."

CLEMENT OF ALEXANDRIA TAUGHT ORIGEN

Origen (ca. AD 185–254) carefully preserved and identified those ancient eyewitness accounts used by the Christian church around the Mediterranean. He was an Egyptian who came to faith and eventually taught at the Catechetical School of Alexandria.[100] He wrote prolifically and penned commentaries for nearly every book of the Bible. Along the way, he quoted all the New Testament books. He did express hesitation about James, 2 Peter, 2 John, and 3 John, but included them in his list of reliable orthodox eyewitness documents. Origen played a pivotal role because he had several students who became important links in the New Testament chain of custody.

PAMPHILUS OF CAESAREA ADOPTED ORIGEN'S WORK

In his later life, Origen fled Alexandria (under the persecution of an archbishop who expelled Origen because he had not been ordained with proper permission) and settled in Caesarea Maritima. Pamphilus[101] also settled in Caesarea Maritima after a long stay in Alexandria, where he became devoted to the works of Origen and even wrote a five-volume treatise called *Apology for Origen*. Pamphilus guarded and defended the work of Origen, and he also accepted the eyewitness accounts of Scripture as authoritative, expressing his confidence in these documents to his own pupils.

PAMPHILUS OF CAESAREA TAUGHT EUSEBIUS

One of Pamphilus's students was Eusebius of Caesarea (ca. AD 263–339), a man who later became an important church historian, church father, and devoted student who documented Pamphilus's career in a three-volume work called *Vita*.[102] Eusebius was a prolific writer, and much of his work survives to this day, including his *Church History*. A close survey of Eusebius's work reveals he recognized and identified twenty-six New Testament books as Scripture. He strongly affirmed Matthew, Mark, Luke, John, Acts, Romans, 1 Corinthians, 2 Corinthians, Galatians, Ephesians, Philippians, Colossians, 1 Thessalonians, 2 Thessalonians, 1 Timothy, 2 Timothy, Titus, Philemon, 1 Peter, 1 John, and Revelation, and less strongly affirmed James, Jude, 2 Peter, 2 John, and 3 John.

This chain of scriptural custody, from Peter to Eusebius, brings us well into the period in which the Codex Sinaiticus was penned and to the doorstep of the Council of Laodicea. The eyewitness accounts and writings of the apostles were collected, preserved, and transmitted from generation to generation during this span of time.

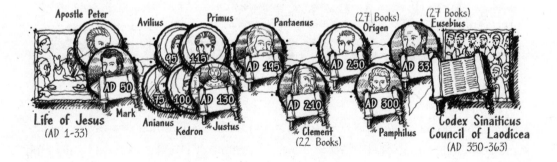

The New Testament chain of custody preserved the primacy and sacred importance of the eyewitness documents and delivered them faithfully to those who would later identify them publicly in the councils establishing our present canon of Scripture. These councils did not *create* the canon or the current *version* of Jesus we know so well; they simply acknowledged the canon and description of Jesus provided by the eyewitnesses.

THE LEAST WE CAN LEARN

Now let's imagine for a moment all the alleged Christian *eyewitness* accounts have been destroyed. Imagine all we have available to us is the written record of a few students of these supposed eyewitnesses. If this were the case, the writings of Mark, Ignatius, Polycarp, and Clement would be our only source of information. This record would certainly be sufficient for us to learn the truth about Jesus; after all, Mark was tasked with chronicling the memoir of Peter and wrote a thorough account. So let's make it a little more challenging. Let's remove Mark's gospel from consideration and force ourselves to consider only the *nonbiblical* letters of the other three students, even though these students made no conscious effort to record the details of Jesus's life and ministry. What would we learn about Jesus from just these three men? Would their nominal description affirm what our twenty-first-century Bible tells us?

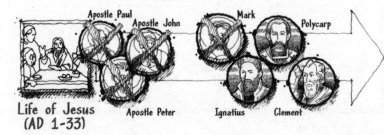

Apostle Paul
Apostle John
Mark
Polycarp

Life of Jesus
(AD 1-33)
Apostle Peter
Ignatius
Clement

Born Miraculously
Recognized as God
Taught Divinely
Died on a Cross
Rose from the Dead
Reigns with the Father

From the earliest *nonbiblical* records, we would learn the following: Jesus was predicted by the Old Testament prophets. He was a man in the line of David, conceived by the Holy Spirit as the only begotten Son of God, born of the virgin Mary, and announced with a star. He came forth from God and manifested God's will and knowledge. He was baptized by John the Baptist, lived a humble, unassuming, perfect, and sinless life, spoke the words of God and taught people many important divine truths (including the principles we recognize from the Sermon on the Mount). Although Jesus was anointed with oil, He was unjustly treated and condemned, whipped, and ultimately executed on the cross. This execution took place during the government of Pontius Pilate and the reign of Herod the Tetrarch. Jesus's death was a personal sacrifice He offered to God on our behalf as a payment for the debt of our sin. Jesus proved His divinity by physically resurrecting from the dead, appearing to Peter and the other disciples, eating with them, and encouraging them to touch Him and see for themselves. Emboldened by their observations of the risen Jesus, the disciples were fearless. They understood their eternal life and resurrection were assured based on their faith in Jesus, who now reigned in heaven and lived in everyone who accepted His offer of forgiveness and salvation. Jesus was (and is) the "Door," the "Bread of Life," the "Eternal Word," the "Son of God," our "High Priest," "Savior," "Master," "Guardian," "Helper," "Refuge," and "Lord." Jesus and the Father are one; Jesus possesses eternal glory and majesty. All creation belongs to Him and is subject to Him. Jesus will judge the living and the dead. Jesus is "God."

We would learn all of this, not based on the gospel accounts, but based on what is described by the earliest first-century students of the gospel writers (and only three of them, at that)! The letters of Ignatius, Polycarp, and Clement confirm the accuracy of the Gospels. Even if, as skeptics, we had some doubt about the minute details in each eyewitness account, there can be no doubt about the major themes and claims of the Gospels. Jesus was described as God, walked with His disciples, taught the masses, died on a cross, and rose from the dead. This version of Jesus is not a late invention or exaggeration; it is the earliest version of the Jesus story. This version of Jesus was witnessed and accurately described by the gospel writers and confirmed by their students. Unlike the man I interviewed, Jassen, whose early story *was not* aligned with the version he provided twenty years later, the earliest account of Jesus's story (as given by the eyewitnesses and their students in the first century) *is* aligned with the version we have two thousand years later.

THE JEWISH RECORDS DIVISION

But how do we know if the other gospel details (not specifically mentioned by the students of the apostles) are accurate? How do we know these portions of the Gospels weren't corrupted in the period spanning from the first century to the inking of Codex Sinaiticus? I came to trust the detective's notes in Jassen's case because I had confidence in the record-keeping ability of my records division. I understood the precise and careful way they copied and preserved the case files. Is there any good reason to believe the primitive, first-century Christians would be equally willing and capable of such preservation?

THE EYEWITNESSES WERE CONSCIENTIOUS AND PROTECTIVE

In chapter 4 we looked at the role the apostles played as eyewitnesses. They clearly understood the gravity and importance of their testimony. The apostles recognized their role in God's plan was simply to tell others about their experiences with Jesus and their observations of His resurrection. People who saw themselves as critical eyewitnesses would be careful to protect the accuracy of their testimony. In the earliest years, their contribution came in the form of verbal testimony. That's reasonable, given the sense of urgency the apostles felt as they eagerly awaited the imminent return of Jesus. But as the months and years passed without the arrival of Christ, the apostles inked their testimony so their observations could be shared with local church congregations. If the Gospels were written early (during the time in which these eyewitnesses lived), it is reasonable to expect the witnesses would *fact-check* the content of their testimony as it was being told to others. If, for example, Mark's gospel was written as early as the circumstantial evidence in chapter 11 suggests, it's sensible to expect Peter would have caught (and corrected) any errors.

THE COPYISTS AND SCRIBES WERE METICULOUS

The ancient Jewish religious culture was already well established in the first century, and it was from this culture the apostles and first believers emerged. It's clear the Jews guarded Scripture with extreme care and precision. From the postexile time of Ezra (and even before), there were priests (Deut. 31:24–26) and scribes (called *sopherim*) who were given the responsibility of copying and meticulously caring for the sacred text. The scribes continued to work in Jesus's day and were mentioned throughout the New Testament by the eyewitnesses who observed them alongside the Pharisees and other Jewish religious leaders. The Old Testament Scriptures were revered and protected during this period, largely because early believers considered them the holy Word of God along with the New Testament documents. Paul described Luke's gospel as Scripture (1 Tim. 5:17–18), and Peter also described Paul's letters as Scripture (2 Pet. 3:15–16). Paul told the local churches to treat his letters accordingly, making them available to other congregations so they could read them during their meetings (Col. 4:16 and 1 Thess. 5:27). It's reasonable to conclude the New Testament documents were handled and preserved like other cherished, ancient Scripture.

It's difficult to know with complete certainty the exact method in which the first-century Christian scribes copied and cared for their sacred texts, but we do know they worked within a religious tradition spanning hundreds of years, both before and after the first century. The Masoretic tradition, for example, gives us a glimpse into the obsessive care Jewish scribes historically took with their sacred texts. Scribes known as the Masoretes (a group of Jewish copyists living and working primarily in Tiberias and Jerusalem) took over the precise job of copying the ancient Scripture and transmitting it for later generations. They developed something now known as the Masoretic Text.[103] These documents are recognized as an incredibly trustworthy replica of the original Scripture, and we've come to trust these texts because we understand the way they were copied. To ensure the accuracy of the Masoretic copies, the Masoretes developed several strict guidelines to guarantee every fresh copy was an exact reproduction of the original. The rules of the Masoretes were every bit as comprehensive as any set of regulations used in modern-day records divisions; they copied and handled their documents with all the precision available to them.

The Meticulous Masoretes

The Masoretes established comprehensive procedures to protect the text against changes:

When an obvious error was noted in the text, it was identified and labeled as a "kethibh" ("to be written") and a correction was placed in the margin called a "qere" ("to be read").

When a word was considered textually, grammatically, or exegetically questionable, dots were placed above the word.

Detailed statistics were kept as a means of guarding against error. Leviticus 8:8, for example, was identified as the middle *verse* of the Torah. In Leviticus 10:16, the word "darash" was identified as the middle *word* in the Torah, and the "waw" located within the Hebrew words in Leviticus 11:42 was identified as the middle *letter* of the Torah.

Statistics were also placed at the end of each book, including the total number of verses, the total number of words, and the total number of letters. By assembling statistics such as these, each book could be measured mathematically to see if there was any copyist error. (Refer to Gleason Archer's *A Survey of Old Testament Introduction*, Moody, 2007.)

History has demonstrated the remarkable accuracy of these ancient scribes who worked under the conviction the documents they were copying were divine in nature. The discovery of the Dead Sea Scrolls in Qumram confirms their amazing ability. In 1947, a Bedouin herdsman found some unusual clay jars in caves near the valley of the Dead Sea. The jars contained several scrolls revealing the religious beliefs of monastic farmers who lived in the valley from 150 BC to AD 70. When this group saw the Romans invade the region, they apparently put their cherished scrolls in the jars and hid them in the caves. The Dead Sea Scrolls contain fragments of almost every book in the Old Testament and, most importantly, a complete copy of the book of Isaiah. This scroll was dated to approximately 100 BC; it was incredibly important to historians and textual experts because it was approximately one thousand years older than any Masoretic copy of Isaiah. The Dead Sea Scroll version of Isaiah allowed scholars to compare the text over this period to see if copyists had been conscientious. Scholars were amazed by what they discovered.

A comparison of the Qumran manuscripts of Isaiah "proved to be word for word identical with our standard Hebrew Bible in more than 95 percent of the text."[104] Some of the 5 percent differences were simply a matter of spelling (like you might experience when using the word *favor* instead of *favour*). Some were grammatical differences (like the presence of the word *and* to connect two ideas or objects within a sentence). Finally, some were the addition of a word for the sake of clarity (like the addition of the Hebrew word for "light" to the end of verse 53:11, following "they shall see"). None of these grammatical variations changed the meaning of the text in any way.

What compelled the ancient scribes to treat these documents with such precision and meticulous care? It was clearly their belief the documents themselves were sacred and given to them by God. When Paul and Peter identified the New Testament documents (such as the gospel of Luke and the letters of Paul) as Scripture, they assured the documents would be honored and cared for in a manner befitting the Masoretic tradition. The first-century Christian scribes didn't have access to photocopiers, microfiche, or digital imaging like modern police-department records divisions do, but they understood the importance of divine record keeping, and they used the first-century equivalent in technology (the meticulous tradition of their predecessors) to carefully guarantee the accuracy of the texts.

CONSISTENT AND WELL PRESERVED

Given the evidence from the chain of custody and what we know about the diligence of the first-century copyists, what is the most reasonable inference we can draw about the accuracy of the Gospels? Unlike Jassen's statement in my cold-case investigation, the message of the apostles appears unchanged over the span of time; it is the same in both the first and twenty-first centuries. Like the notes from the first detective, the details of the first-century account appear to have been adequately preserved. The Jewish *records division* was capable and efficient; they copied and guarded the eyewitness accounts over time.

SO, WHY DO SOME CONTINUE TO DENY IT?

Some are still skeptical of the accuracy of the Gospels, despite the strong circumstantial evidence supporting such a conclusion. Let's see if a little *abductive reasoning* can help us determine if any of the objections of critics are reasonable when they describe the Scriptures as "fictitious."

IGNATIUS, POLYCARP, AND CLEMENT DIDN'T QUOTE SCRIPTURE PRECISELY

Some have argued the writings of the first-century students of the apostles either cannot be authenticated or fail to precisely quote the Gospels. These critics claim the letters attributed to Ignatius, for example, are not truly from this student of John. Many have also argued those passages where these *second-generation* students appear to be quoting from a gospel (such as their references to the Sermon on the Mount) are not precise *word-for-word* quotes; they argue the students were only alluding to vague and unreliable early oral accounts not yet inked on papyrus and corrupted long before they were ever finalized.

BUT ...

While there is controversy related to some of Ignatius's letters, there is no reason to doubt the authenticity of the seven letters we've isolated in our chain of custody. Yes, there are additional letters appearing late in history and falsely attributed to Ignatius, but the seven letters we've referenced are listed in the earliest records of Ignatius's work, and they are corroborated by Polycarp's letter (which refers to Ignatius).

Ignatius, Polycarp, and Clement often referenced passages of Scripture, capturing the meaning of the passage without quoting the specific verse *word for word*. But this was not uncommon of authors at this time in history. Paul also paraphrased Scripture (the Old Testament) on occasion (e.g., 1 Cor. 2:9, where Paul is likely paraphrasing both Isa. 64:4 and Isa. 65:17). Polycarp's and Clement's use of paraphrase is not evidence the New Testament documents didn't exist at the time these second-generation authors wrote their letters any more than Paul's use of a paraphrase is evidence the Old Testament did not exist when he wrote his letters.

Most importantly, the Jesus described by these letters is identical to the Jesus described by the apostolic eyewitness, even if the students of the apostles paraphrased or used their own words to describe Him.

THERE ARE MANY CORRUPTED COPYIST INSERTIONS

Skeptics have also challenged some of the late insertions (artifacts) we talked about in chapter 6. Large artifacts like those I've described there are incredibly rare. More common are single-word variations observed in the available ancient manuscripts. In fact, Bart Ehrman cites these smaller variations and makes the provocative assertion: "There are more variations among our manuscripts than there are words in the New Testament."[105] It does appear some copyists intentionally corrupted the manuscripts they were duplicating either to fill in a detail or make some theological point missing in the original text. If this is the case, how can we trust anything we have is reliable or accurate? If *some* parts of the text were corrupted, *none* of the text can be trusted.

BUT ...

The fact these corruptions are *obvious* should alert us to something. Why are the corruptions and late additions we mentioned in chapter 6 so evident? They stand out to us because we have hundreds of ancient copies of the Gospels to compare to one another.

Let me give you an example of how this process of comparison works. My responsibilities as a homicide detective have often caused me to reschedule events with my family. Imagine I am stuck at a homicide scene on my regular day off and must reschedule a coffee date with Susie.

I message her to tell her I will meet her at the Starbucks on Main Street at 2:00 p.m. I also ask her to order me an Americano with an extra shot of espresso (in case she gets there before me). Using my new smartphone, I shoot her a text, but alas, my first effort is filled with typos and inadvertent auto-corrections:

The message I intended:

"Let's meet at Starbucks on Main Street at 2pm. Can you order me an Americano with an extra shot if you get there first?"

⟵——————— The message she received

This version of the message is confusing, so I try again. In my second effort, I eliminate some mistakes but include a few more, albeit in different locations. Undeterred, I decide to try again, and again, and again. Each time, I correct older mistakes while making new ones:

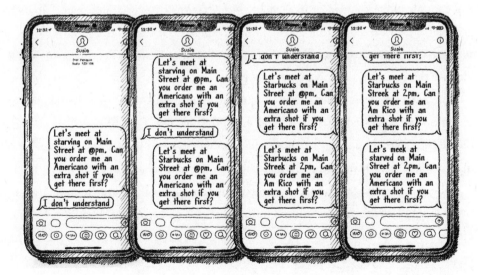

Imagine if I were stubborn enough to send Susie dozens of texts, but inept enough to send even one error-free.

I suspect Susie already knows where and when to meet me (and what I would like her to order), even though I didn't send her a single inerrant text. In fact, there are now more variations between my text messages than there are letters in my message! Yet Susie has had enough and responds, "Stop already!" How can Susie be certain of my original intent, given all these variations? You already know the answer. It turns out the number of variations isn't nearly as important as the number of copies. Susie can compare the copies to identify the variations, remove them accurately, and return sensibly to my original intent.

We have far more ancient New Testament manuscripts than Susie had copies of my text message. That's why scholars (and even skeptics like Bart Ehrman) can accurately identify the variants in the first place. It's also why we can isolate and separate artifacts from evidence to return to the original intent of the biblical authors.

There are no better-attested ancient documents than the New Testament Gospels. As an example for comparison, the Greek researcher and historian Herodotus wrote *The Histories* in the fifth century BC. We trust we have an accurate copy of this text even though we only possess eight ancient copies. By contrast, we possess thousands of ancient copies of the New Testament documents. These copies come to us from all over the ancient world surrounding the Mediterranean. When compared to one another, the diverse manuscripts, coming from several different Christian groups located in a number of different regions, reveal the variations immediately. The textual deviations are obvious because we have a rich treasure trove of manuscripts to examine and compare. With this many copies at our disposal, we can easily identify and eliminate the variations. As a result, we can redact the late additions and reconstruct the original with a high degree of confidence.

MANY BIBLICAL NARRATIVES DIFFER FROM ONE ANOTHER

Skeptics have also observed the different way in which the gospel writers described the same events and have argued these variations constitute irreconcilable *contradictions*. These differences, according to the skeptics, invalidate the accuracy of the biblical account.

BUT ...

We've already discussed the nature of eyewitness accounts in chapter 4, and we now know we should *expect* variations among true eyewitness accounts. These expected variations are not a problem for those of us who are working as detectives, so long as we can understand the perspective, interests, and locations from which each witness observed the event. It's our duty, as responsible investigators, to understand how eyewitness statements can be harmonized so we can get the most robust view of the event possible.

THE MOST REASONABLE CONCLUSION

Let's return once again to the process we know as *abductive reasoning* to determine which explanation related to gospel accuracy is the most reasonable. Once again, we'll list all the evidence we've looked at in this chapter, including the evidence cited by the skeptics. Alongside these facts, we'll consider the two possible explanations accounting for what we have seen so far.

Given the record of the second-generation disciples of John, Peter, and Paul, we can have confidence the essential teachings of the Gospels have remained unchanged for over two thousand years. The first explanation, that the Gospels and other New Testament documents were written early and taught to the students of the apostles, is the most reasonable conclusion, and this explanation is also consistent with the evidence for early dating we examined in chapter 11. The evidence from the chain of custody and the nature of the copyists support the first explanation, and this explanation offers reasonable responses to the challenges offered by skeptics. The second explanation, on the other hand, fails to adequately account for the evidence offered by Ignatius, Polycarp, and Clement. The first explanation is *feasible*, *straightforward*, and *logical*. It *exhausts* all the evidence we have assembled, and it is *superior* to the alternative explanation. It is, once again, the most reasonable explanation.

John's Students Confirm the Accuracy of the Gospels
Paul's Students Confirm the Accuracy of the Gospels
Peter's Students Confirm the Accuracy of the Gospels
The Eyewitnesses Were Conscientious and Protective
The Copyists and Scribes Were Meticulous
Ignatius, Polycarp, and Clement Didn't
   Quote Scripture Precisely
There Are Many Copyist Insertions That
   Are Obvious Corruptions
There Are Many Biblical Narratives That
   Differ from One Another

The Gospels were recorded early and recited to the students of the Apostles.
The texts we have today are consistent

~~The students of the Apostles never wrote any letters and the message of the Apostles was distorted over time~~

PASS ✔
FAIL ☐

THE GOSPELS PASS THE THIRD TEST

We've now evaluated the nature of the gospel eyewitness accounts in three of the four areas in which we evaluate witnesses in criminal trials. The most reasonable inference from the evidence indicates the gospel writers were *present* and *corroborated*. By studying the chain of custody and the way these records were preserved over time, we can now draw the reasonable conclusion they are also *accurate*. Are we ready to say they are reliable? Almost. There is still one final area we need to examine.

Chapter 14

WERE THEY BIASED?

"The one thing we know about the Christians after the death of Jesus is that they turned to their scriptures to try and make sense of it.... How could Jesus, the Messiah, have been killed as a common criminal? Christians turned to their scriptures to try and understand it, and they found passages that refer to the Righteous One of God's suffering death. But in these passages, such as Isaiah 53 and Psalm 22 and Psalm 61, the one who is punished or who is killed is also vindicated by God. Christians came to believe their scriptures that Jesus was the Righteous One and that God must have vindicated him. And so Christians came to think of Jesus as one who, even though he had been crucified, came to be exalted to heaven, much as Elijah and Enoch had in the Hebrew scriptures.... But if Jesus is exalted, he is no longer dead, and so Christians started circulating the story of his resurrection."[1]

Bart Ehrman, New Testament scholar, professor of religious studies, and author of *Forged: Writing in the Name of God—Why the Bible's Authors Are Not Who We Think They Are*

THREE MOTIVES

Everyone has a motive. We tend to think of criminals when we hear the word, but jurors must also consider motive when examining and evaluating eyewitnesses who have testified in a trial. Jurors learn they must think about whether a witness was "influenced by a factor such as bias or prejudice, a personal relationship with someone involved in the case, or a personal interest in how the case is decided." There are two factors at work in a question like this: *bias* and *motive*. Were the disciples lying about the resurrection, as Bart Ehrman claims? Were their claims based on religious expectation or bias? If so, what was it they were hoping to gain from this elaborate lie? If the apostles wanted Jesus to be God, an elaborate lie wouldn't accomplish this, at least for the apostles. Lies might fool those who weren't there, but they wouldn't fool those who knew better. What did the disciples hope to gain if their stories were false? Let's study the issue of motive and finish our journey with an examination of Christian eyewitness *bias*.

In all my years investigating homicides, I've learned only three broad motives lie at the heart of any murder. As it turns out, these three motives are also the same driving forces behind other types of misbehavior; they are the reasons why we sometimes think what we shouldn't think, say what we shouldn't say, or do what we shouldn't do.

FINANCIAL GREED
This is often the driving force behind the crimes I investigate. Some murders, for example, result from a botched robbery. Other murders take place simply because they give the suspect a financial advantage. As an example, I once worked a homicide committed by a husband who didn't want his wife to receive a portion of his retirement.

SEXUAL OR RELATIONAL DESIRE
I've also investigated several murders motivated by sex or relationships. Some sexual attackers murder their victims so they can't testify later. Some murders occur simply because a jealous boyfriend couldn't bear to see his girlfriend dating another man.

PURSUIT OF POWER
Finally, some people commit murders to achieve or maintain a position of power or authority. It might be a rivalry between two people who are trying to get the same promotion. Others have killed simply because the victim dishonored or "disrespected" them in front of a group of peers.

Sex, money, and power are the motives for all the crimes detectives investigate. In fact, these three motives are also behind lesser sins as well. Think about the last time you did something you shouldn't have. If you examine the motivation carefully, you'll probably find it fits broadly into one of these three categories.

The presence of motive doesn't always mean a suspect committed the crime. Someone might have the motive to do something criminal, yet be able to resist the temptation to act. On the flip side, however, defense attorneys often cite the *lack of motive* when they are making a case for their client's innocence. "Why would my client have done such a thing when it would not benefit him in any way?" That's a fair question and one we need to ask as we examine the claims of the apostles.

 ## APOSTOLIC MOTIVATION

Did the alleged eyewitnesses of Jesus's life and ministry have an ulterior motive when writing the Gospels? Do we have any good reason to believe the apostles were driven to lie by one of the three motives we have described? No. There is nothing in history (neither Christian history nor secular history) to suggest the disciples had anything to gain from their testimony related to Jesus:

 ### THE APOSTLES WERE NOT DRIVEN BY FINANCIAL GAIN
There are many ancient accounts describing the lives of the apostles following the period recorded in the book of Acts. Local believers in a variety of ancient communities wrote about the activities of the individual disciples as they preached the gospel across the region. None of these texts describe any of the disciples as men who possessed material wealth. The disciples repeatedly appear as men who were chased from location to location, continually abandoning whatever property they owned and vacating whatever homes they were borrowing. The disciples were accustomed to living in this manner; they decided to leave their homes and families when they first began to follow Jesus. Peter acknowledged as much when he told Jesus, "Behold, we have left our own homes and followed You" (Luke 18:28). The disciples rejected all material wealth, believing the gospel provided eternal life, something of

far more value. Paul described their impoverished financial condition many times, reminding his readers the apostles were "both hungry and thirsty, and [were] poorly clothed, and [were] roughly treated, and [were] homeless" (1 Cor. 4:11). The apostles lived "as unknown yet well-known, as dying yet behold, we live; as punished yet not put to death, as sorrowful yet always rejoicing, as poor yet making many rich, as having nothing yet possessing all things" (2 Cor. 6:9–10). If the disciples and apostles were lying for financial gain, their lies didn't seem to be working. Those who watched Paul closely knew he was dedicated to spiritual life rather than material gain; he "coveted no one's silver or gold or clothes" (Acts 20:33).

The other apostles were in a very similar financial situation. When Peter and John were in Jerusalem in the first half of the first century, they were approached by a poor disabled man who asked them for money. Peter told the man, "Silver or gold I do not have, but what I have I give you. In the name of Jesus Christ of Nazareth, walk" (Acts 3:6). The disciples were consistently described as having chosen a life of material poverty in pursuit of spiritual truth. When James described the rich (as in James 5:1–5), he always did so in the second person. He didn't include himself in their numbers. The apostles never described themselves as wealthy; instead, they warned against the danger of wealth and its ability to distract us from eternal matters. Like the other apostolic writers, James described his fellow believers as joyfully impoverished: "Did not God choose the poor of this world to be rich in faith and heirs of the kingdom which He promised to those who love Him?" (James 2:5).

Motive

Judges advise juries they may consider motive as they assess the guilt of defendants:

"The People are not required to prove that the defendant had a motive to commit (any of the crimes/the crime) charged. In reaching your verdict you may, however, consider whether the defendant had a motive."

"Having a motive may be a factor tending to show that the defendant is guilty. Not having a motive may be a factor tending to show the defendant is not guilty" (Section 370, Judicial Council of California Criminal Jury Instructions, 2006).

The apostles gained nothing financially from their testimony of Jesus's life and ministry. The New Testament letters of Paul were written very early in history to people who knew Paul personally. If he was lying about his financial situation, his readers would have known it. All the nonbiblical accounts related to the lives of the apostles, whether legitimate or legendary, affirm the poverty of the disciples as they traveled the world to proclaim their testimony. The most reasonable inference from the New Testament and nonbiblical record is clear: the writers of the New Testament were as contentedly penniless as they proclaimed. It is reasonable to conclude financial greed was not the motive driving these men to make the claims they made in the Gospels. In fact, they remained impoverished due primarily to their dedication to their testimony.

"Behold, we have left our own homes..." (Luke 18:28)

"...poor yet making many rich, as having nothing yet possessing all things" (2 Cor. 6:9-10)

"Silver or gold I do not have..." (Acts 3:6)

"...both hungry and thirsty, and poorly clothed, and roughly treated, and homeless" (1 Cor. 4:11)

The Gospel authors were not **Motivated by Money**

"Now listen, you rich people, weep and wail because of the misery that is coming on you." (James 5:1-5)

2 THE APOSTLES WERE NOT DRIVEN BY SEX OR RELATIONSHIPS

It's equally unreasonable to suggest the apostles were motivated by lust or relationships. While the New Testament documents say little about the "love lives" of the apostolic eyewitnesses, we do know Peter was married and had a mother-in-law (Matt. 8:14). Paul confirmed this and suggested Peter wasn't the only one who was married when, in his letter to the Corinthians, he asked, "Do we not have a right to take along a believing wife, even as the rest of the apostles and the brothers of the Lord and Cephas [Peter]?" (1 Cor. 9:5). The early-church fathers also suggested all the apostles were married, with the possible exception of the youngest apostle, John. Clement of Alexandria claimed Peter and Philip had children[2] and that Paul, although married, did not take his wife with him when testifying as an apostle:

The only reason why he did not take her about with him was that it would have been an inconvenience for his ministry.... [The apostles], in accordance with their particular ministry, devoted themselves to preaching without any distraction, and took their wives with them not as women with whom they had marriage relations, but as sisters, that they might be their fellow-ministers in dealing with housewives.[3]

Clement suggested the apostles were not only married, but denied themselves sexual contact with their wives after the ascension in order to better minister to those they sought to reach with their testimony. Ignatius also referred to the apostles as married men:

For I pray that, being found worthy of God, I may be found at their feet in the kingdom, as at the feet of Abraham, and Isaac, and Jacob; as of Joseph, and Isaiah, and the rest of the prophets; as of Peter, and Paul, and the rest of the apostles, that were married men. For they entered into these marriages not for the sake of appetite, but out of regard for the propagation of mankind.[4]

Like Clement of Alexandria, Ignatius also claimed the apostles placed their testimony ahead of their personal desire. This was affirmed by another early Christian author named Tertullian, who wrote in the early third century:

[The] Apostles, withal, had a "licence" to marry, and lead wives about (with them). They had a "licence," too, to "live by the Gospel."[5]

The apostles had a right to bring their wives with them on their journeys and some may have done so. In any case, it is clear from both the biblical record and nonbiblical history that the apostles were careful to live their sexual lives in a manner beyond reproach. In fact, while other men within the culture often had more than one wife, the apostles only allowed men to rise to leadership if they limited themselves to one wife (1 Tim. 3:2).

The twelve apostles were not twelve single men in search of a good time. They weren't using their position or testimony to woo the local eligible ladies. If the apostles were motivated by sexual desire, there is certainly no record of it in the ancient writings of the time and no hint of it in their own texts. They were married men (most likely) who held chastity and sexual purity in high regard. Sexual or relational desire was not the motive driving these men to make the claims they made in the Gospels. This is the most reasonable inference, given what we know about the lives of the apostles.

"Many had believing wives"

"They had 'license' to marry"

"They were married men"

The Gospel authors were not
Motivated by Sex

"They took their wives with them"

3 THE APOSTLES WERE NOT DRIVEN BY THE PURSUIT OF POWER

Some skeptics argue the apostles were motivated by a desire to be powerful within their individual religious communities. They often point to the power Christian leaders eventually held in Rome when Christianity became the state-sponsored religion in the fourth century. There is no doubt the popes of the Roman Catholic Church eventually became incredibly powerful both religiously and politically. But when we examine the lives of the first-century apostles, they bear little resemblance to the lives of the Roman Catholic popes.

Power has its perks, not the least of which is the ability to protect oneself. This kind of power was never available to the apostles. The early Christian movement immediately faced hostility from those who possessed power in the first century. Rumors quickly spread claiming the Christians practiced offensive rituals and were unwilling to worship Emperor Nero as divine. Tacitus recorded Nero's response:

Consequently, to get rid of the report, Nero fastened the guilt and inflicted the most exquisite tortures on a class hated for their abominations, called Christians by the populace. Christus, from whom the name had its origin, suffered the extreme penalty during the reign of Tiberius at the hands of one of our procurators, Pontius Pilatus, and a most mischievous superstition, thus checked for the moment, again broke out not only in Judaea, the first source of the evil, but even in Rome, where all things hideous and shameful from every part of the world find their centre and become popular. Accordingly, an arrest was first made of all who pleaded guilty; then, upon their information, an immense multitude was convicted, not so much of the crime of firing the city, as of hatred against mankind. Mockery of every sort was added to their deaths. Covered with the skins of beasts, they were torn by dogs and perished, or were nailed to crosses, or were doomed to the flames and burnt, to serve as a nightly illumination, when daylight had expired.[6]

At this early point in Christian history, leadership within the Christian community was a liability rather than an asset. Prominent believers and leaders who openly admitted their allegiance to Jesus ("pleaded guilty") and refused to recant this allegiance were the first to die. It was during this time in history when Peter and Paul were executed in Rome, but they weren't the only apostles whose prominence as Christian leaders cost them their lives. The nonbiblical histories and writings related to the lives and ministries of the twelve disciples consistently proclaimed the apostles were persecuted and eventually martyred for their testimony. The apostolic eyewitnesses refused to change their testimony about what they saw, even though they faced unimaginable torture and execution. Only John appears to have escaped martyrdom, but he was instead exiled and persecuted for his position as an apostle.

Persecution was the uniform experience of the apostles, long before they were finally executed for their faith. Paul's experience, as he told it in his letter to the Corinthians, was sadly normative for the apostles:

Five times I received from the Jews thirty-nine lashes. Three times I was beaten with rods, once I was stoned, three times I was shipwrecked, a night and a day

I have spent in the deep. I have been on frequent journeys, in dangers from rivers, dangers from robbers, dangers from my countrymen, dangers from the Gentiles, dangers in the city, dangers in the wilderness, dangers on the sea, dangers among false brethren; I have been in labor and hardship, through many sleepless nights, in hunger and thirst, often without food, in cold and exposure. Apart from such external things, there is the daily pressure upon me of concern for all the churches. (2 Cor. 11:24–28)

As the apostles rose to positions of leadership, they made themselves the target of persecution and abuse. The more prominent they became, the more they risked death at the hands of their adversaries. The pursuit of power and position was *not* the motive driving these men to make the claims they made in the Gospels. This is the most reasonable inference, given what we know about their deaths.

If a defense attorney were representing any of the apostles, defending them against the accusation they lied about their testimony, the attorney could fairly ask the question: "Why would my client have done such a thing when it would not benefit him in any way?" Certainly, there was no benefit to any of the apostles in the three areas we would expect to motivate such a lie.

Paul, the writer of more New Testament letters than any other author, held a position of power *prior* to becoming a follower of Jesus, and *surrendered* this position of authority, respect, and leadership to join the small religious sect then known as "the Way." Born as Saul to Jewish parents in the city of Tarsus, Cilicia, in AD 5, he studied the Hebrew scriptures under Rabbi Gamaliel (a

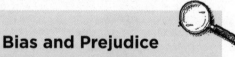

Bias and Prejudice

Bias:

"An inclination of temperament or outlook; especially a personal and sometimes unreasoned judgment."

Prejudice:

"(1) Preconceived judgment or opinion, (2) An adverse opinion or leaning formed without just grounds or before sufficient knowledge" (*Webster's Collegiate Dictionary*, 11th ed., 2009).

leader of the Jewish Sanhedrin with impressive educational pedigree). Saul then rose to a position of leadership that provided him with the ability to arrest and imprison the earliest converts to the Christian faith.[7] He was a zealous Pharisee and a "Hebrew of Hebrews,"[8] a man on the rise within the Jewish tradition and culture.

If a defense attorney were representing Paul against the accusation he lied about his testimony, the attorney could fairly ask the question: "Why would Paul—based on a conscious lie—leave his position of authority, power, and respect with the larger, better established religious community to join a much smaller, less influential, and less powerful community?" If Paul had been motivated by the pursuit of power, he would have been foolish to leave a position of authority, hoping to someday return to what he already possessed, unless of course, he saw the risen Christ and knew Christianity was true.

Pelted with stones

Shipwrecked in the deep

Beaten with rods

Faced danger everywhere

Lashed with whips

The Gospel authors were not
Motivated by Power

Without food or water

FREE FROM ULTERIOR MOTIVE

Motive is a key factor jurors must assess when evaluating the reliability of witnesses. That's why judges advise jurors to ask questions like "Was the witness promised immunity or leniency in exchange for his or her testimony?" (see chapter 4). We need to know if something other than the simple desire to report the truth motivated the witnesses to say what they said. As we examine the motives of the gospel writers, it's clear the forces typically compelling people to lie didn't drive the authors. The apostles were free from ulterior motive.

But what about bias? Even if they didn't possess one of these three self-serving motives, how do we know the gospel writers weren't simply biased? Judges encourage jurors to find out if the witness was "influenced by a factor such as bias or prejudice, a personal relationship with someone involved in the case, or a personal interest in how the case is decided." If a witness held a *preconception* or *partiality* as he or she watched the event, that bias may have influenced how the witness interpreted what they saw. Bias can cause people to see something *incorrectly*. Was this the case with the apostles?

SO, IS THIS WHY SOME CONTINUE TO DENY IT?

Some skeptics base their distrust of the Gospels (and of the nonbiblical accounts of the apostles' lives following Jesus's ascension) on the possible presence of bias. Even though there is no evidence to suggest the apostles were motivated by greed, lust, or power, critics are still suspicious of the gospel accounts. Let's look at the reasons behind their suspicions and include them in our final evaluation utilizing abductive reasoning.

THE GOSPELS WERE WRITTEN BY CHRISTIANS

Skeptics argue the Gospels cannot be trusted because they were not authored by *objective* non-Christians. The New Testament records, according to this view, were written by biased Christians who were trying to convince us of their religious perspective. Critics claim these Christians observed the events through a charged religious lens and then reported the events from this viewpoint. As a result, the gospel narratives are biased and unreliable.

BUT ...

This is not an accurate description of what occurred in the first century as the gospel eyewitnesses observed the life and ministry of Jesus. Let me give you an example from one of my cases to illustrate the point. Many years ago, when I was working robberies, I had a case in which a local bank was robbed. The suspect (Mark Hill) entered the bank in the afternoon and waited in line to approach the teller. He stood in the lobby for two or three minutes, waiting to walk up to the counter, where he eventually gave the teller a "demand note" and flashed a handgun in his waistband. While he was waiting for the opportunity, a bank employee (Kathy Smalley) saw him standing in line. Kathy was working as an assistant manager and had a desk located in the lobby, adjacent to the teller line. She recognized Mark as he waited for his turn. Kathy had attended high school with Mark and recognized him because he was a talented (and popular) athlete. Even though many years had passed, Kathy still recognized him with certainty. Mark, on the other hand, was focused as he waited to rob the bank. He never even looked up to see Kathy watching him. He eventually approached the teller (Debra Camacho) and completed his robbery. Debra gave Mark the money he demanded and then pushed the silent alarm button as he turned to walk away. She motioned quickly to Kathy, who was sitting within her view.

Kathy recognized the fact Debra had just been robbed. She couldn't believe it. She never considered Mark to be the kind of person who would commit a robbery. In fact, she thought Mark got an athletic scholarship after high school and assumed he became a successful athlete and college graduate. When she first saw Mark enter the lobby, she never thought he was about to commit a robbery. After the fact, however, she was certain Mark was the robber. She was now a *true believer* in Mark's guilt. After all, she saw it with her own eyes. You might say Kathy was now a "Mark Hillian" believer related to the robbery. So let me ask you a question. Should I trust her testimony? Isn't she too biased to be a reliable witness? Kathy is not neutral about what she saw in the bank. She has a perspective and an opinion about the identity of the robber. She's a Mark Hillian believer; she is certain he is the man who committed the robbery, despite the other possibilities. If she's this biased, how can I trust what she has to say?

Can you see how ridiculous this concern would be? Kathy didn't *start off* with a bias against Mark or a presupposition tainting her observations. In fact, she was shocked Mark would commit such a crime. She was not a "Mark Hillian" believer until *after* the fact.

In a similar way, the authors of the Gospels were not "Christian" believers until *after* they observed the life and ministry of Jesus. Much has been written about the fact Jews in first-century Palestine were looking for a Messiah who would save them from Roman oppression. They were expecting a military liberator, not a spiritual savior. Even Bart Ehrman admits the disciples found themselves asking the question "How could Jesus, the Messiah, have been killed as a common criminal?" They didn't expect Jesus (as the military messiah) to die, and they certainly didn't expect Him to come back to life.

The Gospels are filled with examples of the disciples misunderstanding the predictions and proclamations of Jesus. There are many examples of doubt and hesitancy on the part of those who witnessed Jesus's life. The skeptical disciples continually asked Jesus for clarification, and Thomas, after spending three years with Jesus, still wouldn't believe His prediction of the resurrection until he saw Jesus with his own eyes and touched Jesus with his own hands. The apostles became convinced of Jesus's deity *after* they observed His life and resurrection. They didn't start off as Christians any more than Kathy started off as a "Mark Hillian." The disciples ended up as Christians (certain Jesus was God) because of their observations, just as Kathy ended up as a "Mark Hillian" (certain he was the robber) because of her observations. The disciples were not prejudicially biased; they were evidentially certain.

 ## THE DEATH NARRATIVES OF THE APOSTLES WERE WRITTEN BY CHRISTIANS

Skeptics also argue little or no weight can be given to the fact the apostles were allegedly martyred for their testimony because the "histories" describing their martyrdom are largely Christian legends written by believers. How do we even know these martyrdoms really occurred if the only records we have are biased stories and legends filled with miraculous tales?

BUT ...

As described in chapter 1, we can't allow the description of miraculous occurrences to automatically disqualify the ancient accounts. If we claim the ancient stories are biased (because they were written by Christians), we cannot reject them with a bias of our own (against supernaturalism). While it is true some accounts related to the martyrdom of the apostles are more reliable than others, we have no reason to reject all of them as historically inaccurate.[9] The deaths of Peter, Paul, James, and John are very well attested, and the remaining martyrdom accounts of the apostles (with the possible exception of Matthias and Philip) are sufficiently documented to provide us with confidence in their claims.

Most importantly, there aren't any ancient non-Christian accounts contradicting the claims of the Christian authors who wrote about the deaths of the eyewitness disciples. It's not as though we have competing accounts related to the testimony of these men. We don't have ancient Christians on one side, claiming the apostles died because they unflinchingly declared the truth about Jesus, and ancient non-Christians on the other side, claiming the apostles eventually confessed it was all a lie. There are no ancient authors claiming anything other than what the Christians described; there are no contradictory accounts portraying the apostles as liars who confessed their lies when pressured. According to the unanimous testimony of antiquity, the early Christian eyewitnesses suffered for their testimony but stayed the course. They didn't flinch, and they never changed their story.

THE MOST REASONABLE CONCLUSION

Abductive reasoning can help us to decide between two possible conclusions related to the bias or motive the apostolic eyewitnesses may have had when writing their Gospels or testifying to their observations. Let's list the evidence one final time, alongside the two possible explanations accounting for what we have seen so far:

The Apostles Were Not Driven by Financial Gain

The Apostles Were Not Driven by Sex or Relationship

The Apostles Were Not Driven by the Pursuit of Power

The Gospels Were Written by Christians

The Death Narratives of the Apostles Were Written by Christians

The Gospel writers reported what they actually observed

The Gospel writers had ulterior motives that drove them to make false claims to accomplish a particular goal

The apostles lacked evil intent. They simply didn't benefit from lying about what they saw. In fact, they would have been far better off if they had kept their mouths shut. What could they possibly have gained from this elaborate lie? It's clear the gospel writers appeared to be more concerned about eternal life than material gain. Could a lie about Jesus make His spiritual claims true? Does it make sense the disciples would forsake everything for spiritual claims they knew were untrue? The evidence from history once again supports the first explanation better than the second. It offers reasonable responses to the challenges offered by skeptics. The second explanation, on the other hand, is simply unable to account adequately for the lack of motive on the part of the apostles. The first explanation is *feasible, straightforward,* and *logical.* It *exhausts* all the evidence we have assembled, and it is *superior* to the alternative explanation. It is, once again, the most reasonable explanation.

THE GOSPELS PASS THE LAST TEST

We've examined the four important areas jurors must consider when determining the reliability of eyewitnesses. The most reasonable inference is the gospel writers were *present, corroborated, accurate,* and *unbiased.* If this is the case, we can conclude with confidence their testimony is *reliable.* We've done the *heavy lifting* needed to determine the reliability of these accounts; we've been diligent and faithful as jurors and have considered the evidence. It's time to decide.

BECOMING A "TWO DECISION" CHRISTIAN

Santiago Ortega turned the key and started his tired 1975 Triumph TR6. The engine sputtered and backfired, spouting smoke into the small parking lot adjacent to the cheap hotel he called home. Santiago was addicted to rock cocaine, and his addiction preoccupied much of his day. He was either smoking rock or trying to find a way to pay for it, and he was increasingly desperate.

He hadn't seen his wife in weeks. His family was scattered across the county and wouldn't offer him refuge, especially now. His father and brother were in federal prison for bank robbery, and sadly, Santiago was following in their footsteps. He'd already committed seven bank robberies in Los Angeles County before he did his first one in our city. I was working on our undercover surveillance team at the time and an informant gave us a tip leading us to Santiago's hotel. We were sitting in the parking lot when Santiago fired up his battered and weary convertible.

While Santiago looked like the man in the bank surveillance photographs, we weren't sure if he was the robber we were looking for. We would find out shortly. He backed out of the parking lot and drove into the city of Long Beach. Our team carefully followed him, five officers and a sergeant trailing our suspect in a series of unremarkable midsized cars. Santiago didn't make it far before he succumbed to his addiction. At the first traffic light Santiago fired up a homemade rock pipe and filled the interior of his small car with smoke. He was nearly invisible in the hazy capsule of the Triumph. Somehow he managed to drive, bathed in smoke, without ever rolling down his windows. He continued for approximately two miles until he came to a Home Savings and Loan.

Santiago parked his car at the edge of the parking lot, just out of view from the bank doors. He exited, smoothed out his shirt, and pressed down his hair. He looked about the parking lot nervously as he walked toward the bank entrance. One of our team members, dressed in jeans and a T-shirt, jumped out of his car and followed Santiago into the business. He communicated to the rest of our team via his portable radio. Like Mark Hill, Santiago was a "demand-note" bank robber. In his past robberies, he never had to show his gun to the tellers; his note was enough to cause them to comply. Today's teller was no exception. She emptied her drawer and gave Santiago the money; he quickly turned and walked from the bank. The customers in the lobby were completely unaware a robbery had even occurred.

But my partner knew. He quickly radioed from the interior of the bank and told us Santiago was, in fact, a bank robber. By this time, Santiago had already run to the Triumph and was now fleeing the parking lot. Our team quickly moved in behind him. In situations like these, we would typically conduct a tactical arrest at the nearest red light, maneuvering our cars into position to prevent the suspect's escape. But Santiago now had a heightened awareness of his surroundings, and he became suspicious of one of our surveillance vehicles. The chase was on.

Intoxicated rock-cocaine addicts and aging Triumphs are a recipe for disaster, especially when they are running from the police. Santiago crashed the car in the first mile of the pursuit. I was the case agent; it was my responsibility to handcuff Santiago and drive him back to the police station for booking. Along the way I was able to talk to him about his life and his future. I began with a simple observation.

"Santiago, you look terrible," I said.

"I know," he replied, shaking his head. To his credit, Santiago Ortega was a broken man, remorseful and repentant about his life and crime spree.

"How long did you think you could go on like this?" I asked the question as a matter of genuine concern. Santiago's eyes were red and infected; he was gaunt and disheveled. He looked like he hadn't eaten in days.

"I knew it was coming to an end, really I did. I don't even know how it got this crazy. I'm not really a bad person. I know better." He was remarkably talkative and honest.

"So why are you doing this?" I asked.

"I'm a junkie. I want to stop. But I always end up back here. You know, I'm married, and my wife is a beautiful lady. She left me when I started up again." Santiago began to cry, and his tears caused him to wince in the pain from his infected eyes. "A couple years ago I went with her to a crusade, and I got saved. She did too. But here I am, still messed up." Santiago told me about his experience at the large evangelistic stadium event he attended. He told me he was moved by what the preacher said, and he accepted the invitation to walk down from the stands and become a follower of Jesus. He thought his decision that night would change his life forever.

"So, I guess you probably think I'm some kind of hypocrite, right? Just another messed-up Christian." He didn't know he was talking to a follower of Jesus.

Santiago decided to trust Jesus for his salvation, but he never decided to examine the life and teaching of Jesus evidentially. Santiago failed to make a second decision to examine what he believed. He was unable to see his faith as anything more than *subjective opinion* as he struggled to live in a world of *objective facts*. As a result, his *beliefs* eventually surrendered to the *facts* of his situation and the pressures of his addiction. He allowed his friends and family situation to influence him, rather than becoming a source of inspiration and truth for his family and neighborhood. Santiago was a one-decision Christian, and his decision was unsupported by a reasonable examination of the evidence.

I wrote back and forth with Santiago in the years that followed. He was ultimately convicted and sentenced to many years in federal prison. He finally found himself in a place where he had the time and opportunity to examine the evidence for Christianity.

DECISIONS, "BELIEF THAT," AND "BELIEF IN"

My journey was just the opposite of Santiago Ortega's. I decided to investigate the claims of Christianity (to see if they could be defended) *before* I ever decided to call myself a Christian. My investigation (some of which I described in section 2) led me to conclude the Gospels were reliable. But this conclusion presented me with a dilemma. When the jury in chapter 4 established Jerry Strickland was a reliable witness, they trusted his testimony related to the identity of the robber. I now had to take a similar step with the reliable gospel eyewitnesses. It's one thing, however, to accept the historicity of locations or key characters in the biblical narrative; it's another to accept what the Gospels were telling me about Jesus. Did Jesus really demonstrate His deity as the gospel eyewitnesses claimed? Did He truly rise from the dead? Did He speak the truth about who He was and about the nature of eternal life? Deciding in favor of the most reasonable inference would require me to release my naturalistic presuppositions entirely. C. S. Lewis was correct: the claims about Jesus, if true, were of infinite importance. This decision would likely change my life forever.

I knew I could never take a blind leap of faith. For me, the decision to move beyond "belief that" to "belief in" needed to be a reasonable decision based on the evidence. I ask jurors to do this every time I present a case—to assemble the circumstantial evidence and draw the most reasonable inference from what they have examined. That's what I did as I assembled the cumulative case for the reliability of the Gospels:

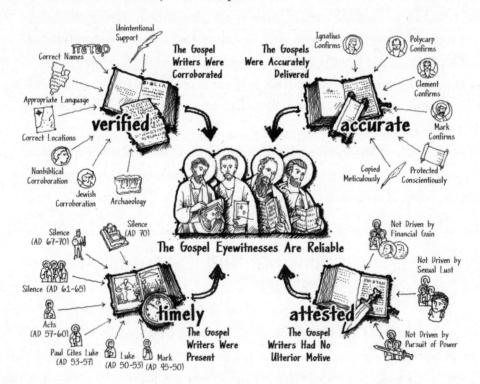

I knew my concerns about the Gospels had always been rooted in the miraculous events the accounts described. Philosophical naturalism prevented me from taking miracles seriously.

But the apostles claimed to see miracles, and when evaluated as eyewitnesses, the gospel authors passed the test.

I can remember the day I finally surrendered my naturalistic biases and moved from "belief that" to "belief in." I was sitting in a church service with my wife. I don't remember exactly what the pastor was talking about, but I remember leaning over and telling my wife I was a believer. Much like Mark Walker, the officer who trusted in his bulletproof vest, in that singular moment I moved from believing *that* the Gospels were reliable eyewitness accounts to trusting *in* what they told me about Jesus.

The gospel eyewitnesses had something very specific to say about Jesus. They did not give their lives sacrificially for personal *opinions* about God; they gave their lives because their claims were an objective matter of life and death. They knew Jesus offered more than a guideline for personal behavior. They understood Jesus was "the way, and the truth, and the life" and "no one comes to the Father but through" Him (John 14:6). The apostolic eyewitnesses gave their lives to help us to understand we, as fallen, imperfect humans, are in desperate need of a Savior. They died as martyrs trying to show us Jesus was, in fact, the Savior who could provide forgiveness for our imperfection. Peter was clear about this when testifying to others:

> You know of Jesus of Nazareth, how God anointed Him with the Holy Spirit and with power, and how He went about doing good and healing all who were oppressed by the devil, for God was with Him. We are witnesses of all the things He did both in the land of the Jews and in Jerusalem. They also put Him to death by hanging Him on a cross. God raised Him up on the third day, and granted that He become visible, not to all the people, but to witnesses who were chosen beforehand by God, that is, to us who ate and drank with Him after He arose from the dead. And He ordered us to preach to the people, and solemnly to testify that this is the One who has been appointed by God as Judge of the living and the dead. Of Him all the prophets bear witness that through His name everyone who believes in Him receives forgiveness of sins. (Acts 10:38–43)

The apostles recognized their message was a life-saving cure for what was (and is) killing all of us; they gave their lives to point us to the Savior, so we could point even more. When

I recognized the power of this message, I moved from "belief that" to "belief in." People started to notice a change almost immediately. It wasn't as though I was trying hard to behave differently or follow a new set of rules; I didn't even know all the "rules" when I first decided to trust Christ. But I did know this: I was grateful. I began to understand not only the true nature of Jesus, but also the true nature of my own fallen condition. It's hard not to see your own imperfection when you are confronted with the perfect God of the universe. As I came to appreciate my own need for forgiveness and what Jesus did to accomplish this for me, I became truly grateful and optimistic for the first time in my life.

I had been a cop for about eight years prior to being a Christian. In that time, I slowly lost my faith in people. I was suspicious; I considered everyone a liar and capable of horrific behavior. Nothing surprised me when it came to the depravity of humanity. I trusted no one and thought of myself as superior to most people I encountered. I was cocky, cynical, and distant. My wife and kids were my entire world. I had a few acquaintances who were also police officers, but few other friends. My heart was shrinking and growing harder with every case I worked and with every passing year. None of this bothered me in the slightest. In fact, I saw my suspicion as a virtue.

That all changed when I put my faith *in* Jesus. As I began to understand my need and the gift I had been given, my compassion and patience grew. As someone who had been forgiven, I now developed the capacity to forgive others. My excitement became contagious. It spilled over into everything I said and did. My partners noticed it, even though I was careful in the early days to hide my conversion from them. My wife was perhaps the most surprised by all of this. She was about to see my life (and hers) change dramatically.

Looking back at it many years later, she is still amazed at the transformation. The truth about Jesus impacted every aspect of our lives as I became consumed by the desire to learn more about Him. I slept less, studied more, worked with more urgency, and loved others in a way I had never loved before. I wanted to share what I had discovered with the people in my world. Everyone I encountered eventually heard about the gospel. I became known as a vocal Christian. I entered seminary, became a pastor, and even planted a small church. Over the past twenty-six years, as I have studied the eyewitness accounts, I have become more and more confident in their reliability and message. This confidence has motivated me to defend and share the truth.

THE IMPORTANCE OF BECOMING A *TWO DECISION* CHRISTIAN

In televised criminal cases, the jurors are sometimes interviewed following their decision. Some make a second decision when approached by reporters. They choose to make a case for why they voted the way they did. Not every juror decides to defend his or her decision, but those who do find they are far more likely to persuade others and grow in their own personal confidence related to their decision. Had Santiago Ortega made the decision to investigate and defend what he believed, I can't help but wonder if he would also have been able to persuade those around him or at least grow in his own personal confidence and ability to resist the influence of others.

When I decided to believe what the gospel writers were telling me, I also decided to become a Christian case maker. The second decision was just as important as the first. I began modestly; I started an inexpensive website (PleaseConvinceMe.com) and posted my own investigations in a variety of areas. When I was a youth pastor, I also posted the lessons and messages I presented to my students. Eventually, I started a podcast. Then I wrote a book. At first, like many Christians, I was uncomfortable defending the claims of Christianity. How would I ever learn enough (or know enough) to be an effective case maker? Don't I need a doctorate in philosophy or Christian apologetics? Shouldn't I be an "expert" of some sort before trying to defend what I believe?

Jurors aren't experts, yet they are required to make the most important decision in the courtroom. In fact, the experts introduced by the prosecution or the defense never cast a single vote. Our justice system trusts that folks like you and me can examine the testimony of experts and come to a reasonable conclusion about the truth. One of the jurors will even become a leader in the jury room. As the "foreperson," chosen by the other jurors, this man or woman will shepherd the deliberations and eventually present the decision to the judge. You don't have to be an expert to serve on a jury or lead the jury as a foreperson. Jurors listen to the experts, carefully evaluate the evidence, and draw the most reasonable inference. Jurors don't need to be experts in the field under consideration; they simply need to be attentive, conscientious, and willing to get in the game.

And that's all we need to be effective Christian case makers: attentive, conscientious, and willing to get in the game. As it turns out, each of us is already an expert of one kind or another.

We have life experiences to draw upon for the expertise we'll need to answer the challenges of skeptics, and we can make the conscious decision to become better Christian *case makers*. It's time well spent and an important part of our identity as Christians.

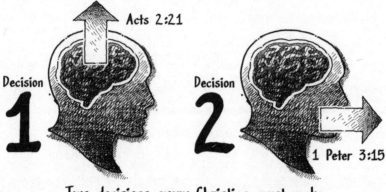

Two decisions every Christian must make

THE DANGER OF BECOMING AN *ABBREVIATED* CHRISTIAN

Many of us have neglected our duty in this area. In fact, we've been unable to see our duty in the first place. We've become *abbreviated* Christians. Let me explain. Most of us understand the importance of evangelism in the life of Christians. Jesus told the apostles to "make disciples of all nations" and to instruct these disciples to obey everything He taught (Matt. 28:16–20). We call this the "Great Commission." We are clearly commanded to make disciples, just as the apostles did in their own generation. As a result, Christians typically feel they are called to evangelism of some sort, even though many of us feel ill equipped to share our faith.

Paul seemed to recognize this and discussed evangelism as a matter of gifting. When describing all of us as members of the church, Paul said God gave "*some* as apostles, and *some* as prophets, and *some* as evangelists, and *some* as pastors and teachers, for the equipping of the saints for the work of service, to the building up of the body of Christ" (Eph. 4:11–12). Not everyone is a pastor or a prophet. Some of us are gifted in this area and some are not.

In a similar way, only some of us are gifted as evangelists; not everyone can share his or her faith like Billy Graham. I've often been comforted by these words from Paul when struggling to begin a conversation about Christianity.

But the New Testament authors, while recognizing not all of us are gifted evangelists, described a responsibility applying to every one of us as Christians. Peter said no one is allowed to relegate his or her duty as a Christian *case maker*. According to Peter, *all* of us need to "be prepared to give an answer to everyone who asks [us] to give the reason for the hope that [we] have" (1 Pet. 3:15 NIV). While only some of us are gifted and called to be evangelists, all of us are called to be *case makers*. It's our duty as Christians. We need to stop thinking of ourselves in an abbreviated manner. As biblical, New Testament believers, we aren't just "Christians," we are "case-making Christians." We can't allow ourselves to get comfortable and relegate the hard work of defending the faith to those who speak or write books on the topic.

Some of us prepare meals for a living. The world is filled with popular and proficient chefs who make a living preparing meals for restaurants or television programs. We recognize these chefs and we can learn something from their recipes and experiences. But even if you aren't a professional chef, I bet you know how to prepare a meal. Meal preparation is an important part of living. Yes, some of us are professional chefs, but the rest of us need to be able to cook if we want to survive. In a similar way, some of us make a living preparing a defense for Christianity. The rest of us can learn a lot from the arguments and presentations of professional "Christian apologists." But that doesn't get us off the hook. All of us, as Christians, need to be able to prepare a defense for what we believe. It's just as important as preparing our daily meals. Our meals may not be as creative or flamboyant as those prepared by professional chefs, but they are typically sufficient and satisfying. Our personal defense of Christianity may not be as robust as what can be offered by a scholarly, "full-time" apologist, but it can be just as powerful and persuasive.

Each of us must answer God's call on our lives as *Two Decision* Christians. If you've already decided to believe the Gospels, take a second step and decide to defend them. Become a *case-making* Christian; work in your profession, live your life faithfully, devote yourself to the truth, and steadily prepare yourself to make a defense for what you believe. I want to encourage you to make that second decision. Start small. Read and study. Engage your friends. Start a blog or host a website. Volunteer to teach a class at your church. *Get in the game.*

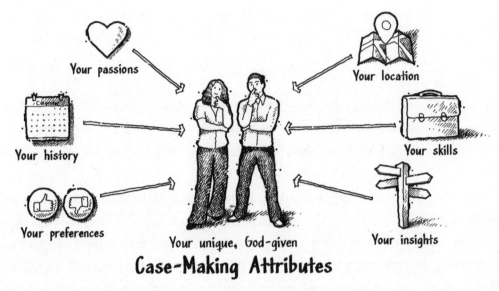

Your passions

Your location

Your history

Your skills

Your preferences

Your insights

Your unique, God-given
Case-Making Attributes

My life as a Christian took flight the minute I decided to become a *case maker*. God cleverly used all my experiences as a detective to give me a perspective I've tried to share with you in the pages of this book. It's my hope the skeptics who read this might at least lay down their presuppositions long enough to recognize there is a substantive circumstantial case supporting the reliability of the gospel authors. It's also my hope Christians who read this book will be encouraged to know God can use you right now, in this very moment, to make a case for the truth.

Afterword

THE CASE CROSS-EXAMINED

In the years since writing *Cold-Case Christianity*, I've had the honor and opportunity to present the case for Jesus and the reliability of the New Testament at conferences and on university campuses. Along the way, we've opened the floor to questions, allowing *Cold-Case Christianity* to be "cross-examined" by students and skeptics. Here are the most frequently voiced questions, concerns, or objections, along with brief responses:

HOW CAN WE BE CERTAIN THE APOSTLES REALLY DIED FOR THEIR CLAIMS?

The deaths of the apostles demonstrated the veracity of their claims related to the resurrection. But some apostolic deaths are better attested than others. Despite this, there are several good reasons to infer the apostles died as martyrs, refusing to recant their testimony about the resurrection of Jesus:

THE APOSTLES BEGAN AN EYEWITNESS TRADITION

The book of Acts provides us with a description of the disciples as eyewitnesses who were unafraid to share what they saw and experienced with Jesus, even when this testimony resulted in their imprisonment or mistreatment. The earliest reliable record of the disciples clearly indicates they were on a path toward martyrdom.

THE APOSTLES BEGAN A UNIFORM RECORD

While the details related to the apostles' deaths may vary from tradition to tradition, the fact they died as martyrs is a point of uniform agreement. Just as important, there are no other competing ancient traditions contradicting the martyrdoms of the apostles. There are no pagan accounts, for example, describing the apostles living leisurely lives along the Mediterranean coast.

THE APOSTLES BEGAN A COMMITTED MOVEMENT

For generations following the life and death of the apostles, the earliest Christian believers sought to emulate the commitment and dedication of the apostolic eyewitnesses. How did they seek to do this? By following in their footsteps and dying for the assertions of the apostles. The early Christians copied the apostles and refused to recant their trust in the eyewitness accounts.

The ancient church acknowledged the martyrdom of the original Christian eyewitnesses. There is more than enough reason to believe the apostles died as martyrs without recanting their testimony. This commitment to apostolic claims is still a powerful testimony to the truth of Christianity.

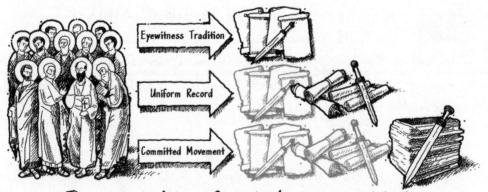

The ancient claims of martyrdom are consistent

DID THE APOSTLES LIE BECAUSE THEY WERE SEEKING THE STATUS PROVIDED BY MARTYRDOM?

Most skeptics agree the apostles gained nothing financially or relationally from their testimony, but there are *also* good reasons to reject the idea the disciples were motivated by the *pursuit of power,* seeking martyrdom as a status symbol:

THE APOSTLES KNEW THE DIFFERENCE BETWEEN MINISTRY AND MARTYRDOM

The book of Acts and the letters of Paul provide us with a glimpse into the lives of the apostles. They were clearly pursued and mistreated, and the New Testament narratives and letters describe their repeated efforts to avoid capture so they could continue their personal ministries as eyewitnesses. The New Testament accounts describe men who were bold enough to maintain their ministry, but clever enough to avoid apprehension for as long as possible.

THE APOSTLES KNEW THE DIFFERENCE BETWEEN A CONSEQUENCE AND A GOAL

These early eyewitnesses were fully aware their testimony would put them in jeopardy, but they understood this was the *consequence* of their role as eyewitnesses rather than the *goal*. That's why they attempted to avoid death as long as possible. While later generations of believers may have wanted to emulate the apostles through an act of martyrdom, this was not the case for the apostles themselves.

THE APOSTLES KNEW THE DIFFERENCE BETWEEN FAME AND INFAMY

It's one thing to be famous, another to be famously despised. Some attain widespread fame based on something *noble* (like Mother Teresa). Some attain widespread fame because of something *sinister* (like Adolf Hitler). The apostles were roundly despised by their Jewish counterparts because of their leadership within the fledgling Christian community. If they were lying about their testimony to gain the respect and admiration of the culture they were trying to convert, they took the wrong approach. The apostles knew their testimony would leave them powerless to stop their own brutal martyrdom.

The apostles did their best to *avoid* martyrdom so they could share what they had seen with their own eyes. Even though they knew their testimony might eventually cost them their lives, they steadfastly continued to proclaim the resurrection of Jesus. Their martyrdom was a consequence of these efforts and clearly not the goal of the disciples.

The Apostles wanted to *avoid martyrdom* to advance ministry

HOW CAN THE GOSPELS BE EYEWITNESS ACCOUNTS IF THEY INCLUDE EVENTS OR FACTS THE WRITERS DIDN'T SEE?

The gospel writers often included information for events they simply could not have personally observed (e.g., the birth narratives in Matthew and several instances in the Gospels where Jesus is alone). How can the Gospels be eyewitness accounts if they include things the authors could not have witnessed? When reading statements from cold cases originally investigated decades earlier, these accounts typically include three kinds of "firsthand" eyewitness descriptions:

FIRSTHAND EXPERIENCE
Events and occurrences they personally observed and experienced.

FIRSTHAND ACCESS
Events and occurrences they did not personally observe but were aware of based on information given to them by someone else at the time.

FIRSTHAND KNOWLEDGE

General cultural conditions and common knowledge of the time, even though they had no direct experience or observation upon which to rely.

Testimony related to what I call "firsthand access" is generally considered hearsay (because the original source for this information is unavailable for cross-examination). But this does not mean information in this category is untrue or invalid. The hearsay standard in criminal trials is narrowly designed to provide the highest possible protection for those being accused of a crime (for more refer to chapter 10). Eyewitnesses provide information from their personal experience and observations, their access to information from other living eyewitnesses, and their intimate knowledge of the culture in which they live. The fact an eyewitness would choose to provide information from "firsthand access" does not discredit what they are providing from "firsthand experience" or "firsthand knowledge."

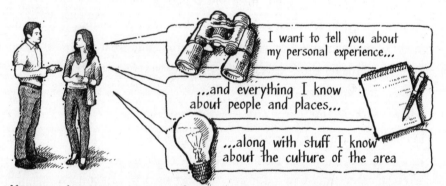

I want to tell you about my personal experience...

...and everything I know about people and places...

...along with stuff I know about the culture of the area

Historical witnesses provide more than eyewitness observations

CAN WE TRUST THE INFORMATION IN THE GOSPELS, ESPECIALLY IF IT WAS FIRST TRANSMITTED ORALLY?

I've assembled a cumulative circumstantial case for the early dating of the Gospels (refer to chapter 11), but even if the Gospels were written promptly enough to have been authored by eyewitnesses, isn't fifteen to twenty years enough time for the authors to forget something important or add something errant, especially if they were only retelling the story *orally*? There are good reasons to infer the gospel information was transmitted accurately, even if this was entirely oral:

PERSONAL REVERENCE

The content of the gospel message was of critical importance to those who communicated it and those who accepted it (and later re-communicated it to the next generation). These folks weren't passing along Mom's meatloaf recipe; they were testifying as eyewitnesses to the greatest life ever lived, and they understood their role as eyewitnesses.

PERSISTENT REPETITION

The first-century culture in which the disciples operated was a culture of oral transmission. Much has been written about this, but my own experience confirms an important truth. I've given the same talks for years now and my kids have attended many of these lectures. My daughter once said she could finish my sentences for me after just a few repeated presentations. She then recited a portion of my talk with perfection. If she could repeat the content of my talks after just a few exposures, imagine what she could accomplish if she accompanied me for three years like the disciples who followed Jesus.

PROMPT RECORDING

The disciples who memorized the repeated teaching of Jesus offered what they remembered to those who recorded it within the lifetimes of the original eyewitnesses. As I described in chapter 11, the early-church bishop Papias claimed Mark recorded the preaching of Peter as he described the life and teaching of Jesus. Like my daughter, Mark sat under repeated teaching until he had memorized it thoroughly. He then recorded the truth about Jesus as Peter delivered it to him. The case for early dating helps us to have confidence this occurred very early in history.

As a Christian, I also believe God protected and guided the preservation of the eyewitness accounts, but even without this protection, there is more than enough reason to infer the observations of the eyewitnesses were faithfully and accurately transmitted into the written gospel record.

Revere   Repeat   Record

WHAT WERE THE DISCIPLES SAYING ABOUT JESUS PRIOR TO WRITING THE GOSPELS?

The biblical eyewitnesses didn't immediately pen their observations about Jesus. Following the resurrection, many years passed before the first gospel was written. In the period between the resurrection of Jesus and the authorship of the first Gospels, what precisely were the disciples saying about Jesus prior to writing the Gospels? Were their oral statements consistent with the gospel accounts? As it turns out, we have an evidential record of the earliest statements about Jesus. They're embedded in the writings of the apostle Paul. In his letter to the Corinthian church, Paul included what most scholars believe to be one of the earliest Christian creeds:

> Now I make known to you, brethren, the gospel which I preached to you, which also you received, in which also you stand, by which also you are saved, if you hold fast the word which I preached to you, unless you believed in vain. For I delivered to you as of first importance what I also received, that Christ died for our sins according to the Scriptures, and that He was buried, and that He was raised on the third day according to the Scriptures, and that He appeared to Cephas, then to the twelve. After that He appeared to more than five hundred brethren at one time, most of whom remain until now, but some have fallen asleep; then He appeared to James, then to all the apostles; and last of all, as to one untimely born, He appeared to me also. (1 Cor. 15:1–8)

Although Paul's letter to the Corinthians is typically dated in the mid-50s, he was referencing information he gave to the Corinthians *prior* to the writing of the letter. When did he first deliver this information to the brothers and sisters in Corinth? Most scholars prefer a dating of AD 51 based on relevant descriptions in the book of Acts and the historical dating related to Gallio.[1] This means Paul communicated the data about Jesus within twenty years of the crucifixion. But when did Paul first see the risen Christ and then receive this information about Jesus? Given what Paul wrote in his letters and what Luke described in the book of Acts, we can reconstruct the following timeline:

> *AD 33*—Jesus was resurrected from the grave and ascended to heaven
>
> *AD 34–35*—Jesus appeared to Paul on the road to Damascus (one to two years after the resurrection and ascension)[2]
>
> *AD 37–38*—Paul received the data about the historicity and deity of Jesus from Peter and James while visiting them in Jerusalem (two to three years after his conversion, depending how you interpret the words "three years later" in Galatians 1)[3]
>
> *AD 48–50*—Paul corroborates the data about the historicity and deity of Jesus with John, Peter, and James in the presence of Barnabas and Timothy (fourteen years after the Damascus Road event or fourteen years after the first meeting with Peter and James in Jerusalem)[4]
>
> *AD 51*—Paul first provided information to the Corinthian church about the historicity and deity of Jesus (during this visit to Corinth, he also appeared before Gallio)
>
> *AD 55*—Paul writes to the Corinthian church and reminds them of the information he previously provided them about the historicity and deity of Jesus[5]

The early Christian creed related to the historicity and deity of Jesus in 1 Corinthians 15 is a written record of the *earliest oral information we have about Jesus*. It represents a view of Jesus expressed within four to six years of the resurrection. There's no reason to believe this view of Jesus was not being communicated even earlier. It would still be several years before any of the eyewitnesses would write a gospel, but the eyewitnesses were steadfast and consistent in their claims related to the historicity and deity of Jesus.[6]

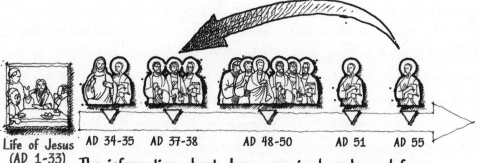

Life of Jesus
(AD 1-33)   AD 34-35   AD 37-38   AD 48-50   AD 51   AD 55

The information about Jesus remained unchanged from AD 37 to the authorship of the letters and Gospels

WHY SHOULD WE TRUST THE NEW TESTAMENT CANON WAS ASSEMBLED CORRECTLY?

The Council of Laodicea (AD 363) simply affirmed the Scriptures followers of Jesus were using for several generations when it endorsed the New Testament Canon we know today (see chapter 13). The earliest believers, hundreds of years before the various councils, preserved the precious eyewitness testimony related to Jesus, continually examining the competing accounts to make sure their collection was authentic and accurate. By the time of the councils, a standard was accepted by Christians to determine which writings were the Word of God (and which were not). There were two important attributes considered by these believers:

EYEWITNESS RELIABILITY

Were the texts authored by an eyewitness or someone with immediate access to the eyewitnesses? (Could the texts be trusted to reflect the truth about what happened? Were they uncorrupted both historically and doctrinally?)

PRACTICAL UTILITY

Did the texts reflect the divine nature and purposes of God to assist God's people in understanding Him better? (Were the texts useful in teaching people about God? Were they understandable and accessible?)

These areas of concern guided the selection process for the earliest believers as they protected and preserved the documents they received from the apostles. These collectors had firsthand access to the men who wrote the Gospels. In addition to this, the *geographic diversity* from which these early leaders emerged further substantiated the authenticity of the New Testament. The disciples of the apostles preserved the testimony of the eyewitnesses and consistently described this testimony in their own correspondence, even though they were separated by thousands of miles:

IN ROME: CLEMENT (AD 95) AFFIRMED THE NEW TESTAMENT

Clement collected many of the New Testament eyewitness documents and held them in high regard. Perhaps more importantly, he believed these documents were already known well enough by his readers to be recognized when quoted or alluded to in his letter.

IN ANTIOCH: IGNATIUS (AD 110–115) AFFIRMED THE NEW TESTAMENT

Ignatius was the first writer of antiquity to use the expression "It is written" when quoting from the New Testament documents; it's clear he thought of them "on par" with the Old Testament. Like Clement, Ignatius also must have believed these documents were already circulated and known well enough by his readers to be recognized when quoted.

IN SMYRNA: POLYCARP (AD 110) AFFIRMED THE NEW TESTAMENT

Like Ignatius, it is also clear Polycarp believed the New Testament documents were Scripture comparable to the Old Testament. In the twelfth chapter of his letter, he wrote, "In the sacred books … as it is said in these Scriptures, 'Be ye angry and sin not,' and 'Let not the sun go down upon your wrath,'" quoting both Psalm 4:4 and Ephesians 4:26 as if they were both equally inspired.[7]

The geographic separation of these three early-church leaders was *significant*. By the end of the first (and beginning of the second) century, Clement, Ignatius, and Polycarp were leading the church in separate regions of the Roman Empire yet were united in their identification of the core letters and Gospels of the New Testament. Even at this early point in history, the New Testament books were already written and accepted as Scripture by the first disciples of the apostles. This generation of believers likely accepted many more of the New Testament writings than they happened to mention in their own letters, but the cited New Testament documents, written by the eyewitnesses (and preserved by their disciples across geographic boundaries), eventually became the core of the New Testament we know today.

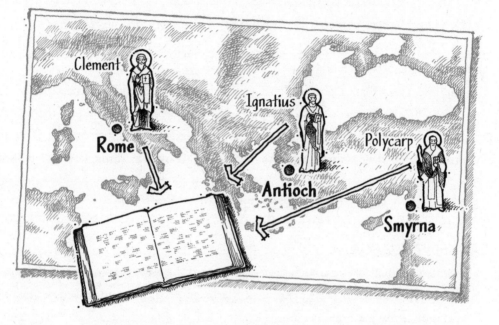

WHY DO YOU THINK THE GOSPELS ARE EYEWITNESS ACCOUNTS WHEN SOME SCHOLARS DISAGREE?

Some scholars question the notion the Gospels are eyewitness accounts, given they aren't written as first-person narratives and the authors fail to identify themselves more directly within the text. It's certainly true the authors of the Gospels took a reserved approach to their own identity within the narrative, but this was not uncommon in ancient literature of the time. In addition, there are several good reasons to believe the Gospels are eyewitness accounts:

ATTRIBUTED STATEMENTS

The New Testament authors repeatedly referred to themselves as eyewitnesses, even if they did not make overt statements including their names. In the last chapter of John's gospel, the author wrote he was testifying, and his testimony was true. Language such as this presumes the author saw something he could describe as an eyewitness. In addition, the authors of 1 John and 2 Peter identified themselves as eyewitnesses who directly observed Jesus (1 John 1:1, 3 and 2 Peter 1:16). While Luke clearly admitted he was not an eyewitness to the events in his gospel, he claimed to rely on the true eyewitnesses for his information (Luke 1:1). The authors of the Gospels considered their work a record of eyewitness observations.

APOSTOLIC STRATEGY

The apostles also behaved as eyewitnesses in the book of Acts, and the strategy they used to share Christianity was consistent with their role as eyewitnesses. When the apostles chose to proclaim the truth to unbelievers in their midst, they did so by describing the resurrection and their status as eyewitnesses. This is consistent throughout the book of Acts. The apostles identified themselves as eyewitnesses, shared the truth as eyewitnesses, and eventually wrote the Gospels as eyewitnesses.

ANCIENT SUPPORT

The earliest writings of the church fathers confirmed the eyewitness nature of the gospel authors. Papias, as noted earlier, described Mark's gospel as a record of Peter's teachings related to his eyewitness observations.

AUTHORITATIVE SELECTION

Finally, the Canon of Scripture reflects the eyewitness nature of the gospel accounts. One of the primary criteria for the selection of the Canon was eyewitness composition. The original Gospels were protected and revered based on their apostolic authorship, and late documents were rejected by the early-church fathers because they were authored too late to have been written by eyewitnesses. The criterion of eyewitness authorship became foundational to the selection process.

While features of the Gospels may still be challenged by those who deny the eyewitness nature of the texts, the best inference from the evidence is the Gospels were intended to be eyewitness accounts.

The Gospels as
Eyewitness Accounts

DO THE NONCANONICAL GOSPELS CHALLENGE THE HISTORICITY OF THE NEW TESTAMENT?

Some skeptics claim the canonical Gospels aren't the only first-century stories about Jesus. They cite additional ancient, noncanonical gospels (like the gospel of Thomas, the gospel of Mary, or the gospel of Judas) describing a version of Jesus very different from the one we accept today. Do these ancient, nonbiblical documents (and their varied descriptions) challenge what we know about Jesus? No. The canonical Gospels are the *only* trustworthy source of information related to the life of Jesus for the following reasons:

THE NONCANONICAL GOSPELS APPEARED TOO LATE IN HISTORY

The Gospels found in the New Testament appeared very early in history (see chapter 11). By comparison, the entire catalogue of noncanonical gospels was written much later in history. (For more on this, refer to my book *Person of Interest: Why Jesus Still Matters in a World That Rejects the Bible*.)

THE NONCANONICAL GOSPELS WERE KNOWN TO BE FRAUDULENT

The earliest disciples of Jesus and leaders of the church knew these late gospels were fraudulent. Early leaders like Polycarp, Irenaeus, Hippolytus, Tertullian, and Epiphanus wrote about most of the noncanonical gospels when they first appeared in history, identifying them as heretical frauds. Irenaeus, writing about the growing number of noncanonical texts, said there were "an indescribable number of secret and illegitimate writings, which they themselves have forged, to bewilder the minds of foolish people, who are ignorant of the true scriptures."[8] Those who were closest to the action knew the late noncanonical texts were *not* to be trusted.

THE NONCANONICAL GOSPELS REFLECTED ULTERIOR MOTIVES

The authors of the noncanonical gospels allowed their theological presuppositions to corrupt their work. Many of the noncanonical texts, for example, were written by Gnostic authors utilizing the pseudonym of an apostle to legitimize the *text* while co-opting the person of Jesus to legitimize their *theology*. As a result, Jesus was often portrayed as the source of hidden, esoteric wisdom communicated in sayings or dialogues with a selected disciple who was privileged enough to be "enlightened." In addition, Jesus was often described as an immaterial spirit without a body, forcing the author to account for the appearance of a bodily death at the crucifixion or other physical appearances described in the New Testament.

We have little reason to seriously consider late descriptions of the life and ministry of Jesus; the noncanonical fictions were rejected by the ancients who recognized their late arrival and understood the self-serving motivations of their proponents.

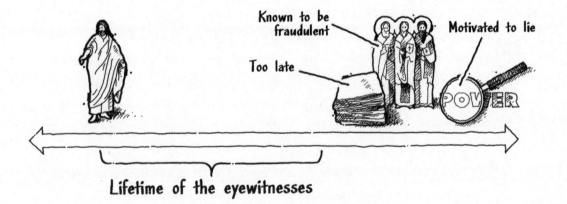

Known to be fraudulent

Motivated to lie

Too late

POWER

Lifetime of the eyewitnesses

WHY DO TEXTUAL CRITICS DOUBT THE AUTHORSHIP OF THE GOSPELS?

Some skeptics question the historical attributions of Mark, Matthew, Luke, or John. Using the tools of textual criticism, many cite variations within the text as evidence of multiple authors. While I am also inclined to examine every word carefully (refer to chapter 5), I am conscious of the limits of this kind of textual criticism. As I employ some of these same tools, I try to keep the following considerations in mind:

CONSIDER THE TIMESPAN IN WHICH THE DOCUMENT WAS WRITTEN

Critics point to differences in language or writing style within a biblical text as evidence of more than one author, but this is often better attributed to the timespan in which the document was written. As a cold-case detective, I regularly open cold cases in which a detective originally authored a "running supplemental report" over a period of time. He or she started writing on the day of the murder and then updated the report over several years as the investigation continued. Looking back at the report years later, it often appears as though several partners worked on the document, when, in fact, only one investigator penned it. As the detective matured, his or her style changed. In a similar way, criticisms of New Testament documents must consider the timespan over which they were written. As we examine the work of the apostle Luke, for example, we must account for the natural changes in his writing style, given the timespan over which he wrote the book of Acts and the gospel of Luke.

CONSIDER THE LIMITS OF THE TECHNOLOGY BEING USED BY THE AUTHOR

When the original detective wrote the supplemental report (prior to computers or word processors), he or she dictated the words to an office assistant who typed them on a typewriter. As a result, detectives seldom returned to earlier portions of the report to modify their language, change punctuation, or correct typos. Instead, they learned to live with their prior language choices and grammatical errors due to the technological limits they faced. I'm sure this was also the case with ancient authors writing with primitive tools or dictating to scribes who used primitive resources.

CONSIDER THE CHANGING INFLUENCES
EXPERIENCED BY THE AUTHOR

As I develop as a case maker and writer, my association with great thinkers and established authors continues to encourage me to improve my own abilities. Along the way, my writing style was influenced by people who mentored me. I find myself including their expressions and style in my work. When I first began writing as a Christian case maker, my articles were much like my professional reports and search warrants. Since then, I've adopted language and styles similar to those case makers who have influenced me along the way. This was likely true for ancient authors as well. If their documents were written over a span of time, without the technology to easily edit earlier portions of the text, we should reasonably expect changes attributed to the influence of those with whom the authors interacted.

CONSIDER YOUR OWN PRESUPPOSITIONS
AS YOU ARE STUDYING THE TEXT

Most importantly, we must carefully examine the underlying skepticism each of us brings to a document. I've worked with defense attorneys who have assumed the worst in the original detective and, as a result, saw deceit and malice in every alteration and variation within the report. Did the nature of the report warrant this response or did the presupposition of the attorney motivate him to see what he wanted to see? In a similar way, we cannot come to a text making claims about the supernatural with a presupposition *against the supernatural*. When this happens, our presuppositions cause us to find fault, error, and deception at every turn.

In the end, we can "read between the lines" to establish authorship or simply rely on the testimony and attributions offered by those who were closest to the action. If we are going to deny the traditional authorial attributions of the Gospels, we should at least recognize the limits of textual criticism.

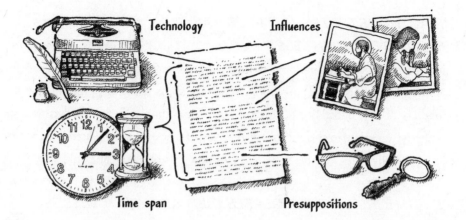

WHAT MAKES THE CLAIMS ABOUT JESUS MORE RELIABLE THAN CLAIMS ABOUT FICTIONAL CHARACTERS (LIKE PETER PAN)?

The mere fact an account may be rooted in some form of true history doesn't mean *everything* in the account is accurate or true. When Scottish novelist and playwright J. M. Barrie wrote the fictional story *Peter Pan*, for example, he set the account in late Victorian London. A thousand years from now, archaeologists may find archaeological evidence confirming the existence of London and may even find evidence that other writers described the Peter Pan story. But the archaeological or manuscript support confirming a portion of the story doesn't guarantee the authenticity of the entire account. The record related to Jesus is far different than the record related to Peter Pan, however:

THE AUTHORS OF THE GOSPELS CLAIMED TO BE EYEWITNESSES

Barrie never wrote *Peter Pan* as a true claim about history from the perspective of an eyewitness. Instead, he first introduced the character in a small section of *The Little White Bird*, a 1902 novel. Barrie never claimed to be writing true history as an eyewitness. The authors of the Gospels, on the other hand, repeatedly identified themselves as "eyewitnesses of His majesty" (2 Pet. 1:16), who described "what [they had] heard, what [they had] seen with [their] eyes, [and] what [they had] looked at and touched with [their] hands" (1 John 1:1, 3).

THE AUTHORS OF THE GOSPELS CAN BE TESTED AS EYEWITNESSES

Unlike Barrie (and other fictional writers), the biblical authors can be tested for their reliability as I've described in this book. When we apply the four-part template described in chapters 11–14, Barrie is quickly exposed as an author of fiction. When we apply this investigative template to the authors of the Gospels, however, they survive as reliable witnesses, especially when compared to other accurate historians of antiquity.

THE AUTHORS OF THE GOSPELS DIED AS EYEWITNESSES

J. M. Barrie and his publishers profited from the story of Peter Pan in several ways. He was motivated to write the fictional account of Peter Pan in a way unlike the authors of the Gospels. The biblical authors never enjoyed the success of a stage play or successful publication. Instead, they suffered for their claims, yet remained committed to their testimony.

Archaeological evidence is one small part of the collective case for the reliability of the gospel eyewitnesses. The story of Peter Pan is a *fictional* claim. The story of Jesus is a *historical* claim. As such, the gospel accounts can be tested to see if they accurately describe the Jesus of history.

Jesus compared to Peter Pan

11 WHY DO YOU TRUST WHAT THE CHURCH FATHERS WROTE ABOUT JESUS WHEN MANY HELD HERETICAL VIEWS?

When tracing the New Testament "chain of custody" to investigate the transmission of the gospel accounts, I typically recount the claims of many early-church leaders (like Polycarp, Ignatius, Clement, Irenaeus, Hippolytus, Origen, Tatian, Justin Martyr, and others) as they described the life and ministry of Jesus from one generation to the next. I am sometimes asked, however, how I can reference these sources, given that some of these church fathers held heretical positions related to Christian doctrines and practices. Can people who hold different (even *heretical*) theological views still play an important role in establishing the historicity of Jesus? Yes, they can:

DIFFERING VIEWS ARE NOT DISQUALIFIERS

In every criminal trial, we summon witnesses who hold theological, philosophical, or political views differing from our own (and from each other). These secondary beliefs are irrelevant because witnesses must limit their testimony to their observations related to the case. Imagine, for example, a witness observes a suspect run to his car, enter on the driver's side, start the engine, but then hesitate just prior to speeding from the location. At the trial, the witness will be asked to describe what he or she saw related to the actions of the suspect. But a question such as, "Why do you think he hesitated before he fled the scene?" is beyond the scope of the witness's knowledge and testimony. It's one thing to testify about what you've seen, it's another to testify about what you think it *means*.

OBSERVATIONS ARE MORE IMPORTANT THAN INTERPRETATIONS

When examining the lineage of historic church leaders, I am more interested in the facts related to Jesus than the interpretations of the church fathers. I want to know what was described about Jesus from generation to generation rather than how each leader developed a theological response. As a result, I am primarily concerned with their descriptions of the Gospels and the details included in these historical narratives. When a church father begins to pontificate on a theological position or interpretation, I recognize this as outside the scope of his testimony. When examining an early-church father, I am only interested in, "What were the facts about Jesus's life you received from those who preceded you?" not, "What do you think all this means?"

One need not agree with every theological position of an early-church father to recognize his value in making the case for the accurate transmission of the Gospels. Yes, even heretics can help establish the historicity of Jesus.

What did John say?   What was John thinking?

12 WHY INVESTIGATE THE BIBLE AT ALL? IS IT STILL RELEVANT TODAY?

This is one of the most important questions anyone can ask about the Bible and my work in *Cold-Case Christianity*. Why write a book defending the Bible? Why would anyone take time to consider the claims of an irrelevant book written two thousand years ago? To answer this question, I typically offer an analogy:

I have a drawer in my desk filled with manuals and instruction guides. Every time I purchase a new device (whether it's an electric garden tool or a smartphone), I store the original instruction manual in this drawer. I occasionally return to these guides when I have a problem or need an answer. But, about once a year, I sift through these documents and throw many of them away. The discarded manuals are still true and skillfully written, but they're now irrelevant; I've mastered the devices they describe, and I'm able to overcome any problem I may encounter on my own. But, while my collection of instruction manuals *shrinks* every year, my collection of Bibles and related study materials *increases*. Why? Because the Bible continues to answer life's most important questions. It solves the most pressing problem we face as humans, a problem we simply can't resolve on our own.

My experience as a cold-case homicide detective is partially to blame for my growing biblical library. The instruction manuals in my desk drawer would never have become part of my collection if they didn't correctly describe the devices they claimed to support. Their *accuracy* is the key to their relevancy. When I first investigated the claims of the New Testament accounts, I knew their relevancy would be similarly dependent upon the degree to which they were *true*. That's why I examined the Gospels using the same skill set I applied to my criminal investigations; the skill set I've described in this book. I became convinced the Gospels were telling me the truth about Jesus of Nazareth. But their reliability and truthfulness were only *part* of the story. The Gospels also accurately described something I observed in murderers.

I've arrested my fair share of cold-case killers, and most of them were law-abiding, upstanding citizens by the time I met them, many years after they brutally killed their victims. The more I spoke with these murderers, the more I realized they were just like … *me*. And *you*. And *everyone else* on the planet. Some had become fire captains, some teachers, some businesspeople. They were good parents, reliable family members, and trustworthy employees. But they were all protecting a dark secret from their past; striving daily to convince a watching world they were good people, even though they had done something unspeakable. None of these killers committed more than one murder, and none would likely commit another. But each bore the burden of knowing who they *really* were, despite appearances.

As I investigated each cold-case homicide, I came to realize these murderers weren't unlike the rest of us. If you think you're incapable of committing such a crime, you've likely *underestimated* the possible scenarios you might face, and *overestimated* how you might respond. Even if you don't think you're capable of such atrocities, I bet there's still some secret you don't want others to discover; we're all moral lawbreakers of one kind or another. The penal code in my state describes crimes as old as human history. In fact, many of our statutes still reflect the biblical language of the Old Testament. Some things change, but our fallen, base desires grudgingly remain. We are moral outlaws to one degree or another.

And *that's* why the Bible is still relevant today. The instruction manuals I routinely discard are still *true*, but they are no longer *necessary*. The Bible, however, is both true *and* necessary.

The New Testament accurately describes the Savior, and it accurately describes our *need* for a Savior. It provides the only solution to the most important problem we'll ever encounter: our separation from a holy, perfect God. We can't solve this problem on our own; Jesus is still the only answer. That's why I'm running out of space for my collection of biblical commentaries, resources, and references, but my desk drawer is more than big enough to hold all my technical manuals. I'll eventually master every device and make the manuals irrelevant, but I'll never overcome my need for a Savior. The claims of the Bible are both true and necessary. The Bible is still relevant today.

WITNESSES AND RESOURCES

Compiling the resources necessary to make the case

Case Files

EXPERT WITNESSES

I've yet to bring an investigation to trial without the assistance of expert witnesses who testified about specific and detailed aspects of the evidence. The following expert witnesses may be called to the stand as you make a case for the claims of Christianity:

Chapter One:
DON'T BE A "KNOW-IT-ALL"

Craig S. Keener
Will testify thoroughly to the credibility of the miracle reports in the Gospels and Acts in *Miracles: The Credibility of the New Testament Accounts* (Baker Academic, 2011).

J. P. Moreland and William Lane Craig
Will testify to the philosophical biases and presuppositions impacting issues of faith and reason in their book *Philosophical Foundations for a Christian Worldview* (InterVarsity Press, 2003).

Michael S. Heiser

Will testify to the supernatural worldview described in the biblical texts in his book *The Unseen Realm: Recovering the Supernatural Worldview of the Bible* (Lexham Press, 2019).

Chapter Two:
LEARN HOW TO "INFER"

Gary Habermas and Michael Licona

Will testify to the *minimal facts* and evidences related to the resurrection in their book *The Case for the Resurrection of Jesus* (Kregel, 2004).

Jake O'Connell

Will testify to the resurrection as the best explanation of the facts (compared to the claim the disciples hallucinated) in his book *Jesus' Resurrection and Apparitions: A Bayesian Analysis* (Resource Publications, 2016).

Lee Strobel

Will testify to alternative explanations for the resurrection as he interviews various experts in the field in *The Case for Easter: A Journalist Investigates the Evidence for the Resurrection* (Zondervan Publishing, 2004).

Chapter Three:
THINK "CIRCUMSTANTIALLY"

J. Warner Wallace

I will testify to the cumulative case for God's existence from eight features of the universe in my book *God's Crime Scene: A Cold-Case Detective Examines the Evidence for a Divinely Created Universe* (David C Cook, 2019).

William Lane Craig

Will testify to the causal evidence related to the cosmological argument in his book *The Kalām Cosmological Argument* (Wipf & Stock, 2000).

John Leslie

Will testify to the fine-tuning evidence related to the anthropic principle in his book *Universes* (Taylor & Francis, 2002).

Neil Manson

Will testify to the design evidence related to the teleological argument in his book *God and Design: The Teleological Argument and Modern Science* (Routledge, 2003).

Paul Copan and Mark Linville

Will testify to the moral evidence related to the axiological argument in their book *The Moral Argument* (Continuum Publishers, 2013).

Chapter Four:
TEST YOUR WITNESSES

Richard Bauckham

Will testify to the nature of the New Testament Gospels as eyewitness accounts of the life of Jesus in his book *Jesus and the Eyewitnesses: The Gospels as Eyewitness Testimony* (Eerdmans, 2006).

Bruce Metzger

Will testify to the early collection of the eyewitness accounts and their formation into the New Testament in his book *The Canon of the New Testament: Its Origin, Development, and Significance* (Oxford University Press, 1997).

Mark L. Strauss

Will testify to the differing renderings of Jesus provided by the gospel authors, examining them as the work of different artists describing the same subject (Jesus of Nazareth) in his book *Four Portraits, One Jesus: A Survey of Jesus and the Gospels* (Zondervan Academic, 2020).

Chapter Five:
HANG ON EVERY WORD

J. Warner Wallace

I will testify in more detail to the role of forensic statement analysis in assessing statements and claims in my book *Forensic Faith: A Homicide Detective Makes the Case for a More Reasonable, Evidential Christian Faith* (David C Cook, 2017).

Craig Blomberg

Will testify to the "forensic" methods of "textual criticism" used to study the Gospels and discuss some of the conclusions drawn from this effort in his book *The Historical Reliability of the Gospels* (InterVarsity Press, 2007).

Daniel B. Wallace

Will testify to what can be learned "forensically" about the early transmission of the New Testament documents in the compilation *Revisiting the Corruption of the New Testament: Manuscript, Patristic, and Apocryphal Evidence* (Kregel, 2011).

Chapter Six:
SEPARATE ARTIFACTS FROM EVIDENCE

Michelle Brown

Will testify to the early formation of the biblical text, while exhibiting a number of ancient biblical manuscripts, in her book *In the Beginning: Bibles before the Year 1000* (Smithsonian, 2006).

Philip Comfort

Will testify to the nature of the early New Testament papyrus manuscripts and the methodology used to re-create the original accounts in his book *Early Manuscripts & Modern Translations of the New Testament* (Wipf & Stock, 2001).

Timothy Paul Jones

Will testify to the methodology of the early transmission of the New Testament and respond to many of the skeptical claims of Bart Ehrman (as mentioned in this chapter) in his book *Misquoting Truth: A Guide to the Fallacies of Bart Ehrman's "Misquoting Jesus"* (IVP Books, 2007).

Chapter Seven:
RESIST CONSPIRACY THEORIES

Sean McDowell

Will testify and provide a comprehensive, reasoned, and historical analysis of the fate of the twelve disciples of Jesus in his book *The Fate of the Apostles: Examining the Martyrdom Accounts of the Closest Followers of Jesus* (Routledge, 2018).

William McBirnie

Will testify to the nature of the lives and deaths of the apostles who claimed to see the resurrection of Jesus in his book *The Search for the Twelve Apostles* (Tyndale, 2008).

E. A. Wallis Budge

Will testify to the history and legends (from Ethiopic sources) related to the lives, martyrdoms, and deaths of the disciples of Jesus in the book *The Contendings of the Apostles: Being the Histories and the Lives and Martyrdoms and Deaths of the Twelve Apostles and Evangelists* (Kessinger Publishing, 2010).

Bryan M. Litfin

Will testify to key early Christian martyrdom stories in his book *Early Christian Martyr Stories: An Evangelical Introduction with New Translations* (Baker Academic, 2014).

Chapter Eight:
RESPECT THE "CHAIN OF CUSTODY"

Mark D. Roberts

Will testify to the historical manuscript evidence and early appearance of the biblical record in his book *Can We Trust the Gospels?: Investigating the Reliability of Matthew, Mark, Luke, and John* (Crossway, 2007).

Mike Aquilina

Will testify to the writings and teachings of the early-church fathers in his book *The Fathers of the Church, Expanded Edition* (Our Sunday Visitor, 2006).

Peter J. Williams

Will testify to the historical reliability of the Gospels, including how the New Testament texts were handed down throughout the centuries, in his book *Can We Trust the Gospels?* (Crossway, 2018).

Chapter Nine:
KNOW WHEN "ENOUGH IS ENOUGH"

David Wolfe

Will testify to how we come to "know" something is true in his book *Epistemology: The Justification of Belief* (InterVarsity Press, 1983).

William Rowe

Will testify to the classic atheist presentations of the "problem of evil" and the classic defenses (theodicies) offered by theists in his book *God and the Problem of Evil* (Wiley-Blackwell, 2001).

Bobby Conway

Will testify to the nature of doubt and belief, trusting in the strength of the evidence, and moving from unbelief to trust in his book *Doubting toward Faith: The Journey to Confident Christianity* (Harvest House Publishers, 2015).

Chapter Ten:
PREPARE FOR AN ATTACK

Craig Evans

Will testify to the assumptions, theories, and tactics employed by skeptics to discredit the Gospels in *Fabricating Jesus: How Modern Scholars Distort the Gospels* (InterVarsity Press, 2006).

Gregory Koukl

Will testify to successful and reasoned approaches employed by those who seek to defend the Christian worldview in *Tactics, 10th Anniversary Edition: A Game Plan for Discussing Your Christian Convictions* (Zondervan, 2019).

Nancy Pearcey

Will testify to the nature of truth as a concept and how the public/private, sacred/secular divide in culture impacts our perception of truth, including the truth of Christianity, in her book *Total Truth: Liberating Christianity from Its Cultural Captivity* (Crossway, 2008).

Dave Sterrett

Will testify to strategies and practical approaches Christians can apply in conversations with those who reject the authority of the Bible in his book *Jesus Conversations: Effective Everyday Engagement* (Tyndale House Publishers, 2021).

Chapter Eleven:
WERE THEY PRESENT?

Jean Carmignac

Will testify to the Semitic origin of the synoptic gospels and how they were formed amidst the Jewish culture of the first half of the first century in his book *Birth of the Synoptic Gospels* (Franciscan Herald Press, 1987).

John Wenham

Will testify to an alternate theory about the early dating of the Gospels (placing Matthew ahead of Mark) by comparing the Gospels to one another and to the writings and records of the church fathers in his book *Redating Matthew, Mark and Luke: A Fresh Assault on the Synoptic Problem* (InterVarsity Press, 1992).

Jonathan Bernier

Will testify to how quickly early Christians wrote the seminal texts and Gospels of the New Testament in his book *Rethinking the Dates of the New Testament: The Evidence for Early Composition* (Baker Academic, 2022).

Chapter Twelve:
WERE THEY CORROBORATED?

J. Warner Wallace

I will testify to the corroborative evidence available in the history of the Common Era (the period known as AD) in my book *Person of Interest: Why Jesus Still Matters in a World That Rejects the Bible* (Zondervan, 2021).

Titus M. Kennedy

Will testify to the archaeological discoveries corroborating Jesus's birth, ministry, crucifixion, and resurrection in his book *Excavating the Evidence for Jesus: The Archaeology and History of Christ and the Gospels* (Harvest House Publishers, 2022).

Peter Schafer

Will testify to the ancient Jewish references to Jesus scattered throughout the Talmud in his book *Jesus in the Talmud* (Princeton University Press, 2009).

R. T. France

Will testify to the nonbiblical ancient sources corroborating the existence of Jesus in his book *The Evidence for Jesus* (Regent College, 2006).

John McRay

Will testify to the archaeological corroboration of the New Testament in his book *Archaeology and the New Testament* (Baker, 2008).

Shimon Gibson

Will testify (as an archaeologist) to the archaeological evidence corroborating the final days of Jesus's life in his book *The Final Days of Jesus: The Archaeological Evidence* (HarperCollins, 2009).

Chapter Thirteen:
WERE THEY ACCURATE OVER TIME?

Michael Holmes

Will testify to the writings of the students of the apostles in his book *The Apostolic Fathers: Greek Texts and English Translations* (Baker, 2007).

Justo González

Will testify to the early history of Christianity and many of the characters who played a part in the "chain of custody" in his book *Story of Christianity: Volume 1, The Early Church to the Dawn of the Reformation* (HarperOne, 2010).

Nicholas Perrin

Will testify to the transmission (and copying) of the gospel accounts in his book *Lost in Transmission?: What We Can Know about the Words of Jesus* (Thomas Nelson, 2007).

Chapter Fourteen:
WERE THEY BIASED?

C. Bernard Ruffin

Will testify to the lives and martyrdoms of the apostles in his book *The Twelve: The Lives of the Apostles after Calvary* (Our Sunday Visitor, 1998).

Josh and Sean McDowell

Will testify to the reasonable conclusions drawn from the testimony of the apostles in their book *Evidence for the Resurrection* (Regal, 2009).

W. Brian Shelton

Will testify to the stories and contributions of the apostles, describing their lives, legacies, and impact on the growth of the early church, in his book *Quest for the Historical Apostles: Tracing Their Lives and Legacies* (Baker Academic, 2018).

Case Files

ASSISTING OFFICERS

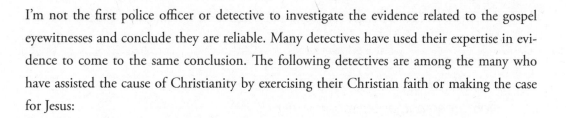

I'm not the first police officer or detective to investigate the evidence related to the gospel eyewitnesses and conclude they are reliable. Many detectives have used their expertise in evidence to come to the same conclusion. The following detectives are among the many who have assisted the cause of Christianity by exercising their Christian faith or making the case for Jesus:

Sir Robert Anderson
Assistant Commissioner (Deceased), London Metropolitan Police (England)

Sir Robert Anderson was a theologian and author of numerous books, including *The Coming Prince*, *The Bible and Modern Criticism*, and *A Doubter's Doubts about Science and Religion*.

Mary Agnes Sullivan
Lieutenant and Homicide Detective (Deceased), New York City Police Department

Mary Sullivan was a devout Catholic and a pioneer in law enforcement in New York City, where she became the first woman homicide detective in the history of the department. She was also the first woman inducted into the NYPD Honor Legion.

Alice Stebbins Wells
Police Officer (Deceased), Los Angeles Police Department

Alice Wells was one of the first groundbreaking female police officers in the United States. Prior to becoming a police officer, she served as a minister and was a member of the Women's Christian Temperance Union.

Robert L. Vernon
Assistant Chief of Police (Retired), Los Angeles Police Department

Bob Vernon is a speaker, writer, founder of Pointman Leadership Institute (http:// pliglobal.com, offering leadership training to police forces globally), and author of *L.A. Justice: Lessons from the Firestorm* and *Character: The Foundation of Leadership*.

Josh Cook
Police Officer in Maryland (foot patrol, patrol, plainclothes enforcement, and academy instructor)

Josh Cook is the cofounder of the Enter the Lion ministry to police officers (www.enterthelion.co), a ministry that "seeks to embolden and equip those who have been called to a life of service by their Lord and Savior Jesus Christ."

Travis Yates
Police Major in Oklahoma

Travis Yates is a teacher, speaker, and editor with *Law Officer Magazine* (www .lawofficer.com). He is one of the most prolific writers in law enforcement, authoring hundreds of articles for various publications. He is also the author of *The Courageous Police Leader: A Survival Guide for Combating Cowards, Chaos, and Lies*.

Michael "MC" Williams
Chief Detective (Lt.), Colorado State Criminal Investigator (Retired)

Michael Williams is an instructor, speaker, and former national vice president of the Fellowship of Christian Peace Officers (www.fcpo.org) who now serves as the director of safety and security for a large Christian high school. He is also the director of the Centurion Law Enforcement Ministry (www.thecenturionlawenforcementministry .org), a national ministry created to bring officers to a saving knowledge of Christ, equip Christian officers to grow in their faith, support law-enforcement marriages, and reduce the very high levels of police suicide.

Michael Dye
Deputy Sheriff, Volusa County Sheriff's Office (Retired), and Marshal with the United States Marshals Service in Los Angeles (Retired)

Michael Dye is a speaker and the author of *The PeaceKeepers: A Bible Study for Law Enforcement Officers*. Michael has also served on the board of directors for the Fellowship of Christian Peace Officers (www.fcpo.org), a ministry providing support and accountability to Christian officers to help them become more effective witnesses for Christ as they disciple and train others to carry out the Great Commission.

Frank C. Ruffatto
Police Detective, Prince George's County, Maryland, Police Department (Retired)

Frank C. Ruffatto is a LCMS pastor and the executive director of Peace Officer Ministries (www.peaceofficerministries.org), a Christian law enforcement chaplaincy ministry providing direct help for those exposed to high-risk events.

Mark Kroeker
Deputy Chief (Retired), Los Angeles Police Department, and
Chief of Police (Retired), Portland Police Department (Oregon)

Mark Kroeker is a speaker and writer. He founded and served as the chairman of the World Children's Transplant Fund (http://wctf.org), a nonprofit organization dedicated to the development of pediatric organ transplantation around the world.

Tony Miano
Investigator and Officer (Retired), Los Angeles County Sheriff's Department

Tony Miano is a sheriff's chaplain, the founder of Cross Encounters with Tony Miano (https://crossencountersmin.com), and the author of *Take Up the Shield: Comparing the Uniform of the Police Officer and the Armor of God.*

Sir Robin Oake
Chief Constable (Retired), Isle of Man, and Chief Inspector to the Metropolitan Police and Superintendent to the Assistant Chief Constable in the Greater Manchester Police (England)

Robin Oake, a recipient of the Queen's Police Medal, is a speaker and author of *Father, Forgive: How to Forgive the Unforgivable* and *With God on the Streets.*

Dave Williams
Assistant Chief of Police (Retired), Portland (Oregon)

Dave Williams is founder and chairman of the board of trustees for Responder Life (https://responderlife.org), an organization dedicated to supporting the families of first responders.

Conrad Jensen
Deputy Inspector (Deceased), New York City Police Department
Conrad Jensen was a speaker and author. He served as a captain in the 23rd Precinct and founded an evangelical organization working with the youth gangs in East Harlem. After his retirement in 1964, the American Tract Society asked him to write a book, *26 Years on the Losing Side*, in an effort to "stimulate concerted prayer that our nation under God might return to the Scriptural foundations upon which it was built."

Randal (Randy) Simmons
SWAT Officer (Killed in the line of duty), Los Angeles Police Department
Randal Simmons was a minister for Carson's Glory Christian Fellowship International Church (California). His legacy of service to troubled youth in his community inspired the formation of the Randal D. Simmons Outreach Foundation (www.randysimmonsswat.com/foundation), a nonprofit organization designed to serve, empower, and encourage families and individuals in underserved areas.

Case Files

CASE NOTES

Detectives become copious note takers, collecting information and documenting their progress along the way. Use the QR code or URL below to access the notes referring to the materials cited in each chapter.

https://coldcasechristianity.com/casenotes/